LIFE IN LARGE FAMILIES

Views of Mormon Women

Howard M. Bahr
Spencer J. Condie
Kristen L. Goodman

Family and Demographic Research Institute
Brigham Young University

UNIVERSITY
PRESS OF
AMERICA

HQ
762
.U6
B33
1982

Copyright © 1982 by

University Press of America, Inc.

P.O. Box 19101, Washington, D.C. 20036

Library of Congress Cataloging in Publication Data

Bahr, Howard M.
  Life in large families.

  Includes bibliographical references.
  1. Family size--United States--Religious aspects--
Mormon Church. 2. Women, Mormon--United States--
Attitudes. 3. Women in the Mormon Church. I. Condie,
Spencer J. II. Goodman, Kristen L. III. Brigham Young
University. Family and Demographic Research Institute.
IV. Title. V. Title: Large families: views of Morman
women.
HQ762.U6B33 1982   306.8'7   82-45005
ISBN 0-8191-2551-2
ISBN 0-8191-2552-0 (pbk.)

We affectionately dedicate this work to mothers everywhere, whether their families are large or small, and to the children who make mothers what they are.

ACKNOWLEDGEMENTS

We sincerely acknowledge the kind assistance and cooperation of the forty-one mothers included in this study who willingly responded to hundreds of questions during interviews sometimes lasting six hours. We are indebted to them for their candor and their gracious hospitality which made this project both possible, and, in our estimation, very fruitful. To assure the confidentiality of their responses none of their names appear in this work. Whenever a mother, her husband, or a child is referred to by name in this book, that name is a pseudonym.

Thanks and appreciation are also extended to Ruth Barlow, Robin Mason, Joanna Rhoades, Debbie Weinheimer, Susan Lisonbee and Mary Stark, of the Brigham Young University Family and Demographic Research Institute, for transcribing hundreds of hours of taped interviews, and to Peg McGeever for preliminary editing of many of the transcripts. We are also grateful to Marilyn Webb, Supervisor of the Faculty Support Center, Gail Cozzens and Kimberly Williams for their invaluable and competent service in preparing the final manuscript for publication.

This project was supported by a research grant from the Brigham Young University Research Division, and we wish to thank Vice-President Leo Vernon for his faith in the project and his willingness to lend substantial support to this enterprise. To all of our colleagues who have given timely advice, criticism and encouragement, we also extend our heartfelt thanks.

TABLE OF CONTENTS

PREFACE

With the possible exception of two television programs, The Waltons and Eight is Enough, both of which have now achieved archival status, modern American Society offers few public glimpses of life in large families. Indeed, the countervailing pressures of the Women's Movement, Zero Population Growth, and intermittent double-digit inflation all operate to reduce the number of large families. In an era when abortions have outstripped tonsillectomies as the most prevalent medical procedure, it is anomalous to find a coterie of well-educated American women who share a belief that a sixth, an eighth, or a tenth child is more of an asset than a liability.

This study focuses upon women whose lives exhibit truly championship qualities, but who often see themselves as inadequate for the challenges they confront. They lament their lack of patience and their problems in "getting organized." At the same time, they are firmly committed to the large family as a quality setting for human growth, and they are assertive about the importance of their chosen roles of mother and wife and the "housework" that necessarily accompanies those roles.

The mothers of large families in this study, for the most part, shared the philosophy of the Nineteenth Century author, Mary Howitt, who wrote, "God sends children for another purpose than merely to keep up the race--to enlarge our hearts; and to make us unselfish and full of kindly sympathies and affections; to give our souls higher aims; to call out all our faculties to extended enterprise and exertion; and bring 'round our firesides bright faces, happy smiles and loving, tender hearts."

Chapter I

INTRODUCTION

* * * * *

This is what I wanted to do. I could have had a career; I am a college graduate. But this is what I wanted to do. . . . I think there will be a time, if I ever wanted to hit the career scene, I can. I think there is a time and a season for everything. . . . I don't think there's anything more exhilarating than just having a baby, that's just neat. You really feel you have done something worthwhile.
> --Heather,[1] mother of seven children, aged 3 to 16

My own philosophy is that you shouldn't deny yourself having children. I think that's the greatest happiness you can find.
> --Sarah,[1] mother of ten children, aged 2 to 20

This study of large families began with two main assumptions. First, that if "large" families continue to exist in a society where small families or childlessness has become the accepted pattern, there must be some advantages and rewards to life in large families. Second, that a look at the dynamics of large family life, that is, at how the family roles and activities are enacted in the context of higher-than-average family density, may yield some useful insights about family life in general as well as an understanding of how certain large families function.

---

[1]Throughout this book, all personal names of respondents are pseudonyms.

1

LIFE IN LARGE FAMILIES

We shall look at large families in the Latter-day Saint subculture. The Church of Jesus Christ of Latter-day Saints is one of several religious subcultures which officially encourage large families. While many of the insights we explore are relevant only in the Mormon setting, we suspect that other findings also apply to large families in other ethnic subcultures.

In the past quarter century there has been a dramatic decline in family size in American society. According to the Census Bureau's Statistical Abstract of the United States, in 1950 over 6.2 percent of all births to white women were sixth or subsequent births. By 1977 only 1.3 percent of births were to women who already had had at least five children. In some sections of the country, particularly in metropolitan areas, one may accurately speak of "the passing of the large family." In Utah also, there are fewer large families than there used to be, although Utah families continue to be larger than the national average.[2]

Several studies of larger families suggest that parents of many children are less happy than other parents and that children from large families have lower IQs, are less likely to succeed in school, and are more likely to be maladjusted than other children.[3] Some of these findings reflect the oft-reported linkage of family size and poverty. Generally the poor have had larger families than the well-to-do, and it is very difficult to sort out which negative consequences for children and parents derive from poverty and which are consequences of family size. Studies of high fertility in middle- or upper-income families thus become especially inter-

---

[2]See Arland Thornton, "Religion and Fertility: The Case of Mormonism," Journal of Marriage and Family, 41 (February 1979), pp. 131-142.

[3]For examples of this research, and some critiques of it, see R. B. Zajonc, "Family Configuration and Intelligence," Science, Vol. 192, 1976, pp. 227-236; R. B. Zajonc, "Dumber by the Dozen," Psychology Today, Vol. 8, 1975, pp. 37-43; Darwin L. Thomas, "Family Size and the Children's Characteristics," pp. 137-158 in Howard M. Bahr, Bruce A. Chadwick and Darwin L. Thomas, eds., Population, Resources, and the Future, Provo, Utah: Brigham Young University Press, 1972; and Richard C. Galbraith, "Sibling Spacing and Intellectual Development," Developmental Psychology, in press.

esting for sorting out the impact of family size as opposed to economic status.

Some people must think that the advantages of large families outweigh the disadvantages, for in this era of widely available information about contraception, of high literary and educational attainment, of inflation and truly staggering costs per child, some families continue to bear many more children than their educational level and economic status would lead us to anticipate.

It is questionable how much of the high fertility of these families can be attributed to social pressure. For instance, in the present-day urban Mormon community, a family of five is "large," and there is little social pressure for higher fertility than that. Five children represent sufficient conformity to the community norm that fertility is good. Nevertheless, there continue to be families of eight, nine, or ten children.

It is also problematic whether we can explain these larger families in terms of adherence to a religious norm which is tied to rewards in the hereafter. For there is no sure, clear pronouncement in Mormon theology that in the hereafter seven children are more rewarding than five, or for that matter that five are more rewarding than three. Consequently, even among the Mormons, we must look to the family itself, to its dynamics, and to the personal values and reinforcement matrices of the people involved, to explain the perpetuation of the large family in modern society.

If in today's society a family of five children is seen as large, what then explains the presence of families twice that large? More importantly, how do such families get by? What are the anticipated rewards that lead a mother of seven children to bear an eighth and then a ninth? It may be that these rewards do not exist, that large families in today's society are highly stressful and less effective than smaller families in rearing well-adjusted, creative children. On the other hand, it may be that in some communities, despite the stresses and costs involved in rearing a very large family, there are sufficient personal or social rewards to guarantee the continuation of such high fertility.

How the Study Was Done

Our method is exploratory rather than experimental. We propose to illustrate the kinds of rewards and costs that accompany life in large families. Our informants were mothers who had had at least seven children, including a birth recorded in Utah County, Utah, in 1977. In an effort to distinguish effects of low economic status from the consequences of having many children, we decided to limit the sample to women who had completed college and who were married to college graduates. In effect, this meant that the sample contained only middle- and upper-income families. Apart from this criterion which kept low-income families out of the sample, there was no attempt to select ideal or "showcase" families; no measure of family efficiency or stability was used to determine which families would be studied.

We want to be very clear about the atypicality of the women interviewed in this study. They were selected because they possessed certain characteristics, not because they were representative of Mormon women or Utah mothers. In the first place, they had seven or more children (or at least had had at least seven recorded births), and that makes them atypical. According to a statewide survey of married people conducted by the Brigham Young University Family and Demographic Research Institute in 1980, only about nine percent of the ever-married women in the state have had seven or more children. Moreover, women who have graduated from college and had seven or more children are very atypical. According to that survey, among ever-married women, one in four had graduated from college, but only one out of ten women with seven or more children had finished college. In other words, about one percent of the ever-married women in Utah had completed college and had at least seven children. Thus the mothers interviewed represent, at best, only one percent of Utah's women. In fact, they are slightly more atypical than that because of the third criterion for inclusion in the sample, that husbands also have completed college.

Among births recorded in Utah County in 1977, there were 48 instances in which the mother was having a seventh or subsequent birth, had completed college, and was married to a man who had completed college. These 48 comprised the sample of our study. We later discovered that one of these 48 women had, in fact, had only five children, and she was dropped from the sample. Another woman who had not personally borne seven but who, in a second marriage, was mother to seven was included because she was responsible for managing the household and the children even though all were not her own children.

The mothers were first contacted by mail, in a letter which introduced them to the project and explained that they had been selected "from a list of mothers who recently gave birth to a child in Utah County." The letter continued:

We will be talking informally about women's opinions and experiences. In particular, we wish to learn about the way mothers deal with the many stresses of modern family life; with how large families are organized so that members' needs are met; and with how mothers view themselves and their opportunities. We are trying to learn, from the actual experiences of Utah Valley mothers, about the successes and failures of family organization, what things you have found to "work," and what patterns have proven less successful. We are especially interested in your family's day-to-day experiences.

Potential respondents were assured about the confidentiality of the data to be collected. Also, because we were requesting an in-depth interview which they might find too lengthy or too personal, we explicitly suggested that they decline to participate if they felt they would not enjoy the experience:

We recognize that many things about family life are personal, and want to assure you that all interviews are totally confidential. Although most women have found this experience to be very satisfying, please feel free to decline this invitation if you feel you would not enjoy talking about your family life. When you agree to participate, you are, of course, free to answer only those questions you wish. [emphasis added]

We also attempted to provide a fairly realistic estimate of the time commitment involved, noting that at least an hour or two would be needed, and leaving the maximum length open-ended. The letter concluded with a statement that they would soon be contacted by telephone:

Since understanding the family and its overall relationship to the community is so important, we do not want to hurry anyone or get only a partial story. Although we cannot estimate how long our meeting will take, we anticipate a visit of at least an hour or two. Our interviewer . . . will telephone you in the next few days. We hope it will be possible for you to talk to her and to make an appointment for a future

visit. Most women have found these sessions interesting and rewarding, and we look forward to meeting and
talking with you.

The telephone call was supposed to take place a day or
two after the letter was received, although sometimes it was
later than that. Additional explanation of the nature of the
study was sometimes necessary both by telephone and at the
beginning of the interview. Most of the mothers were willing
to participate once they understood the nature of the study:
41 of the 47 potential respondents were interviewed, and in
36 cases there were multiple interview sessions. Typically a
session ranged from one to two hours, and usually was
tape-recorded. Twelve of the women had a third session.
Total interview time ranged from two hours in one of the
single interview sessions to more than six hours, with the
average being between three and four hours.

All of the interviewing was done by one interviewer,
thereby providing relative consistency in the way questions
were asked and the kind of probing that was done. The
interview guide was basically a list of questions or topics to
be covered. The interviewer was not required to treat the
topics in the order given on the schedule, but rather to
conduct the session as naturally as possible. Interspersed
among the open-ended questions were several pages of
structured items, including questions on the demographic
characteristics of the family, and various standard indicators
of attitudes. The structured items had to do with marital
satisfaction, feelings about coping with duties and
organizations, and characteristics of the home environment
(quiet-noisy, organized-disorganized, warm-cold, and so on).

Characteristics of the Mothers and Their Families

All of the wives and their husbands were middle-aged
whites. The mothers ranged in age from 31 to 46, with a
median of 38. Their husbands were between 31 and 51 years
old, with a median age of 41.

Residential history. The 41 mothers were long-term
residents of Utah County. Over 40 percent of them had lived
in the county a decade or more, and the median length of
residence in the county was 15 years. They were
predominantly Western women: four out of five were from
Western states or Canada, with 18 native to Utah, seven
native to the Pacific states (Washington, Oregon, or
California), six others from the Mountain states (Arizona,

Colorado, or Idaho) and three from Canada. Their husbands were even more native to the West. Only one of the 41 husbands was born in a non-Western state, and 26 were native Utahans.

The mothers were also fairly long-term residents of their present neighborhoods. Only one in four had lived in her present family home less than five years, and the median number of years in residence in the present dwelling was seven. Two-thirds of the mothers said that before they had moved into their present home, they had lived elsewhere in Utah.

Marital history. All of these mothers had been married only once, and 40 of the 41 were still living with their husbands. The exception was a mother who had been divorced between the time of the birth of her last child and the time of the interview. She was functioning as a single parent, and all of her children were living with her.

Thirty-nine of the 40 women in the intact first marriages were married to men who were also in their first marriage. The one exception was married to a man who had been previously married and divorced.

Forty of the marriages had been performed under religious rather than civil auspices, with 38 out of 41 couples being married initially in a Latter-day Saint temple marriage. Two other couples who were first married by civil authority had subsequently married "for time and eternity" in a Latter-day Saint temple ceremony.

Education, occupation, and income. According to the records from which the sample was drawn, all of the husbands had completed college. According to the women, all except one husband had finished college, and that man had completed three years of college. Thirty-four of the women said that their husbands had taken post-graduate education of some kind. The median years of schooling completed by husbands was 18, compared to 16 for the wives.

The county statistics used in selecting the sample proved slightly in error about the mother's educational attainment also. According to the mothers themselves, 39 had completed college, one had finished two years and the other three years of university education. Nine of the mothers had completed at least one year of post-graduate schooling.

Judging by the husbands' occupations, the effort to limit the sample to middle- and upper-status families was successful. Thirty-five of the 41 husbands had professional occupations, and only two had blue-collar occupations. The families of teachers were overrepresented in the sample. Half of the husbands were teachers at either the university, secondary or elementary level, and most of these (14 of 20) were university teachers. In part, this overrepresentation of teachers is a reflection of the predominance of the education industry in Utah County. The non-teachers were essentially a cross-section of professionals, with accountants, engineers, physicians, dentists, journalists, and musicians represented. Other husbands were businessmen, insurance and real estate agents.

Four of the 41 mothers were employed outside the home at the time of the interview. Some others had home-based jobs. Eight women (20 percent) listed themselves as having an occupation, the most frequent being teacher at other than university level (four women) and writer, artist, or entertainer (two women). About one-third of the mothers said they had worked for pay sometime during the past year, and all but five had been employed at some time during their marriage.

Nine out of ten mothers reported a family income for the previous year (1978) of over $15,000, and half located their family income between $20,000 and $30,000. Only one family in six had an income of over $40,000. Plainly these are middle- and upper-middle-income families, and not upper-class families.

Religious participation. Forty of the mothers were Latter-day Saints, and one belonged to a Protestant denomination. None of the marriages was religiously mixed. All of the mothers were active churchgoers; 40 said they attended church services at least weekly, and one went at least monthly. Husbands' church attendance as reported by their wives was about the same as the wives' attendance, with 40 husbands attending at least weekly and one reported as attending several times a month. Thus, insofar as church attendance is defined as an indicator of religiosity, our respondents may be described as highly religious Latter-day Saint mothers who are the wives of highly religious husbands.

Thirty-nine of the mothers held a position in their church at the time of the interview, the most common being Visiting Teacher (13 women), and Spiritual Living Teacher in the Relief Society (four women). Sixteen of the mothers held at least two church positions. Their husbands were also active church leaders; all of them had some church position, with the most frequent being Stake High Councilman (six husbands), Bishop (four), Scoutmaster (four), and Sunday School Teacher (six).[4] Many of the remainder were counselors in bishoprics or priesthood quorum leaders. Twelve of the husbands held two or more church positions.

Fertility history. With the exception of the mother who had married a divorced man who already had several children and then had three children of her own, all of the respondents had had six[5] or more children. The number of children ever born to these women ranged from 3 to 12. All but one of the mothers had at least five children still living at home. The median number of children ever born to these women was eight, and the median number presently living at home was seven.

The mothers' experience with pregnancy is greater than the figures on family size indicate. Twenty-nine of the 41 mothers had had miscarriages or stillborn children. One mother in three had had one miscarriage, one in five had had two miscarriages, and five of the 41 mothers had had three or more miscarriages.

The median age at which these mothers had their first baby was 23; the range was from 19 to 31. Seven of them had not begun childbearing until age 25 or later.

Voluntary organizations. Most of these mothers did not claim membership in any voluntary organizations apart from

---

[4]Visiting Teachers belong to the Relief Society, the women's organization within the LDS Church. These teachers are assigned to visit other women in the congregation at least once a month. Spiritual Living Teachers teach lessons dealing with religious matters during the weekly Society meetings. The offices of Stake High Councilmen, Bishops, counselors in the bishoprics, and priesthood quorum leaders are considered responsible leadership positions within local church units.

[5]According to county records, all of the respondents were women with at least six children who had a seventh or subsequent birth in 1977, but two of the mothers said they only had six in all, excluding miscarriages.

their church. The seventeen who did belong to an organization were primarily involved in organizations related to their children's activities: 11 mothers said they belonged to parent-teacher associations, and two worked in 4-H Clubs. Ten of the women belonged to at least two organizations, and there were three "joiners" with three or more affiliations.

Marital satisfaction. Our respondents seemed to be very happily married. In fact, on several standard measures of marital satisfaction, they proved to be more satisfied than married women generally, despite the strains and challenges that presumably accompany life in large families. When asked to describe the happiness of their marriages on a five-point scale ranging from very unhappy to very happy, 29 (71 percent) selected the highest possible "very happy" category, and the rest marked the next category, "happy."

In interpreting these figures it must be remembered that most married people regard their marriages as happier than average. Even so, the 71 percent figure for "very happy" is extraordinary. In the 1980 statewide survey of married persons mentioned earlier, 43 percent of Utah wives described their marriages as "very happy," and an additional 37 percent checked the "happy" category.

The finding that these mothers of large families are more likely than married women generally to indicate high satisfaction with their marriages is corroborated in comparisons of their responses and statewide figures for two other items. Asked to rate how satisfying they thought their marriage was in comparison to the marriages of most other people, 27 (66 percent) selected the highest satisfaction category, "much more satisfying." In contrast, among married women in Utah in 1980, 40 percent said their marriage was "much more satisfying." Finally, both our survey on large families and the statewide survey contained the question, "If you had to do it over again, would you want to marry the same person?" Thirty-six of the mothers of large families (88 percent) checked the unqualified "yes, definitely" response, compared to 66 percent of married women in the statewide sample.

The remaining chapters of the book will deal with why these women have large families, how their households are organized and what actually happens in the home. Additionally, we shall explore the mothers' perceptions of themselves, their husbands, their marriages, and current women's issues.

Chapter II

DESTINY AND CHILDBEARING:

THE IMPACT OF RELIGIOUS BELIEF

* * * * *

Lo, children are an heritage of the Lord: and the fruit of the womb is his reward. As arrows are in the hand of a mighty man; so are children of the youth. Happy is the man that hath his quiver full of them. . . .

Psalms 127:3-5

Do not run faster or labor more than you have strength. . . .

Doctrine and Covenants 10:4

In many parts of the United States, families of six or seven children are a curiosity. For one thing, they are statistically deviant; there are not many families that large. They are sometimes also seen as deviant because the parents seem not to share the prevailing preference for "stopping at two." When large families travel outside of Utah, they are frequently subjected to various types of harrassment which boil down to the message, "You have too many children." Even in Utah, where large families are more common, there are often responses from friends or relatives which tell the mothers that they are having too many children or having them too close together.

In addition to the social pressures, which in Utah may favor large families but which in the rest of the country usually do not, there are the economic and emotional pressures which seem to generally favor the small family. Living space, parental time, and family finances must all be divided more intensively in a large family. Most of the disadvantages of large families mentioned by the mothers are variations on the theme that the ecological pressures--demands for space, time, money, organization, and effort--are more challenging in large families.

The mothers in our study identified two general advantages of large families. First, the large family was seen as a superior environment for human development in all its essential dimensions; and second, it was seen as a more enjoyable environment. It was claimed that large families are the ideal settings for the development and transmission of the traits of personal responsibility, tolerance, cooperativeness, patience, love for God and others, and the essential skills for successful living. Mothers described their lives in large families as a source of personal growth as well as a superior setting for their children. However, for most of the mothers, whether large families are more fun or better contexts for learning life's lessons are not the main reasons for their having many children. The main reasons are generally more religious in nature.

Religious Beliefs That Encourage Large Families

The mothers are almost unanimous in their statements that not every couple ought to have a large family and that decisions about the number or spacing of children are private and sacred and should involve only the couple and God. Although most of them would not prescribe their own priorities as suitable for all couples, they said they believed that they themselves ought to have large families. In fact, they are so convinced that their primary mission is rearing children that many of them, despite their large families, have also welcomed foster children into their homes.

The primary basis for the mothers' commitment to large families is religious. It was expressed in one or more of the following principles: 1) families have a destined number of children, determined by God or by agreement between God and the parents and the children involved,[1] and couples should continue having children until they receive a positive witness that they have completed their "assignment"; 2) Church authorities have counseled the Saints to have large families, and the obedient will do so; 3) birth control is

---

[1]Mormons believe all of mankind lived together as spirits in a premortal existence.

wrong (related to this is the idea that human procreation is ultimately in the hands of God, and people conform to His will by <u>not</u> interfering with the reproductive process and by <u>accepting</u> what comes); and, finally, 4) good families should have many children because otherwise, spirits are forced to come to earth in less desirable circumstances. We shall next consider each of these principles in more detail.

<u>Achieving one's destiny</u>. The sense of destiny, that there are a certain number of children meant for a couple, a number that one <u>should</u> have had, was voiced by several of the mothers. Laura, mother of eight children all under the age of 13, plus a teen-aged foster child, said she knew that if she had fewer children she could give more help to the ones she had in their schoolwork, extracurricular activities, and with enrichment activities such as family vacations. Nevertheless, she said that she had borne children that she was supposed to have, and that there would be compensations for whatever enrichment her children might have missed. Laura's physician had suggested she should stop after she had her sixth child. While she was carrying her eight, she told her husband, "I am going to quit after I have this one unless I have a real strong feeling that I <u>shouldn't</u> quit." She said she hadn't had any such feeling:

> We're through. It wasn't my choice--it was because we had to. I would have loved to have had more, but we had to quit. . . . I think it would have been easier [to have had fewer children or spaced them differently] but I don't think it would have been right, because I think that the way they came is the way they were supposed to come. And I just think, I keep saying, my time will come when I can do the things that those people do. And it will come. I just hope it doesn't come too late for the older ones.

Sometimes the feeling of destiny is more specific. One mother said that during their marriage ceremony, she and her husband were told "that the spirits that would become our children were in our presence in that sealing room in the Salt Lake Temple and awaited the consummation of our marriage." They were not told how many children to expect, but a vital sense of divine mission was imparted to them. This mother, now in her mid-forties, has eight children between two and twenty years in age and said she didn't expect to have any more. However, each of her past three children had initially been defined as perhaps the last one: "We've had three cabooses in a row. Each time we've had a new child we wondered, 'Now why is it that we had that child?' and we have seen the profound effect that that child has had on our growing, maturing family." In this mother's mind, all three cabooses had been intended to come to her family.

Another mother we interviewed had seven children between the ages of two and sixteen and was expecting her eighth. She said that she and her husband had never decided to have any set number of children, and that both of them were willing to exercise faith with respect to having them and caring for them. Her husband, she said approvingly, felt that "if the Lord wants us to have another one, He'll find a way to provide." She took the position that she really had no choice about the spacing and number of her children:

> I don't want you to misinterpret, but we haven't been given a choice as to how long we have between children. . . You just take what comes and do your best with what you've got. I didn't "plan" to have any. Planning hasn't been part of our family, I regret to say. No, I don't regret it. We are expecting another one. They all come as a surprise to us, even with birth control methods they come as a surprise to us. So we figure if it's going to happen, we'll take them. If they've got them, we'll take them.

Emily has ten living children, lost two others, and has had two miscarriages. She said she believed that her children were friends in the pre-existence, "And as we have brought new babies home there have been occasions where the veil is very thin and I think they have renewed old friendships."

Another mother who acknowledged the possibility that her children had known each other in the pre-existence, said she encouraged the children to do their share of the family work by trying to establish individual "friendship" ties with each of them:

> Their favorite story is about how we were all friends in the pre-existence, and we wanted to be friends together on earth, so even though I am their mother and they are my daughter or son, we're all good friends and you help your friend. I find that that works a lot better than coercing them to do things for me.

14

The sense of a destined number of children was also expressed by another mother of seven, who had recently had a miscarriage: "I would like to have another one; I guess because of the miscarriage I had, I feel like there's one more there for me at least."

Another statement of the notion that there are a certain number of spirits waiting to join a particular family was given by a mother who has ten children aged thirteen and under, plus a foster child. She said that she and her husband had once planned to have eight children, but now they had ten, and she thought they might have more:

> I'm one of those people who can get pregnant any time. Well, see, we had it all planned--we were going to have four girls and four boys, and we had four girls and three boys. Then along came a daughter and goofed up the whole thing. Then we had to have our other boy. Then we had to have another girl to go with our youngest girl because she was getting to be such a spoiled little brat down there in the middle of all the boys. So now I don't know what we'll do, but as long as I have good health and we can support them and what not, there is no reason why we shouldn't. You see, we always say that there is a log up in heaven and here sit all of these little spirits waiting for the Lord to put their ears on so they can be born. We just don't know how many there are still up there sitting on the log, but every one of these kids we have known. Even if I was still kind of tired from the last one, I have known that it was time to get pregnant again.

This mother said that she believed that in the pre-existence she promised, "to bring these children down here and to give them the safety of a good, strong home where they can be taught." She said her husband had had a dream which he interpreted to mean that "we must have promised the entire family we would bring these children in here." And as a result, she said, "We just seem to know when we're supposed to have another one or if we're not supposed to have any more."

One mother said that she thought that the Lord took care of the spacing of her children and said she hoped her own children would have as many children as they could because "they ought to have as many children as they can have, because in my personal belief, I think that is what the Lord wants us to do, whether you can afford them or not."

LIFE IN LARGE FAMILIES

This mother had nine children between ages two and seventeen, and at the time of the interview was expecting her tenth. She described her view of the Lord's assignment for her this way:

> Well, we're still going to have all that's possible. We're just not going to have twenty. I had two or three miscarriages, so that took a while. We're still planning on having all the Lord has for us, but I for one am hoping He doesn't have very many more. I was hoping He didn't have any more after our last one. In fact, I never ever in my prayers managed to say that I was willing to have another one until just before I got pregnant this time. Before that I said, "I really don't want any more." So, I guess the Lord was just waiting for me to be willing.

A mother who had eleven children between the ages of two and nineteen described some of the negative reactions she had received from relatives and then emphasized the religious motivation behind her decision to have a large family:

> My philosophy is, I would love to have as many as the Lord wants me to have, and that He'll help me to take care of. So it's a religious thing, it's kind of a spiritual thing with me. It's more of an emotional thing with my husband. I mean, he's had a hard time with the last few wondering if he could financially take care of us all. . . . He can see that if there's a never-ending amount of children, that it would be . . . it has been a little harder for him that way.

Later in the interview she again affirmed her feeling that her choices about childbearing had been in line with God's wishes: "I would do exactly the same because I was really inspired to do the way I was doing. But because of the difficult situations that arise in your marriage, sometimes you look back and you think, "Oh, do I have to have this burden, or do I have to have this cross to bear?" Later she amended her statement slightly, saying that if she could have, she would have had more children.

An illustration of the need to learn that one had "done one's part" was given by a mother with seven children aged fifteen and under. She said she had at one point thought they would stop at five, then she and her husband made it a matter of prayer, and now they were convinced that seven children was the right number for them:

When I had five children, I decided that that's all I could handle. I didn't want anymore, and I prayed about it for a long time, and I didn't feel good for--didn't have much energy or strength--for about six months after I had my fifth one. . . . I had the attitude then that if I had any more kids, I just might as well go out and shoot myself. I really, really felt like I was up to here with it. Then I got an answer as to how many more children I would have and what they would be, and this surprised me because I was praying whether or not I should have six or if I should stop at five, and I was told that I would have seven. So that's why I feel like I've got my seven and I'm through.

Maybe I'm being too personal, but there was a time when I thought you were really committing a sin if you ever had a tubal ligation. My sister had it done after her fifth one, and for many years I thought she had really done the wrong thing, and looking back on it now, I can see that her nerves cannot take any more children than five. And as it turned out, about a year after she had this done, she couldn't have any more children anyway, and she knew when she was going in for that surgery that it was the wrong thing to do. She had some physical problems. . . .

Like I was recently talking to a doctor. "When you decide that you're through having your family," he said, [then she should come see him]. "I know . . . [a prominent local Church official's] wife who came in and had a tubal ligation because they decided five was all they wanted, and they're not going to be excommunicated for stopping at five."

If that's what they want, and that's what they feel best about, they've gone to the Lord and talked it over and got an answer as to how many children they should have and so on, then fine. It's a personal matter. It's a sacred matter. If someone wants to stop at three and it's the right thing, then they're doing the right thing. I don't think that Mormons should say, "Well, hum, they only have three children, what's wrong with them? Why aren't they living their religion," or something like this.

The mission of fertile motherhood was beautifully exemplified in the life of a mother of ten children who told how, after their second child was born, she and her husband were counseled by a physician to not have any more children. So they had some foster children come to live with them, and soon her physical health had improved to the extent that they were able to have another child of their own. She defined the coming of her later children as the result of a Priesthood blessing:

> We were given the blessing that there were other spirits that were to bless our home, and that through our faithfulness they would come to us, so that's how they came.

She said that after her last child was born, her husband said to her that he had a strong feeling that they were not to have any more children, and that she herself now felt content that there weren't any more children that were meant to come to them:

> So I've had a lot of pregnancies and I've had all the problems. . . . I feel like we each have a mission here on earth to perform and I feel like anything short of the ten children that I have would have been short. For someone else, maybe they don't have the qualities of patience and the ability to cope with some of these circumstances that are necessary in a large family situation, but on the other hand, they have time to serve in ways that I will never serve.

<u>Church leaders recommend large families.</u> "The Prophet says it's a good thing to have a family," said Judy, "but you do what you can. And I think he makes it clear it's an individual thing according to the mother's health. You decide if it is a good thing to have a family and if you can have more, then that's fine. So we're trying to do our best to follow the counsel of the Prophet." Judy's "best" was eight children between the ages of two and eighteen. "As far as the Gospel is concerned," she said, "we're trying to do what we feel is right. . . . When I look at other mothers having children close together, I think they are doing the right thing."

For some, the ideal of the large family takes on the force of a commandment. One of the mothers said, "We're kind of thinking about ten, or what works out. We've got seven now." She went on to say that she'd like her children to have large families, partly because she herself enjoys large families, and partly because:

It's a commandment for one thing. I just really feel like if they can, they should. I think that many blessings can come from having large families.

This same woman included in the statement of the large-family ethic a more overriding priority to do the Lord's will as it applied in one's own specific situation:

You don't know all the circumstances so you can't say people with smaller families aren't good Mormons. Maybe they are completely, and Heavenly Father has told them not to have more, you don't know.

Two other mothers expressed similar concerns about inferring someone's righteousness from the number of children she had:

I worry sometimes in that the number of children we are having might be a label that we're looking for as far as righteousness' sake, or whatever. We might be using this large family as a means of saying, "Look, I'm following advice," or "I'm following the counsel of the Church," or "Look at me, my family's larger--I'm a better person." I hope that we're not doing that, but sometimes I question.

I know we somehow equate having all the children you can with gaining exaltation or something like that in this Church. . . . [There is the idea that] unless you are gung ho about it and try to have as many children as you can, you might not make the Celestial Kingdom. . . . It's kind of a funny attitude we have, and again I still say it's a prayerful matter for the parents to decide how many children they should have.

Another mother of seven expressed the cultural value, "I know we should have large families," but she was sure that her seven fulfilled both the letter and the spirit of the law, and she said she didn't think they would have any more:

I think I've bitten off just as much as I can handle. If I had any more I'd be surprised, although my husband keeps saying, "Do we want to raise him [the baby] all by himself?" and I say, "He's not all by himself. He's got all these other kids." But the youngest one before him is five, so he is kind of off by himself. But I'm forty now and I'm getting up there and I feel like I've multiplied the earth quite a bit. I've done my share.

Birth control is wrong. The perceptions of an official anti-birth control ethic were best expressed by a mother who described her "conversion story." At the time of the interview, she had nine children, the eldest being thirteen. She said that she and her husband had waited three years before having their first child, then two years before having another. Then they moved to Utah County:

> We came back to Utah, and because I can take a class [at the University] without having to pay for it, I do that. I take an evening class each semester, and those classes that I got into, I was being bombarded with information against birth control. I was just getting statement after statement. I don't know how I missed that growing up, but I did, and it concerned me. I struggled through it because I still had this idea in my head that I ought to be able to choose. I could not let myself go and not know what was going to happen. I wanted that control over my life. But I still knew what all of these statements said, and I had quite a collection. I've kept it.
>
> I prayed about that over a period of months, that the Lord would help me be in tune with what He wanted for me, that I wouldn't try to rationalize or intellectualize, that I would see and that I would feel. More importantly, that I would feel, not just have a surface conviction, and I really did. I felt that change, and our third baby came fifteen months after the second. The next was fifteen months after that, and sixteen, and eighteen, and back to fourteen. I no longer worry about that at all. It is almost a complete change, that I put so much worry into thinking, "What will I do if I have ten children?" I realized that I never would have ten children from two; you don't go from two to ten or from three to ten, you just add one at a time. All of that worrying was so silly because it is a very natural increase, not all of a sudden, having something that you had never been prepared for.

This mother summarized her conversion by saying that she hoped to have more children, because "where we are right now is that we have planned not to plan." She is fully convinced that what she is doing is the right thing, and she told how whenever they had a new baby they emphasized to their other children how fortunate they were, so that their children would appreciate large families and not be taken in by the media statements favoring small families or childlessness:

> What would we do without our new baby? Everybody relates to that. What would we do if we didn't have so-and-so, or so-and-so, or so-and-so? What if we only had three children, then we would not have this child. Whenever we see anything like that, or whenever anybody expresses negative feelings about families, we talk about how that is Heavenly Father's plan for us. Families are the place to be happy. It is the way it is meant to be. Heaven is families. But I don't know other than praying about it, how we can get the girls they [the boys] are going to marry to be taught the same way. I hope there are other people, and I am sure there are, but I hope there are enough of them to go around.

Helping the spirits come. Sometimes the idea surfaces that parenthood was performing a service to an eternal being. Said one mother: "I have an opportunity to help someone else by bringing a child into the world, by bringing a spirit."

Lana, who had eight children between the ages of two and eighteen, was expecting her ninth at the time of the interview. She stated her view of the Church philosophy about families this way:

> Generally, we feel that it's the LDS philosophy that there are spirits that need bodies and that we should have as many children as we can physically and emotionally handle. We think about the alternatives--if a spirit didn't come to our home, it might have to go to this home, or this home, or this part of the world, or in this situation. Having travelled a fair amount, the children have seen different situations, and looking at the alternatives, they welcome them into our home and are willing to share.

As a result of that philosophy, Lana said that she planned to have more children, and that she would encourage her children to have as many as they could. Lana's children are approximately two years apart. She said that if she could relive her married life, she would like to have "a few more children."

LIFE IN LARGE FAMILIES

A mother of nine children, all under age thirteen, was expecting her tenth when we interviewed her. She said that if people felt guilty about having only a few children, maybe there was a reason for them to feel defensive, "Maybe they are fighting their own conscience or something." However, no one had a right to criticize:

> You can't just say, yes, she should feel guilty; she is not doing her share of getting all the spirits down here or something like that. Nobody has a right to say that to anybody else.

But while the size of each person's "contribution" to the job was left open, the nature of the job was not. Motherhood meant doing one's part in "getting all the spirits down here."

Another woman, who had had seven children within a ten-year period and was expecting her eighth at the time of the interview, illustrated how personal coping capacity interacts with feelings that one ought to provide bodies for all the spirits one can. Her statement also suggests an underlying anxiety that perhaps there is some kind of shortage of earthly bodies, either generally or in specific types of families, such that some of the waiting spirits are "really desperate to come."

> We have about as many as we can handle for a while. . . . Eight really is a nice, even number. . . . Hopefully we are about to the end of having children, although we would hate to turn anyone away who was really desperate to come. But we feel like we are just about to the point where we are overwhelmed--can't handle any more. Actually, we feel like we've passed that point. So that in five years, hopefully, as I would visualize it, we would no longer have a baby in diapers, which would be a very unusual thing.

The Validity of Personal Differences

Despite their own sense that a large family is a part of their destiny, that the Church encourages large families, and their belief in a theology which suggests that many spirits wait anxiously to be born into good homes, most of the mothers are quite careful not to generalize their "mission motherhood" perspective to others who are not suited by temperament or family situation to manage large families. These mothers may believe that motherhood is better than non-motherhood and that many children are better than few children, but most also believe that couples should exercise their own agency in deciding how many children to have. The consensus is that being a parent in a large family is not a role prescribed for everyone.

Large families are not for everyone. Many statements about whether people ought to have large families were provoked by this story:

> After a Relief Society lesson about the benefits of a large family, Mrs. Hawkes was defensive about having only three children, adding that she and her husband felt that was all they should have. Should she have felt guilty? How do you feel about women who have three children?

The typical initial response was that Mrs. Hawkes should not feel guilty, that her family size was a personal marital decision. A few mothers went on to say that maybe her defensiveness was an indication that she was not convinced in her own mind that three was all she should have. Although most said they thought she shouldn't feel guilty, they felt people should have their children for the right reasons. If Mrs. Hawkes was at peace with herself, then it was no one's business how many children she had, and she should not take the lesson personally. Many of the mothers went on to say that they believed there were many women whose personal make-up or marital situation was such that it would be a mistake for them to have many children.

For instance:

> I think it is a very personal matter, and some people can cope with it and roll with the punches and some can't. I think the secret is to be content with what you have, be it many or few. We just happened to be blessed with ten.

> I think it's terrible to have children just because somebody else thinks you ought to have them. That's not a good reason. If you only want three children, fine.

> The blessings from having a large family are really great, but it depends on how much you can tolerate. The pressures of big families are just hard--I am not kidding.

Children are a great thing, but you can overdo it if
you have too many and you don't properly train them.
There are some families that, whether big or small,
they haven't taken time to teach their kids what's
right or wrong and to discipline their kids as they go
along. And they end up with a lot of problems. The
kids don't have happy lives.

The mothers we talked to, with only one or two
exceptions, did not feel that the Church was pressuring
people to have more children than they ought to have. But
many of them did say that the people in the Church sometimes
took things as blanket statements applying to everyone when
they were meant to be interpreted according to each family's
individual situation. They said they knew people who felt
pressured to have large families, and they didn't think that
was right.

A mother who has eight children between the ages of two
and seventeen, and who said she would like to have another
baby, said that she didn't feel that a large family was
appropriate in many situations.

The mother's health, the financial situation, not only
her physical health, but also her mental health . . .
and the place where they're rearing the children [all
should be considered]. Trying to cram a lot of
children into a little home where they don't have many
benefits, I don't think that's right either, and I
don't think our Church is teaching us how many
children to have. It has to be an individual thing.

Other mothers repeated the same theme:

I think it's sad for people to feel like maybe they're
pressured by the Church. The Church says to have big
families, but maybe there are some people who just
emotionally can't handle a lot of children, and it
would be sad for children if they weren't well cared
for in a home that was happy. I don't know--I can see
where there are people who probably shouldn't have a
lot of children.

If a woman has found that she is taxed having three
children, then I don't think it is a blessing for
those three children or herself or her family to have
any more, and I don't think she should feel guilty. I
don't think the commandment we are given to multiply
and replenish is a blanket statement. In fact, I

think if people would read closely the statement that
is given out by the First Presidency about birth
control, they state that it should depend on the
woman's emotional health. They say that. And they
take other things into consideration about people.
Because I just can't believe that the Lord intended
for us to have more children than we are capable of
handling. It doesn't do anyone any good to have a
mother who is falling apart, having a nervous
breakdown.

What these expressions boil down to is that most of the
mothers accept family planning in principle, although perhaps
not for themselves. That is, they think people should have
as many children as they <u>want</u>. None of them thought it
would be a good thing for an unwelcome child to be born into
a family, and almost universally they said that decisions about
family size were the couple's responsibility and that others
should not interfere. In their own experience, however, a
substantial number of these mothers had the attitude that
they were willing to accept and welcome as many children as
the Lord was willing to give them. Several remarked that
they didn't plan their babies; they just had them. This
almost fatalistic acceptance of whatever happened in the
matter of their own fertility as being God's will, was not the
majority view, but it was not uncommon.

Many of the comments about people's differing capacities
to handle large families had to do with how rapidly a mother
had children, rather than the total number of her offspring.
Of course, the two concerns are closely related; other things
being equal, mothers who have births one after another will
end up with larger families than mothers who space their
births two or three years apart.

<u>Attitudes on how many, how often</u>. Ideas about how
often a woman should bear a child, and perceptions of social
pressure which either encouraged or discouraged additional
fertility were obtained in the mothers' reactions to this story:

The Browns have had six children in eight years and
some of their relatives think they have had too many
children too fast. Mrs. Brown's mother suggests to
her daughter that maybe they should "slow down." What
do you think of this situation?

Most of the responses emphasized that people were different
and that what the daughter should do depended on her
assessment of her own personal and family situation. Here is

a typical reason: "I think it's possible for six children in eight years to be emotionally devastating to a family, but I don't think it always is. I don't think six children in eight years is too much for everybody."

Another woman noted that people have different thresholds of tolerance for handling children, and whether a set of births is too fast or too slow depends on the parental personalities and family characteristics. She said that some of her friends had hit that tolerance threshold at three children, some at five, some at twelve, and some she wasn't sure would ever hit it.

Statements affirming the differences among women in the capacity to deal with a large family included a reference to one woman's sister who "simply doesn't have the nerve control to handle any more [she had four]," to people who would "just crack up over the situation." One mother put it this way:

> I think that some people shouldn't have any children.
> Some people should only have two or three because that is all they are capable of [having and] being calm. I probably should have only had two or three [but she had eight]. You know, we have different personalities. You should think about economics, but the main thing is your emotional state. I don't think you should say, "I'm a Mormon and we have big families, therefore, I am going to have a big family." That is just ridiculous to me. I've seen too many awful things happen where a mother has a nervous breakdown or has to be completely taken away from the children just because that isn't her thing.

Another echoed these sentiments:

> It is wrong to have children one couldn't care for. And I mean take care of the children, not have a big family and then push them off on somebody else to take care of, but take care of them, teach them, love them.

"Right" reasons for having children. Most mothers said that it was not right to have children unless you were willing and able to care for them. At least half explicitly excluded financial pressures as valid reasons for limiting one's family. Others thought it appropriate to consider physical as well as spiritual and emotional resources in the decision to have a baby.

Although not every mother dealt with financial resources
specifically, among those who did, most seemed to feel that in
America in the present economic situation, one should have
children and have faith that one would be able to support
them. Several recognized that people in other nations might
face more difficult circumstances and might be justified in
having fewer children. It should be remembered that most of
these mothers have husbands who are employed in
professional occupations, and their statements about financial
pressures must be interpreted from their middle- to upper-
income perspective.

"I believe that you should have the number of children
that you can have for the right reason," said one, "I mean,
if we had decided to limit our family because of financial or
convenience kinds of things, I'd feel we were guilty."
Talking about whether her children might have large families,
a mother revealed her own priorities:

I know I would be disappointed if I felt they were
willingly limiting the size of their family because of
reasons other than extremely bad health or something
like that. I don't think there are financial reasons
for limiting family size.

Another mother said that a shortage of money wasn't
enough reason to put off having more children, because "I
don't think you can ever know what you are going to have in
money."

The space problems experienced by many of these
families are related to financial problems. If they could
afford it, many of them would have larger homes. One woman
explained how she rationalized away her need for more living
space:

My husband settles my worries every once in a while
when I speak about this particular problem, when he
mentions that the pioneer parents raised their
families in a log cabin, which was a one-room home.
Their children for the most part were very excellent
and well-behaved, good citizens. They seem to have
had a lot less problems than most of the children you
see nowadays. And so I can't use that as a real
disadvantage. The roof over my head not being big
enough isn't really that big of a problem.

In direct contrast is the mother who responded to the story about the woman having six children in eight years with this statement:

> If they can't handle them in their situation, if their living situation isn't good, if their home is too small and all these things, then I'm saying that they shouldn't have had them that fast. . . . You've got to be able to take care of them. If you can't take care of them, then you shouldn't have that many. . . . A lot of people will have that many and they can't take care of them really like they should--keep them dressed right and train them right and do all these things.

One of the mothers whose family was well-off financially approached the issue of finances from a different perspective. She said that both the need to make enough money and for self-fulfillment were critical elements in being able to manage a large family. One of the most desirable characteristics for a husband to have, she said, was to be able to support his family.

> I think that's really important, since we've got friends and it's really rough on them because he just can't, and he never has. They're always in debt, in the hole, and it's terrible. Then you look at that and you think, "I really appreciate the fact that my husband can go out and really earn enough money."

A thoughtful commentary on the kinds of factors people should consider in making family-size decisions was given by Charlotte, a mother of seven children aged fourteen and under:

> I think that sometimes women think it's their obligation to have a baby every so often, and I don't think this is right. I really don't, because you don't realize, now, when these six children are eight and younger, their demands are different. But with children, the demands keep on, and when your kids are teenagers, the demands are different. What am I trying to say? I think that you can handle all of those little babies at once, but then they get harder. Then when you've got all of this and then _more_ little babies to handle, it becomes really hard on the mothers--really, really hard on the mothers. It depends on the husband, too, and how many demands he

expects. Husbands are a lot of work, and they take a lot.

Charlotte went on to say that in a case where a husband was really willing to pitch in and work right beside his wife, it might be possible to have six children in eight years and have it come out beautifully. But she advised couples to be sure that was the kind of relationship they had. She especially thought that a competitive situation in which the number of children was seen as some kind of a mark on the spirituality of the family was a mistake.

> I think a lot of times that being a parent becomes a competitive thing--I really do. It becomes a competitive thing between women, and then the children suffer. In too large a family, you watch those oldest children, and they're out of the home by age sixteen and seventeen. It is not fair to those older children because there is no way you can do it alone, and so they start part of the parenting role--they have to. I don't think that's good. That's not fair to them; it's not fair to the other ones. . . . I think you have to be really careful about it and definitely not make it a competitive thing. Some women's temperament--some women are easier going, but I think you have to be really careful because I don't think you give [enough when there are too many children]. A child's needs, their physical needs are a lot, but it isn't the whole, total thing. They need schooling, they need to be encouraged, and you've seen all of these big families. I know there's a big family--this lady had a lot of children--but I never saw her to a ball game with one of her boys. That's just not fair. It's not fair to have more children than the situation can handle.

Child-Spacing: Attitudes About Birth Intervals

The women generally stated one of three main notions about how one's children should be spaced. They were: (1) parents should exercise little or no control over the spacing of their children; rather, just let them come as they come; (2) it is better for parents to have all of their children fairly quickly, with relatively little space between births, so that the children know each other well and grow up as a cohesive group, and the child-birth years, while intense, do not stretch out too long; (3) it is better to have one's children more gradually so that the pressures on the parents and on the siblings are minimized and mothers have more time to devote to each new child.

Laissez-faire child-spacing. Some of the attitudes about leaving matters of family fertility totally to Providence were illustrated in the sections above on "achieving one's destiny" and "birth control is wrong." We will not treat them in detail here, except to quote some of the mothers who took the position that they did not consciously space their children:

> I never planned any child I've had. I don't do that, I just have them.

> I didn't plan on having the number I got. I just got them and I will probably do the same thing with any that come. I take them as they come. . . [Asked if she would change anything if she had to do it over again] I didn't have any control over it in the first place so I don't think I would control it in the second.

> Where we are right now is that we have planned not to plan.

The rapid-sequence approach. The high density approach to having a large family is to have children as rapidly as possible, or nearly so, so that a couple arrives at the number they define as "their share" or their destiny, and yet the parents are still relatively young. The reasons given for this approach include the idea that younger parents are physically more capable of dealing with the stresses that come with a houseful of children; that it is easier to meet the children's needs if they are two years or less apart; that it is better for the children to have brothers and sisters near themselves in age rather than to have three or four year gaps between them; and that the parent's life consists of several well-defined stages rather than having grown children, teenagers, grade school children and preschoolers all at the same time. There is also the argument that the parents are young enough, because they had the children quickly, to share in the recreational and social pursuits of the children to some extent. The idea is that family solidarity is enhanced because the size of the "generation gap" between parents and their children is minimized. The rapid-sequence approach also implies that the last child is grown up and out of the home by the time the parents reach late middle-age.

Here are two mothers' justifications for the rapid-sequence approach:

> Our decision to have a large family was our own and they're close because my husband didn't want to be older when he was trying to play with the boys and do things with the boys, and we felt very strongly about that, so that's just our own opinion. We didn't want to stretch having 7 or 8 children out over 20 years. A lot of people do that. I like to have them when I'm healthy and I can be with them and do things with them, and then stop.

> Some people have said, "Oh, isn't it hard to have them that close?" To me, it would be much harder to have them spaced three, four, or five years apart, because you would already be moving into an area of new freedom, and you would maybe begrudge a little bit having to do things that you didn't have to do just a short time before. I have heard people talk about that: "I hated to get out the diaper pail," or "I hated to be confined to my home when I wanted to do this." I haven't felt that . . . I know everybody can't have it that way. It was not meant to be that way for some reason, but I am quite happy it is that way in our family.

One argument given for the rapid-sequence approach is that it allows a couple to have their babies while they are able to, rather than waiting until some future time when circumstances may have changed, perhaps because of the death of one of the parents or the onset of disease. The basic idea seems to be that one should have the children as fast as one can because one may not always be able to have them. Several of the mothers were very concerned that the consequences of procrastinating childbearing often were that one doesn't have children at all, or has fewer than one could have had. Here is one expression of this statement:

> I think as I observe people that sometimes they space them and put it off and they get to the point where they can't have them or something. There's things that you don't know beforehand that you can't predict that are real tragedies . . . Have your family while you're young because it is a strain on your health. It taxes everything, and so have them while you're young, and have them so they can be together and enjoy each other's companionship. . . . We have had them close, some of them think they all just hatched

31

together. They don't remember anyone else being a baby or something like that. They have just always been together, and so we didn't have any trouble with jealousy of one child when another one was born.

The gradual approach. An alternative view held by some was that mothers should continue to have children throughout the child-bearing years, but having a space of two or more years between children. This more gradual approach to the childbearing was seen as better for the mother and the children, because it provided more individual time for each new baby, and was more likely to produce a situation where there were older children competent to help. The mothers who favored this approach also viewed it as reducing the stress on the parents, because they were less likely to have several children in any particular age range.

There was also a perception that even though many mothers might be able to handle large families, some couldn't manage it if the children came too quickly. Responding to the story about the mother who had six children in eight years, one said: "Some mothers can handle it. I don't know that I could handle having children that fast. I don't think I could, even though I'm rather calm I think it would be very hard."

Here are some corroborative statements:

I think two years is just about right, unless the mother's health is a problem, because they are close enough to be close to each other and yet not so close that you've got two little tiny ones to worry about at the same time. If they get too close, then it is awfully hard on the mother to have two babies tugging at her and another one in her arms. I think it would be hard emotionally on the mother although some people are capable of doing that. You know, some women it doesn't phase them at all to have three or four little ones, preschoolers. I think that if it is too much then the kids don't feel close to each other.

I think it is possible to have too many too fast. You can't meet all their needs. We find that, and ours are two years apart. But sometimes you simply can't react to each person and fill their needs as they should be met . . . I'm not saying how many, but just spread them out.

A woman who had both teen-aged children and very small children concluded:

> I'm glad I had them spaced like it was, I really am, although a lot of people think it is better to get them all over at once like it's a drudgery. I think it makes your life feel fulfilling to have the different ages. Like having a second family. I like it like that. It's neat when these younger brothers look up and have this older brother on a mission and they are learning so much from them.

* * * * *

The mothers in our sample were generally happy with the number and frequency of their children and felt they were doing the "right" thing from a religious point of view. Most were quick to add, however, that the choices they had made and the large family situation in which they found themselves was not necessarily right for everyone. They reaffirmed all couples' right and responsibility to choose for themselves their family size and to feel good about the choice.

Chapter III

SOCIAL PRESSURES AND CHILDBEARING:

"IT'S NOBODY'S BUSINESS"

* * * * *

After all, children are not just transients in the
world's boardinghouse, to be welcomed or turned away
at the convenience of the older boarders. And if it
is true that every newborn child should have a right
to its share of food, it is also true that those who
control the food supply should think twice before
declaring that they no longer have enough for
strangers and newcomers. In other words, the essence
of the population problem--so far, at least--is not
that mankind has propagated too many children but that
it has failed to organize a world in which they can
grow in peace and prosperity.

--Otto Friedrich[1]

[Physicians should] discourage fertility itself . . .
in order to diminish the amount of adult stupidity,
which itself is a form of social pollution, and a most
dangerous one. It may be difficult for an
obstetrician to bring himself to discourage exuberant
fertility among his patients, but his civic
responsibility is clear.

--Garrett Hardin[2]

---

[1]Time, Sept. 13, 1971, p. 59.

[2]Everybody's Guilty: The Ecological Dilemma," California
Medicine, Vol. 113, (November, 1970), pp. 45-46.

"Today," said the teacher, "we have a special activity. We're going to have a survey and find out how many brothers and sisters we all have. First, how many have no brothers and sisters?" There was a scattering of raised hands across the third-grade classroom. "How many have one brother or sister?" Many more hands went up. "Fine. How many are from families of three children, how many have two brothers or sisters?" Now there were only a few raised hands. Even fewer responded that they had three brothers or sisters. When the teacher asked about families with five children, the same hand went up.

Thus targeted, the child from a Mormon family of six children found herself the object of cutting questions and negative comments. She remembered, as she explained the experience to her parents, that both the teacher and the other children had said things like, "Oh, how terrible." Her mother said that the incident provoked a family crisis, and the child became physically ill.

> You know, they were asking her like she was some kind of really weird, awful person and she came home and vomited and was really, really upset. We spent a lot of time with her. I thought that we had resolved the problem but the next day she came home and said, "Guess what? The teacher did that in all the classes and I wasn't the worst one. There was one that had eight." So even after all the time we had spent, she called herself the worst--almost the worst--because we had six. You know, little kids in the second and third grade would say to them, "How many do you have in your family?" even though they knew how many. They would be their good friends, and just kind of harass them.

This kind of negative pressure against large families was one of the reasons this mother and father moved from California to Utah. After moving here, they had two more babies.

Social Pressure Discouraging Large Families

The mothers share the view that the nation as a whole, and much of the world, is prejudiced against the large family. Most of the mothers we interviewed would agree with the one who said, "Society, in general, really frowns on a large family . . . they think you're crazy or something, or they think you're not conserving resources, or you're unpatriotic."

LIFE IN LARGE FAMILIES

Most of the mothers said they encountered thoughtless, anti-large family attitudes--"There are always people around who feel that some families are too large"--but they were most aware of the negative attitudes when they traveled outside the state.

Encounters while traveling. For many large families, a long trip with all of the children along is a severe financial and sometimes emotional trial. As a result, many large families do much less traveling and vacationing in distant places than they would prefer. Almost every large family that does travel encounters people who are prejudiced against large families, and others to whom large families are a curiosity. There were reports that "if you go into a restaurant and take all of the children, you are aware that people are looking at you, you become a little uncomfortable with the whole flock with you." People on the freeway, driving alongside, turn around and very obviously try to count how many children are in the car. One father got into the habit of holding up his fingers to show the number of children, so that the straining onlookers, the "counters," wouldn't have an accident.

None of the mothers suggested that prejudice against the large family was universal either in other states or in foreign nations. Many people were remembered as being supportive and helpful. Sometimes the mothers expected to receive negative reactions and were pleasantly surprised when they didn't. But prejudice against large families, like other forms of prejudice, need not be universal or even a majority view, to hurt.

Another mother described the vacations with the children:

> I have seen people stop and just count them and shake their heads and things like that. In Utah we have seven and that really isn't a big family. Here it is 12, 13 and 14 kids that are considered a large family, so we feel like we fit in. That was one of the reasons we left California, was that we had four children, and people just couldn't understand--I was pregnant with the fifth--what we were doing with that many kids. We do tend to take them a lot of places.

Many parents reported similar experiences. A family took six children on a tour of England, and "people looked us all over; they just wrenched their necks driving down the road." In midwestern America one family was not served at a restaurant because they had too many children. Children in this same family, living in a midwestern state, felt the stigma of being from a large family to the extent that the oldest son came home from school and told his mother, "If you have another baby, I'm leaving."

Large families are a focus of attention whether they travel "in style," using motels and restaurants, or "rough it." A mother of nine said that on camping vacations people in the campground will hear about them and come visit their campsite just to be sure. They make comments like, "I have never seen so many people in one car."

While living for a time in a foreign country, a husband was told by his wife's physician, "Your wife is not a machine," and he lectured her, "you had better slow down." Later, back in Utah, following her seventh child in ten years, her physician said she was healthy and had no apparent problems. She interpreted the foreign doctor's statements as deriving from his attitude about large families. She said that in the foreign country people would stare at them, treat them as a novelty, but also there were frequent positive remarks, such as "what beautiful children." They received much stronger negative pressure in California.

Local social pressures. In Utah there are at least two kinds of pressures related to family size. First, there is a social expectation that parents will have several children. A family of four or five children seems to be the acceptable middle ground between too little and too much fertility. There are many larger families but parents of eight, nine or ten children begin to experience another kind of social pressure. If they have their children fairly close together, the mothers in particular, are often subject to advice from their own mothers or other close relatives that they should slow down. Most of the mothers we interviewed had had more children than their own mothers had had, and so by generational standards, their own families were defined as very large. Sometimes on seventh and subsequent pregnancies, the mothers reported that they began getting negative comments not only from relatives and friends who lived outside of Utah, but even from people within their own neighborhoods and wards [church congregations]. Often the comments are couched in terms of concern that a family will be able to care for all of its children, or that a mother will be able to maintain her physical and mental health. Whatever the underlying motivation, expressions such as "maybe you shouldn't have gotten pregnant" or "maybe you should have waited" are viewed as offensive by many mothers. Some respond to the perceived pressure from parents and other associates by putting off announcing their pregnancy as long as possible, or by not taking their youngest baby with them on errands or visits lest the young age of their baby and visible pregnancy provoke negative comments.

On the other hand, if a couple put off having children, or have a gap between babies of more than three or four years, then some people make comments about "not doing their share" or "having a crop failure." Outside of Utah, the pressures are seen as being much more uniform. There is a single dominant message. Small families are preferred. Anything beyond two children is apt to be seen by some as "excess fertility."

Most of the mothers said that the Utah County region is very supportive of large families, but at the same time, almost everyone had received pressure from relatives, both in Utah and elsewhere, to slow down their childbearing. A mother of ten told us that every time she is pregnant, her mother-in-law says things like, "Don't you think you should slow down? You have so many children that you can't give them the opportunities in education . . . you won't be able to have them all take piano lessons, and they'll be deprived." As a result, this mother says, "Every time I get pregnant, that's the worse thing I have to do is tell my mother-in-law. I don't like to tell people I'm pregnant; that's the worst thing." When she finally does confront her mother-in-law, she says something like, "I'm pregnant; there's nothing you can do about it."

A mother of seven children said of her friends and of her sister, "They think I'm having too many." She also gets negative feedback when she leaves her seven children and "gets away" on trips for a few days with her husband. She said her children and her parents-in-law accept her new pregnancies, but "my mother doesn't think it's fine. She is from the school of 'You should have two children and that's probably it; how can you afford it' kind of stuff. She gets very upset when she finds out I'm having another baby."

Another mother of seven children said that she and her husband were both from small families:

> So when we had ours, just one right after the other, we
> have always gotten lectured. To me it is nobody's
> business besides my husband's and mine. If we feel
> like we can handle it, and we can love them and can
> afford them, then we should have as many as we want. I

38

would never think of telling his mother that I thought three was such a low number, that I think she should have had six or seven. It is none of my business.

She copes with the problem by asking her mother-in-law questions like, "So, which of the children would you like me to send back?" Also, she says she doesn't tell her mother-in-law she is pregnant until it shows.

Another woman, who has eleven children ages twelve and under, said she received the worst negative pressure from her mother. "She thinks it is terrible that I have so many kids." She said she dealt with her mother by not telling her--she lets someone else tell her and her mother calls and says, "I hear you're pregnant again," and the woman responds, "So what?" She said she gets "lots of reactions here in Utah Valley" from people who think she has had too many children too fast, but so have her relatives who live in the East and in California. People say things like, "Well, you've got your two; you've got your share." Her sister in California, she said, had considerable negative pressure when she became pregnant with her third. That same sister decided not to have any more children until their family moved back to Utah because "it was just not worth all the ostracism they were having, even from their ward [Church congregation] in California."

Many of our respondents reacted to the story about the mother encouraging her daughter who had borne six children in eight years to "slow down" by saying, "sounds like us." One mother estimated that judging from her own experience, in 99 out of 100 couples a mother who had six children in eight years would be pressured by her parents or relatives to slow down. This mother had nine children. She said that in her family such advice stopped with their seventh birth. Before that she had been pressured by her mother, who had difficult pregnancies and thought her daughters couldn't handle more children than she herself had had.

Then there was the mother of eight who had had a miscarriage a few months before the interview. She said that after the miscarriage her mother came to her and said that perhaps she shouldn't feel bad about not having any more children, that maybe she already had too many to care for. The woman said, "I can remember being offended, thinking, 'that really isn't your business to tell me that.'"

Some reactions that are not explicitly negative are still defined as nonsupportive by mothers of large families.

39

Comments such as, "How do you do it? I can't keep up with my two," "That many kids would just drive me up the wall," or "I'm glad they're yours and not mine," are not defined as complimentary. A mother of 11 children said that after her fifth pregnancy her parents began to say things like, "Oh, again?" and "Are you going to try to populate the whole world by yourself?" At one point the parents tactfully asked, "Do you know about birth control?" Beyond her seventh child, she said people realized she was impervious to their criticism, and at that point the pressure ended. Having "given up" or "adjusted," she says others' reactions are now more positive: "I think that if I had ten more that they'd be just as happy and thrilled about it."

Negative reactions from relatives are more likely when a family is beset by economic pressures. A mother whose family income was among the lowest of the families we studied said she often was asked, "Are you sure you want to have another child now?" and she was convinced that if her family were better off financially such comments would not have been made. When interviewed, she was expecting her tenth child, and she said people kept asking her, "Why are you having another baby?" Her reaction was, "I think they should go jump in the lake." Because that kind of pressure bothered her, she said she kept her condition a secret as long as she could: "I'll tend not to tell anybody I am pregnant, just because I don't want to hear some people's comments."

Not everyone experienced or recognized social pressures affecting family size. One mother said that she hadn't felt any stress from other people to have a lot of children, or negative pressure because she was having too many (she had had nine children in 13 years), but she said some of her friends in the neighborhood felt they had received some pressure. In another instance, a mother commented that after she and her husband had four children, her mother was upset, "just shocked that we were really going to have another baby." However, since that time, that "watershed" of the fifth child, her mother has just accepted whatever happened.

According to the testimony of several mothers, parental efforts to encourage sons and daughters to have smaller families and/or to space their children more exhibit a fairly standard pattern. Several of the mothers said that their relatives had suggested that they postpone or prevent future pregnancies. Suggestions were said to continue up to a certain family size, ranging between four and seven children. Beyond that point, said the mothers, the relatives trying to exert the influence begin to realize that their advice will be ignored, and often then give up giving advice. The summary message is that while respect for one's parents or kindred may dictate that people listen to unwanted suggestions, a couple should continue to do whatever they themselves think is right. After four or five children, sensitive relatives will finally get the message that their advice is inappropriate and ineffectual, and most will stop offering it.

Coping with prejudice. In dealing with the prejudice and discrimination they sometimes encounter, large families use many of the same defense mechanisms used by members of ethnic minority groups to cope with prejudice and discrimination. Avoidance behavior is sometimes used: parents will avoid taking all of their children with them in public, or pregnant mothers will avoid some gatherings because they want to avoid having to face negative comments. Some families resort to the verbal counterthrust, devising "snappy comebacks" which protect their own egos and bring a potentially painful discussion to an early conclusion. Another defense mechanism, also familiar to students of minority behavior, is the attempt to overcompensate, to prove the detractors wrong by having one's children better-behaved, better-educated, better-prepared for life than children raised in smaller families.

One example of avoidance behavior practiced by our mothers is the case of the expectant mother who decided not to attend her class reunion because she would get so many questions about why she was expecting her eighth child. In another instance the mother said, "I have gone through being very embarrassed, being pregnant, and holding a baby; when you get to that point, you stay home as much as possible." Hiding the fact that one is expecting a baby is another form of avoidance behavior. Apparently just announcing the forthcoming event is sometimes very difficult: "The very worst job we had each time was to tell her (mother-in-law) I was pregnant. But as soon as they (each baby) were here she just adored them and has really loved them."

Here is the statement of a mother who said she had resisted the tendency to avoid church meetings while she was pregnant:

> The only time I have been sensitive to that (negative comments about her having too many) is when I'm actually pregnant and people make snide remarks about my size, (or ask), don't I know where babies come from. There are lots of very cutting, cutting remarks. And

41

with one or two of my children, I have dreaded Sunday;
I just didn't want to have to face the comments. But
after the children are here it has been no problem at
all . . . once in a while you take the brunt of jokes,
but that's life.

She went on to say she had adopted the philosophy that no
matter what she did, she wasn't going to please everyone,
someone would always criticize her, and so she decided that
others would not decide what the rules of her home would be:

They weren't going to determine whether or not I was
going to have more children; they weren't going to
determine how clean or dirty I kept my house; they
weren't going to determine what I did or didn't let my
children do.

Another form of avoidance is to receive negative
communications but not to react to them. One couple has
faced negative pressure most of their marriage, from parents
who thought they should postpone having any children until
the husband graduated from professional school, and then
were continually disturbed that the number of grandchildren
kept increasing. The mother learned to deal with the
unwanted advice by not paying any attention to it:

It bothered me at first and I wondered why people are
telling us what to do, but after a while we just
ignored it. We listen out of respect and say,
"MmmHmm," and then you just do what you wanted to
anyway.

Quick and witty replies to questions are another way of
coping with negative reactions. Among the snappy comebacks
the mothers say they use is an answer to the query, "Are
you sure you can take care of them?", to which the mother
responds, "Well, my children are so lucky now, they couldn't
have come into a better home." One mother answers
questions about "How can you have so many?" with "How can
you have so few?" (However, this mother emphasized that
she only uses such a biting reply on people who refuse to
mind their own business: "People who are willing to live and
let live," she says, "I am willing to, too.") An approach
that is guaranteed to help the parent of a large family to
respond to the gaping stares and obvious counting of children
by the tactless is to say, "Well, this is only a few, you
should see the ones we left at home." Many of the mothers
had at some time been asked, "Don't you know where babies
come from?" A useful response to the question was said to

be, "I sure do. Isn't it marvelous!" One of the mothers had visited Europe not too long before the interview. Attending church in France, she created a small sensation when people learned that she had eight children. Everyone turned and looked at her, she said, and someone primly inquired, "But what do you <u>do</u> with them?" She replied, "Well, I just take care of them and that sort of thing."

The method of coping with possible negative reaction by overcompensation is illustrated by the mother who said she had to prove that a very large family could be successful. She said that she had learned to be careful not to express her ideas about family size to most people.

> Because of the fact that I have found that some people are offended, and as I was expecting my eighth, ninth, and tenth, many comments were made to me, "Don't you know how to quit?", those kinds of things, and I felt like one of my purposes was to prove that it is possible to have a large family and a good family . . . .

The kinds of pressures she said she feels are "like some people are looking for a failure," because she has so many children. As a result, she said she thought her children had to be overly kind and to achieve more than they might have if they had been from smaller families. Of course, the choice to deal with negative pressures by overcompensation places additional strains on top of the usual demands of a ten-child household.

Another instance of overcompensation is the visit to Disneyland described by one of the mothers. She dressed her large family in matching, clean outfits, hoping that bystanders would be positively impressed.

The mothers see the local setting as mostly supportive and family-oriented. Nevertheless, most of them confront people who say that their families are too large or too small, or that their pregnancies are too close or too far apart. Most of the mothers seemed self-confident and committed to what they were doing, and consequently able to endure the occasional negative comments and discriminatory encounters. However, many said that negative comments bothered them most when they were pregnant, and made suggestions about how people who want to be supportive and sensitive to the feelings of expecting mothers might watch what they say and how they say it, lest they hurt or offend.

First, the mothers say, a more positive, supportive attitude to the expectant mother would be appreciated:

> I think people who are having a lot of children really could use a little more of a positive approach. My sister-in-law and my sister, when they get pregnant, call me because they know I am the one person who will say, "Oh, I am so happy for you," and they don't get that from a lot of other people. They get, "Oh, can you handle it?" That doesn't make anybody feel too happy.

> My mother really does suffer when she sees her daughters having children readily because she knows she never could have handled it. I don't believe she could have. I think she is absolutely right, she couldn't have. But on the other hand, the fact that her daughters have decided that they will take children as they come, just as long as health permits, it would be so much nicer if there were more support from the parents instead of the concern. It is genuine concern; it's not negative, it's fear. But I think people who are having a lot of children really could use a little more of a positive approach.

There was a general consensus that what the expectant mother needs is to have people say, "It is great to have a family, it is great to have this opportunity," instead of the frequent negative comments. Rather than being told that she is having babies too fast, when a young mother gets pregnant shortly after she has had a baby, she needs to be told something like, "I am so glad you are having another cute little baby." One respondent described her conversation with a close relative who had received many negative comments about her "too frequent" pregnancies. She told the relative that she thought it was nice that she was going to have another baby. The woman replied gratefully, "Oh, it is so good to hear somebody say that. Everybody is always telling me we are having them too fast."

The mother justified her statement supporting the near-relative's pregnancy this way:

> I just feel if a girl tells you she is pregnant, the least you can do is to help her and not make her feel guilty about it and not make her resent the pregnancy. I mean, it is one thing if she comes to you and says, "Should I get pregnant?" Now, if she wants to come to you and say, "I wonder if you think I ought to get

pregnant," then you can say, "Well, you may want to
wait." But if she comes and says, "I am pregnant," to
tell her she is having her babies too fast, that is
just going to make her resent being a mother and to
hate her job. She is already pregnant.

Another mother offered essentially the same advice:

I think that just after the baby is born is a nice
time to say, "Now you ought to take it easy and maybe
wait a couple of years before you have the next one,
you have a large family." When you find out your
daughter-in-law is expecting, it is not a time to say,
"Oh, no, how could you do this again?" because once it
is there, what are you going to do? You might as well
enjoy it.

Social Pressures Favoring Large Families

Surprisingly, some mothers identified the local pressures
favoring large families as problems they had to deal with.
One said, "I think that sometimes women think it's their
obligation to have a baby every so often. I don't think this
is right." Another said she had received mostly positive
reactions about the size of her ten-child family, although she
said some people she knew seemed to feel guilty that they
didn't have more children. One way of dealing with the
problem in social situations is not to ask people how many
children they have, because it makes many people defensive
"especially if they could have and didn't." One woman said
sometimes when people find she has nine, they are apologetic
that they only have three or four.

Many of the mothers said they recognized that there may
be different pressures on people with small families. Several
of the women explained that they were trying to do their part
to minimize these pressures:

I am trying to be less critical of some of my pet
peeves because I realize that all people have feelings
and all people have circumstances that aren't the same
as mine. I know of a young mother who had two children
whose husband was very active in the Church and gone
most of the time. She simply one day could take it no
longer and wrote a note and said, "I'm leaving," and
she left her husband and children and went her own way.
She broke the hearts of her immediate family and
parents and brothers and sisters and everything else.

I look at her and think, where did we fail when we let
those pressures build until they exploded in that
mother? And, how do you teach your own children to
avoid that pitfall?

Several years ago if a person had had only three by
choice, I might have judged them. I don't do that
anymore because I learned that people are so different
that I really do not know what they are inside and what
kinds of pressures they have and what they can take and
what they can't. I see my job as to be more of a
support to people. I do see my job as to do a bit of
proselyting, and I do that. I have done it with my
sisters quite successfully [and] with my sister-in-law.
But I don't pressure her at all because she is very
different from me. I just support her and encourage
her in a very low key. She is not having any children
right now, and I simply say . . . I don't say anything
unless she brings it up, and then I say, "Well, you
know when you'll be ready," because I really feel that
this is the best thing to say to her.

I know people who feel bad in the Church . . . They
feel unworthy because they only have two or three
children or one child. I don't know why they're made
to feel that. There are some built-in guilt feelings
that are much more apparent here than in other places.

The woman quoted in the preceding statement went on to say
that people with small families sometimes perceived the
pressure even when it wasn't intended:

I've had to work at making friends with some people who
have just a couple of kids and who feel that I am in
judgment of them. I mean, I've had to consciously let
them know . . . that I believe it is their business and
not mine because I think they've been burned
enough . . . I think that's a general attitude, that
people with smaller families feel discriminated against
in Utah Valley.

She also noted the positive social support for her own large
family, saying that she has received much praise and
attention.

The countervailing social pressures which affect some
Utah families were illustrated by the mother of seven who told
how she and her husband had their first three children, and
then for several years didn't have any more. After a time,

46

"Everyone kept telling my husband he had a crop failure; three children is a crop failure in Utah, and you've got to have more than three. So now we don't have a crop failure." But being "in step" with her Utah neighbors has put her out of step with her mother:

> She just acts like she's embarrassed to tell anyone that her only daughter has seven children. That makes me feel bad, but she does love them. I know that, but she gets very nervous when she comes, and she doesn't come very often, and she doesn't stay very long.

There were also those who were encouraged by their relatives to have large families. A mother with seven said that her mother was encouraging her to have her eighth because in years to come the children would be her greatest joy. She said she had received no criticism about the size of her family at all; in fact, some people had said they were envious of her having seven.

Somewhat negative definitions of families that have three or fewer children are implicit in a few mothers' comments. One argued that if a woman had only two children and was healthy, then "I think she ought to feel guilty . . . but that's completely up to her." Another mother's reaction to mothers of small families was that she didn't want to hear them complain about all the things they had to do. In some families, the parents had warned their children against judging people with small families: "We've talked about being tolerant of other people that look like they ought to have more children that haven't, because there may be hidden reasons why they can't."

Finally, several mothers questioned the priorities of those who had small families:

> I have a cousin who has just three and her reason is, she says, "I just can't take it. My nerves just won't take it." I said to her one time, "I'm as nervous as anybody else, but I'd sure hate to be without that little curly-haired blonde girl. I'd rather have the nerves than be without her."

Perceived Advantages and Disadvantages of Large Families

We asked the mothers if they sometimes wondered if they could have given more advantages to their children if they had fewer of them. Many agreed that there might have been some slight economic advantage, but they said that financial advantage was not nearly as important as the experiences that life in a large family provided in mutual tolerance, self-reliance, cooperation, and getting along together. They said the challenges, if met successfully, taught the children important lessons that were not as easily learned in smaller families.

On balance, the mothers weren't sure that the material advantages of a family with fewer children were very important. Nevertheless, a large family strains available resources more insistently than a small family. Usually, parental time, household space, and money are all in limited supply. The very existence of these incessant pressures means that the large family must organize to meet them. The process of meeting the challenges of overcrowding, or of a limited family financial base, were not seen as harmful to the children.

In addition to the religious reasons for wanting to have many children, the mothers identified several practical advantages. These advantages, expressed in a variety of ways, may all be summarized in two: large families are more fun, and they are a superior environment for raising children. Several of the mothers had fairly strong prejudices against the one- or two-child family, defining them as not fair to the children. Sometimes they told how deprived they had felt as children because they were only children, or had been separated from their nearest brother or sister by a several-year gap.

The large family may be a superior environment for teaching children how to get along with others, but is is also a more challenging situation. The larger the family, the greater the pressures upon the family income. The financial pressures usually translate into problems of work and space. It is harder to keep a house clean when there are many children. It is also harder to maintain order and keep the peace. The parents of large families have the same amount of personal time as do parents of small families, which means that they must spread themselves thinner. Many of the mothers reported that they felt they ought to spend more time with their children on an individual, one-on-one basis. They also expressed many unmet needs of their own, because mothers of large families usually deal with the heightened pressure by devoting time they might spend on themselves to household and family matters.

If she is to provide a minimal level of support for her children, the mother of a large family must delegate more tasks to others, or must be much better organized than a woman with fewer children. All of these pressures--on parental time, available space, and family finances--are easier to manage if a family has substantial economic resources. With only a few notable exceptions, the families where mothers were coping best with the challenges they faced, and where those efforts at coping were producing visible results of an orderly, well-managed home without apparent undue pressure and strain on the mother, were families in the upper-income categories. To say the same thing another way, large families that seemed to be having the most difficulty in meeting the personal needs of both the parents and the children tended to be those families in our largely middle-class sample that had the lowest income. Other things being equal, a higher income seems to help.

Most mothers defined it as an advantage of large families that older children had to help care for the home and teach younger children. A few said that occasionally the older children had missed opportunities in their own lives because they had to work at home. Whether it is an advantage or disadvantage for the elder children to be responsible for part of the socialization of younger children, depends on a mother's perspective and the child's needs and attitudes.

There are also some statements that on the face of it seemed, like the cliche about "cheaper by the dozen," to be paradoxical. For example, one mother argued that ten children were no worse than two. In fact, she said, ten were better because the elder ones tended the younger ones. Thus, the necessity of delegating some of a mother's responsibilities to the older children was turned into a virtue. The fact that the older children helped out was seen as beneficial to them, good for the family, and good for the mother.

Another advantage ascribed to the large family was that children have ready-made playmates. They are rarely found without someone to play with, because there are other children of roughly the same age in the same family. Furthermore, several mothers said that having a large family forced the mother to teach the children correct principles of family organization. With one or two children, it was thought possible for children to have sloppy personal habits, and yet for a family to function because parents followed up, doing things for the children they should have done for themselves. With eight or ten children, however, a household becomes chaotic unless the children have at least minimal skills in caring for their own needs.

The same kind of built-in requirement for effective parental teaching applies to getting along. A small family can afford (or tolerate) a self-centered, recalcitrant or obnoxious child in a way that a large family cannot. Almost every mother mentioned that having many children helps to teach the children love and concern for others, not to mention teaching the parents patience and selflessness. Even the financial pressures of large families were sometimes seen as advantageous to children in that it forced them to earn their own way, to choose carefully, or to do without some things. That kind of self-denial, whether by choice or not, was seen as often beneficial. Children from large families were said to be less selfish than children in small families whose parents were able to give them every advantage. One mother said that in her large family her children were getting things of lasting worth--an education, shelter, food, clothing, and learning how to get along with people--and she wasn't sure they really needed anything else. Other mothers said that their own children had more luxuries and more opportunities than they themselves had, and while they might not have as many material advantages as children in some families, what they had was sufficient. In sum, the contrast was often made between the values of the world and eternal values; the parents of large families felt that, with respect to eternal priorities, their children were as well off, if not better off, than children from smaller families. As one woman put it:

> I think the best thing that we could do for our children is to help them learn to love one another, to love a lot of children, to want to have a lot of children themselves, to want to bring them up so that they can have eternal families. I think the way we are, we have a better chance of doing that with a larger family than with a smaller one.

A few mothers said having a large family was an advantage to them because it forced them to focus their attentions on matters of most worth in the long run. One said that if she had fewer children, she would have more outside interests, and the children might not be given as much of her time and attention as they now receive. "But with a large family, I know I have a full-time job, and so I zero in on that." Further, not only did the large family force her to pay attention to her mothering above all else, but it required everyone to give and take, to express love and learn to be sensitive to others' feelings.

Another perceived advantage was that the large family was useful because it made it very difficult for parents to do too much for their children--they are spread too thin--and, therefore, the children learn independence. In sum, children in large families don't have too much free time, they learn how to work, they are not overpampered, and they must learn to get along with each other.

The disadvantages of large families were generally problems that the women had found they could deal with, either by changing their expectations or the way they organized things. Almost everyone mentioned the continuing challenge of trying to keep a house clean when there was a great deal of human traffic through the house, of trying to keep a peaceful, orderly environment in a household containing between nine and fourteen people, most of them young children. Noise, confusion, conflicts between children, and an enormous amount of housework were almost universal problems at least some of the time.

A mother of eight said that "the laundry is just astronomical for ten people." She continued that while the blessings of a large family were "really great," parents had to build up their tolerance levels to manage. Most mothers expressed concern that they were not as organized as they ought to be, and many said that they felt tired or frustrated. Most of them have more to do than they can squeeze into each day, and they say they cope by becoming more relaxed, or changing their standards on things that they decide are relatively unimportant. They end up working mainly to handle the really important things.

Most of the mothers recognized a disadvantage of large families in that parents may have less time for some of the important but not vital aspects of family life, but they have concluded that that is a trade-off worth making. Let us illustrate some of the disadvantages expressed by a series of brief quotations. Many of these ideas will be considered in more detail in the subsequent chapter on how mothers of large families organize their daily activities.

If I worried about my house all the time, I would go nutty. I would scream and be after the kids all the time. There are a lot of things that are more important.

I sometimes get kind of upset because of just the general mess. You mop the floor and at the end of the day it looks like it hasn't been mopped for days. I guess that's just part of having a big family, is that there's more traffic and wear-and-tear on your house.

When everyone comes home, they immediately want Mother, and they want to tell what has happened, so I have maybe six people vying for my attention at the same time. It gets extremely noisy.

We are people who like quiet, peaceful rest, but with ten people under one roof, there are rare moments when everything is at peace. To have ten people with their lives completely in order and everything happy, all at the same time, is unusual.

One of the worst parts of a big family is the noise. Sometimes you just want to get away from it all, so you go into your bedroom and shut the door and hope that nobody comes in.

Sometimes I feel there are far too many children in this house . . . when everyone is misbehaving and not getting anything done, and when the house is a mess, or I feel like I'm not getting anything done.

They have so many little things to do . . . when you have a few kids, that's hours of running around and meeting everybody's schedules. I think that's the most annoying thing to me.

There's not enough time to give to each child [to meet] the individual needs that they have. Sometimes we have to, more often than not, we have to group them together.

There is always continually a child needing something from me, or even being in the same room sometimes, where I'm never alone, just me. That is very stressful to me sometimes, especially when it goes on all day long and I can never sit down and organize myself.

For the last two months I've thought about getting a pair of sandals but it doesn't seem like I can ever get to the store long enough to find me a pair of sandals. But I've been to the store 50 times for baseball shirts and hats and that kind of thing, and it seems to me when I come home, if I were more organized I would be able to do that better or I would be able to take care of my things as well as their things.

Biases against very small families. Almost half of the mothers came from families of four or fewer children, and eight of the 41 were from one- or two-child families. Eighty-five percent of the mothers had more children than their own mothers had, and three-fourths of them had more children than either their own or their husbands' parents had had.

Several mothers complained that they had been separated from their closest brother or sister by several years, and so had missed the experience of having a near age-mate. Most of these were committed to giving their own children the experience that they themselves had missed of having a close brother or sister. Widespread support for the idea that large families are more fun also surfaced among women who themselves had been raised in large families. Often they contrasted the variety of enjoyable things that had gone on in their homes as they were growing up with the less inviting situations in the homes of their friends and relatives who had only a few children. Explained a mother who had seven brothers and sisters, "We had cousins, there were only two in their family, and we always used to laugh and comment that they would come and spend the holidays with us because we had so much fun."

Sometimes the experience of growing up in a one- or two-child family was seen by the mothers as not preparing them psychologically for their mother role, although it did create in them the desire to have more than one child. A mother said that, "I am an only child and that is why I am just delighted to have such a large family . . . I didn't want to be here all alone, and now I've got myself really busy and I never get bored." She does get rattled at the commotion in her house, however: "I just can't stand fighting, maybe that's because being an only child, I just never had that commotion and whenever they start fighting, I just try to get it stopped right now."

A mother who was an only child had married a man who was also an only child, and they agreed that in their home they would not have the "unnatural situation" they had both experienced while growing up. "We knew that what we had isn't exactly the ideal situation, and we wanted the warmth that is brought into the home with lots of children, and we've never regretted any of it."

LIFE IN LARGE FAMILIES

Another mother lamented her own childhood, because she had been enough older than her baby brother that "I hardly know him at all." She said that while she was growing up, she wasn't involved very much in "children-type things," and now, looking back, she is sad about that:

> I really missed something. When they talk about what memories . . . you have of your family, I don't even remember half of my family. So I've had them [our children] together, so they can be companions to each other.

This sense of having missed something by not having a close sibling appeared several times. There were statements that one felt "kind of deprived," that one had missed a feeling of closeness, that one missed the companionship of a sister, or never got to really know one's brothers and sisters. "I never felt my sister was my friend," said one mother, and another echoed, "I was always the little sister underfoot, and she was always the big one giving orders."

Contrasting her children's situation with her own upbringing, a mother of seven explained that she thought her own children were more sharing by necessity, more giving, more open to the feelings of others around them, and less self-centered than children in one- or two-child families usually were. "They have to intermingle so much, that really their friends, particularly up until they are twelve or so, are right here within the home and they become very much aware of feelings because they're dealing with them all the time."

A mother of nine said that she thought being an only child would be an unfortunate thing: "If you were an only child, you would have so many problems it would be terrible." She described a relative who was an only child, saying, "No way does he want just one child, because that's the worst thing that ever happened to him." This mother then described what she thought were problems with families of size two and three children:

> If you only had two and you could have more, I think it would be unfortunate because two are very competitive, and I think this can be difficult. And if you have three and you could have more, then that would be unfortunate too, because the third one is always left out. Although there are advantages of three, you've got a bigger family. I think four is more like a family, and there are two people to share when you've got four. Four is a nicer number, because

you have somebody to be a playmate with and there's always somebody else. So, if you have to have a smaller family, I would think four would be about the smallest you'd like to end with, if you have a choice.

Professional Mothers "I Have Them Because I Want Them"

The dominant message about large families which the mothers conveyed was that, while children were a lot of work, they were the most rewarding thing in the world. Although many mothers described in painful detail the extent of the personal sacrifice and extraordinary effort involved in bearing and rearing many children, they consistently affirmed that they had large families because they wanted them. They said they were what they were by their own choice, not by accident. Remember that these women were college graduates, many had married late, several had begun professional careers before opting for the wife and mother role as their primary identity.

Here are some of their personal statements about how they feel about that choice:

I really feel that our family is different and we have had an advantage because both my husband and I were older when we were married. We had both had years of being alone and I was ready to be a mother. I don't consider it a sacrifice because I know that, after ten years of teaching and being something else, that's not all that wonderful either. I know how good I've got it.

We didn't accidentally have eight children. We chose to have eight children. We feel that others should have that privilege.

You shouldn't deny yourself having children. I think that's the greatest happiness you can find. I wouldn't have anything in life important to do if I didn't have kids. I really feel that way. I don't think being a nurse or anything would contribute to civilization or to my own personal development. I think that maybe my family is going to.

The challenge, I think, is to be happy in spite of the stress and the strain and not let it get you down . . . . One of the things I do is to tell myself I am in a situation because I chose to be here. Now, there are stresses that come with a large family. But I chose that, so I don't spend my time and energy feeling sorry and wishing things were different . . . . I'm here by choice and I'm doing what I want to do . . . . I really like what I'm doing, I really enjoy it. I love spending time with the kids. I love doing what I am doing and I love it to the point that it is not hard for me to make choices between others that would put demands on my time that would pull me away from home and away from children.

I don't think there will ever come a time when I won't want a baby. I think there has got to come a time when I've got to face the fact that there won't be anymore babies at our house, and I've shed a few tears over that. As I watch the baby and she sits up, and I say, "Don't sit up yet," and as she starts to walk, I say, "Don't walk yet, lie down," this kind of thing . . . People keep telling me I'll get to the point where I'll be relieved not to have to worry about being pregnant again. I haven't reached that point, and I don't know where that point is. Some women hit it sooner than others . . . . So I've got to face the fact that when you're forty-four and you've had fourteen pregnancies, the old body just won't hack it anymore, and it's not wise for it. It's not wise to push yourself beyond that, and I think the way I cope with that in the back of my mind; I say, "Well, maybe, maybe I can handle one more," instead of saying, "No, this is it, and that's the very end."

It is not an easy life style. Many of the mothers agree that it wasn't meant to be easy. But most feel it is the life pattern they were meant to have. For those who are less than positive about whether they were foreordained to have a large family, it is a life pattern they have chosen, either explicitly or implicitly, by following what they believe is good advice about how life ought to be lived in families that have the advantages they see themselves as having.

There is so much around us that pulls at us, that is negative. I keep thinking the world is "too much with us, late and soon." I think that is one-hundred-percent of the problem. My sister-in-law said yesterday that a couple of friends had called her and they were very low because they were both pregnant and they had three children already. That just seemed to me like another of these areas where all perspective was lost. We seem to view having families a lot in the same way that the world does, as something to hold us down, as a hinderance, as something to interfere with your freedom. And not to see it as the grand design of the whole creation, the entire reason we are here, to develop ourselves and to give other spirit children the same opportunity and advantages to grow and to become all that we are capable of becoming.

Several mothers said that the emergence of the women's movement had motivated them to examine their own life styles and motivations. The typical result of the assessment was, "I like what I'm doing and I'm doing it because I want to." One response to a question on the women's movement was:

I'm perfectly happy in my home and I think they're [the women's movement] wacky for wanting to get out of it . . . I have been known to write "mother" when they say occupation [in a questionnaire] and invariably they'll cross it out and write housewife or even homemaker. They don't understand what a mother is in my book.

She views her motherhood as a chosen profession and has consciously rejected alternatives as less satisfying: "I can't see why women would want to work outside the home except they don't know how to get satisfaction out of being a mother."

Another mother said that though raising a large family was difficult, and there were plenty of stressful times, she was doing precisely what she wanted to do:

I feel liberated. I feel like in my position of me being myself, I could do anything I wanted to do. Because if I wanted to I could hire somebody to come in and tend the children, and I could go out and be a career woman, because it's available out there, or I could go to school . . . I think being a woman is just terrific, I love it.

A third mother described herself as a professional mother. There was no profession in the world that was more important, she said. She had continued to read and study and take classes, trying to learn how to be a better mother and to keep her home a happy one. As a result, she felt she knew what she was doing: "It's not a home in which children come and we don't know what we're doing, and I suppose that makes a difference."

A fourth perspective was that if a woman could succeed at being a mother of a large family, she could succeed at almost anything:

> I think that to get really on top of a house is the hardest thing, the very hardest thing a woman could do if there are a number of children . . . . You could go be a secretary; you could go be an executive; you could go do anything and be on top. So, I feel very satisfied in my mind's eye. When I am on top of things, I feel very good. You know, I feel like I could do anything at that point.

A variation on the same theme cropped up in a mother's expression of concern about the future and the impact of some of the current anti-family values upon her children:

> I wonder how many girls will grow up strong enough to believe that motherhood is a good option for them, as fulfilling as something that would give them a lot more worldly acclaim . . . I think that would take tremendous amounts of self-esteem when all around you people were saying, "Oh, anybody can be a wife and a mother. If you really want to make your mark in the world you have got to do more than that." As if there could ever be any more than that.

One woman made the point that her large family, consisting of seven children ranging from less than a year to almost 12 years old, was not a result of her responding to a religious ethic: "I don't feel any pressure from the church to have kids. I have them because I want them . . . ."

> I feel like kids are the best product that we have in this world. They are our only hope. They are the only salvation that we have, but yet what we need to try and do is to turn out quality children and not quantity.

This woman's husband was a physician, and she described his experiences with some LDS (Latter-day Saint) women who he thought continued to have children because of social pressures rather than because they really wanted them:

> It is so sad. They come in crying. I don't know. I just can't imagine crying because I'm pregnant and being unhappy, yet I just feel for that person. Having five or six at home and just barely hanging together and because their church says no birth

control should be used, they show up with number seven
or eight and they are just devastated. My husband's
heart just aches for them. It is not his place to
tell somebody, "you should only have this many." You
can only form your own opinions. He is supportive of
them and does everything he can to help. There are
quite a few who come in like that.

We hasten to add, as the last paragraph makes plain,
that there are many mothers of large families who are not as
affirmative about their situation as the well-educated women
we interviewed. Also, we recognize that there may be a
certain amount of rationalization involved in some mothers'
statements that if they had their lives to live over again they
would make the same choices about the number and spacing of
their children, because at this point in their lives most of
them really do not have many realistic alternatives to
continuing their role as "professional mothers."
Nevertheless, the indications from their behavior suggest a
deep commitment to continuing parenthood and child
nurturance by the mothers in our study. Three of these
behavior indicators are 1) the sizable proportion who have
voluntarily brought foster children (usually American Indian
children) into their homes, thereby adding a new potential for
stress on top of the challenge posed by seven or more
children of their own; 2) the continuing fertility of the group
as indicated by the number of mothers who were again
pregnant at the time of the interview, even though they had
been selected for the study because they had recently borne
a seventh or subsequent child; and 3) the fair number of
women who, although they had very large families by
community standards, nevertheless expressed desires for
another child or two, or lamented a lapse in fertility at some
point in their married life. These behaviors corroborate the
women's words, revealing a continuing commitment to the
large family ideal as their life style by choice.

One of the mothers who had seen both sides, the career
and life as a mother, described how she had chosen the latter
role with her eyes wide open:

It is kind of like becoming whole. I was half before,
and I am whole now . . . I have been single, I have
done my thing. I am now happy to be where I am, and
it was my choice to be where I am. I am very glad, I
am very happy to be known as a housewife, except I am
not a housewife, I am a homemaker. To me there is a
difference—not a wife to a house. I make a home,
yes. As my mother said, "He makes the living and she

makes it worth living," . . . . I think to be a real
fine homemaker, a wife and mother is far more than any
career that you can have, as far as I am concerned.
My teaching career is important to me, yes, and I have
enjoyed being able to teach, but I wouldn't want to do
it all of the time. I really wouldn't, because I
would hate to have missed the opportunity to be at
home, to be able to see my kids for awhile, to watch
my kids grow up.

Chapter IV

SELF-PERCEPTIONS: I KNOW WHO I AM

* * * * *

. . . yea, they had been taught by their mothers, that
if they did not doubt, God would deliver them. And
they rehearsed unto me the words of their mothers,
saying: We do not doubt our mothers knew it.
                                        --Alma 26:47-48

And now, he imparteth his word by angels unto men,
yea, not only men but women also.
                                        --Alma 32:23

Our information on how the mothers see themselves comes
from answers to three sets of questions. One sequence began
with "How would you respond to the question: Who am I?",
followed by items asking for the adjectives they would use to
describe themselves and how happy they were with their
identity. Then we asked, "How does your husband see
you?", followed by probes such as "How would he describe
you?" and "What adjectives would he use?" Then there was
the item, "What do you think are the major strengths and
capabilities which you contribute to your marriage?", and its
counterpart, "What about weaknesses and shortcomings?"
Also, in the course of the interviews the mothers sometimes
made offhand comments which further illuminated their images
of themselves.

The typical response to the "Who am I?" question was an
answer that affirmed spiritual identity and emphasized kinship
to God. Usually, it was some form of the "I am a child of
God" concept. After that, the most frequent answers
referred to identities as mother, wife or homemaker. Almost
half of the women mentioned mother or wife (and often these
were mentioned together) as their dominant role.

LIFE IN LARGE FAMILIES

No other specific role was mentioned by very many of the women. They sometimes identified themselves by name, or claimed a kinship role, such as daughter or sister. Or they referred to certain activities or attributes, for example, stating that they were good companions, or that they were normal persons. But there were no dominant identities, apart from wife and/or mother, and daughters of God.

This is not to say that they lacked terms of self-description. An identity, however, involves a role--a position with prescribed expectations and linkages to other positions--as well as attributes. Thus, to be a companion is to occupy a role. To have a sense of humor or to be irritable are considered to be personality traits rather than roles.

The most frequent adjectives chosen by the women to describe themselves were (1) "happy," and its synonyms; (2) terms for various good qualities, especially those that go along with being a warm and supportive mother; and (3) "intelligent." Also frequently mentioned were the personal qualities of optimism, diligence, and persistence.

A striking aspect of the mothers' answers to questions about their identities is that so many of them said that in their roles as wife and mother they were doing what they ought to be doing at this time in their lives. Expressions of uncertainty about personal identity, or about the value of what they were devoting their lives to were quite rare, and so were overt statements of dissatisfaction with their roles. That is, most of these mothers said they knew what they were supposed to be doing in life, and that they were doing it, if not superbly, at least acceptably.

Moreover, despite times of strain and difficulty which most of them accept as integral to marriage and motherhood, they say they are happy. They seem convinced that they find purpose in life and that their lives have meaning. Most of them said they would not change the roles that they occupy even if they could. If they are dissatisfied, it usually is dissatisfaction with the way they play the parts of wife and mother, rather than with the roles themselves. Even the most dissatisfied were generally optimistic about their own progress toward being better persons, mothers, and wives. To the query, "Are you happy with your identity?", most said yes.

I Am a Child of God

Sometimes a mother admitted that her initial, almost reflexive response to the "Who am I?" question was a standard cultural response, an LDS cliche. Some labeled it "a pat answer," or referred to the children's song that reinforces the phrase. Said one, "the first thing that comes to my mind is the Primary song, "I am a Child of God." Another acknowledged the statement as overused but used it anyway: "I could give you the trite sentence that I am a child of God, but I really believe that."

The sense of divine mission seems to imbue the mother and wife roles with dignity, at least when the women think about things in long-range perspective. Their affirmative stance involves a sometimes bristling rejection of the view that homemakers are "nobodies."

> That question requires the answer "I'm a child of God" to me, because then your focus just isn't on today, but it is on yesterday and tomorrow. What I've done is important, what I am today is important, and what I plan to be tomorrow is very important. Who am I? I am a person who feels like time is very important. The time I have here I will use to be best, to accomplish everything I can. I'm a mother and that's very important to me.

> The most critical thing I am now is a mother, but that doesn't mean that's all I am. . . . I'm a daughter of our Heavenly Father and I think that makes a difference in how I feel about being a mother and being a wife, an eternal companion. I think that I am going to have just as much work to do after we die, in the Hereafter, as I do now, and I think I have an obligation spiritually to become the best individual I can.

> I know who I am and I know where I'm trying to get, so I don't feel that I am a nobody or a lost soul or anything like this.

> Who am I? I am _____, mother of seven and wife of one fine gentleman. A homemaker, maid, chauffeur. I guess mostly I am a child of God . . . . It frustrates me sometimes because I don't live up to who I am.

I am a child of God. In the way I feel, I'm an important person to Him. And I'm a mother and a wife and a sister and a daughter and all those other things. I don't know. I guess I'm an important person to a lot of people.

Oh, I know who I am. You have to come to a certain point in life where you say, "Who am I? and what is my role? and what is my stewardship? and where am I going?" And if you can't find this out through the spirit, I think you are really lost. I mean, there is no way, if I didn't know exactly what my stewardship responsibilities were and how they were defined through the spirit, I certainly wouldn't be doing what I am doing.

Despite the tendency to at least begin their response with the pat answer, the cliche, several mothers shared some of their feelings about the struggle to achieve a personal identity unique to themselves, independent in part from their roles as wife and mother. Said one:

Who am I? Now years ago I may have said that I was Mrs. Jones, but you know we have all been affected in certain aspects as to Women's Liberation. At least we've been thinking about it and perhaps [it has] made us question who we are. I wouldn't say that I am necessarily just Mrs. Jones, because I am still an independent thinker. I take ideas from my husband, very much so, and we are in one thought in many ways, but I don't feel that I am that dependent on my husband. I know some women who would perhaps be completely devastated if they lost their husband. I don't feel that I would be. I feel that I could pick myself up pretty well. Now perhaps that accounts because of the education I have had. I feel I could fall back on that pretty well and maybe it's the time I have been spending without my husband. It has been a great deal of time, but I am able to make decisions by myself, so I don't necessarily have to have that "Mrs." attached to my name. I won't say that I am "Ms." I'm not that liberated, but who am I? I'm just me. I can function both independently and as a wife and mother. I'm satisfied.

Here is another response to the "Who am I?" question which reveals someone struggling for identity:

Who am I? Here again, I think we just have to be on
faith. In the Church we have been so brainwashed
about who we are that we have never really had the
chance to sit and think who we were. You know,
sometimes when you are told who you are all your life,
you never really sat and thought, "who am I?", where
somebody from another faith not having people tell
them who they were, may have sat and pondered and
pondered about it. I think the childlike faith--you
just have to keep trying. I think age grows you out
of faith. You have a lot of faith when you are
little, and then you grow out of it and the older you
get, you lose it because you get so smart. You think,
"Oh, how could I be that important? You know, this
big, fat old world, all those old worlds; and I'm just
teeny-tiny me." I just think those things are
detrimental to your mind. You have to just not think
about those things. I know one thing that has really
helped me and I know it has. I used to not like to
read the scriptures and I would really get irritated
when I would go to Primary (children's meeting) and
they would say, "We are having a reading program and
everybody is supposed to read one chapter a
day. . . ." But you know, I started reading the Book
of Mormon this summer. . . . I really enjoy it and
that is a heck of a lot different than having somebody
make you do it or assign you to do it.

Reading the scriptures, she said, had helped her sort out
her personal identity.

I Am Intelligent

As might be expected in a population of college
graduates, many mothers saw themselves as bright, creative,
and intelligent. Over one-third of them referred to
intellectual pursuits or their own intelligence as an essential
part of their self-image.

They view themselves as interested in knowledge,
well-endowed intellectually, imaginative, perceptive, and
constantly learning. Here are references to this dimension of
self-image:

I am a fairly fun person to be around and fairly
intelligent--not super intelligent, but interested in
a lot of things.

I'm a bookworm.

I always have to have some things I do just for me like going to school . . . . I'm intelligent, but sometimes I think I'm too smart for my own good.

I'm curious, I'm imaginative. I like to try to be creative and do things in maybe a different way than the usual.

I'm fairly easy-going and I'm reasonably intelligent and I'm quite practical.

I think I am smart, intelligent. I did well when I was at school, but in some ways I'm kinda' stupid too, when I stop to think about it.

I am a woman of varied interests, with high ambition, tending to be independent.

I am a woman with lots of desires to learn, to grow. I like to discover new things. I like learning.

To me, I feel like I want to constantly be learning and constantly want to be doing something even to the point--I push this too much on my children. I get excited about something and I want to do it. I really feel good about it. I want my children to get excited about something.

Who am I? I am intelligence from the beginning. I am one of God's children and therefore, inside of me somewhere, even if I don't see it, I've got super potential. I guess my main goal is to be able to find it, express it, let it out in creative and different ways. But as a person, I am good. Everyone is. I think that I have a place in this life and I feel like I've got a lot of things to accomplish, and I'm excited about doing them.

I'm Always Trying

If the strengths mentioned by most mothers can be defined as prerequisites for successful life in large families, then the capacity for hard work must rank near the top of the list. Whatever weaknesses they thought they had, these mothers said they had developed, perhaps out of necessity, the ability to work hard. Added to that is the related attribute of persistence, even though the almost ritualistic persistence was sometimes accompanied by discouragement and depression. In sum, the mothers' views of themselves contain a strong segment of, "We keep going, come what may."

I keep trying, after I fall many times or I get knocked down by--psychologically I get knocked down by many problems. I keep trying, I'm always trying. I'm always trying new ways and new methods of doing things and making things better and I think that's about the biggest thing I can say, because I've got a lot of faults."

Here are other instances of the supportive, hard-working mother, determined, diligent, and practical:

Well, I think we both work really hard and just are able to fill up the day with a lot of good things. It's hard to say about yourself. Well, I think that my children come first in my life. There aren't any outside activities that really interfere. I think that turns into an advantage, that I'm most always available.

I've also learned not to cry. It doesn't help. It doesn't do anything but give you a headache, and I don't like whiners. I used to have a neighbor that would come over and whine and sniffle and I just couldn't be bothered. Maybe I'm not as tolerant as I think I am. You just have to decide within yourself that you can do whatever it is you want to do and then do it. And there are so many things to do that it only strikes me as ridiculous for people just to sit around and whine and say they can't.

I think I'm really dedicated and I try really hard. I'm not as organized as I should be but I keep going.

I'm industrious, I'm quite independent, I'm quite thorough. I can be demanding, sometimes maybe too much. I'm too critical sometimes, sometimes I'm overbearing.

I'm a persistent person, and I see things through to their finish even when they're not pleasant or when they're difficult and it seems like I don't want to go on. I'm a persistent person so that I see that things are completed and done. I try to be a person that's aware of what's going on so that I can discuss with my children intelligently when they want to discuss things with me and even when they ask things that would be maybe seem unsettling or embarrassing. . . . So I try to keep myself abreast of the current events and happenings.

A mother who fit into the "always working" category in her image of self said, "I want to try, kind of enduring. I'm a good worker, I know how to work long hard hours. That's kind of hard to do." This woman had concluded that the challenges she faced were as difficult as those faced by earlier generations:

> I want to go ahead on and to do these things as best I can so that I can get them over with, to go and meet the next thing that comes along, and I just really have a desire to help everyone. Just keep that steady flow going forward day to day. I consider myself a very lucky, very blessed individual to just be in this day and age and this dispensation. I think it's hard. I think my challenges in a way are as hard as some of the pioneer challenges. Some of theirs were very difficult and maybe I couldn't have done what they could have done, but I think in a way that some of the things that I've met here have been very difficult to overcome. I'm happy today. I don't know what's going to happen tomorrow, but today I'm happy, and I'm happy that it's a day that I can be happy. I just hope that the day that I can't be happy, that I'll be able to cope with it.

I Am Organized, To A Degree

The amount of "organization" a family seems to exhibit necessarily depends upon some standard or ideal image of organization against which the family may be compared. A well-organized large family may differ in many ways from a well-organized small family, or from the model household visualized by writers of "Home Beautiful" magazines, or even from the ideals held by the parents themselves. Part of the necessary organization consists of assigning priorities, and if a mother assigns housework a lower priority than some other activity, say helping her children with homework or creating an intellectual environment or carrying out creative activities with her children, then her home may not <u>appear</u> as organized as she would like or as her neighbors might expect. Many mothers of large families do not spend as much time on personal grooming as they would like. Similarly, many do not keep their houses as clean and uncluttered as they would if they were not busy with other things to which they give higher priority.

A consequence of her choices about priorities is that the mother of many children often finds herself in the position of having to apologize either for the way she looks or for the way her house looks. She, or it, do not come close enough to the image she holds, and that she assumes others hold, of what ought to be. Even if she is tough-minded enough to refuse to apologize aloud for conditions that are to some extent beyond her control, the fact that she doesn't look as good as she thinks she should, or that her house isn't in exemplary condition, affects her self-image. She accuses herself of not being a good housekeeper, or if not being organized enough, or of letting herself go.

Thus we have the paradox that mothers of large families both recognize their own talents at organization and at the same time lament the fact that they do not organize as well as they could. The situation is the same for patience. Most of the mothers recognize patience as one of their positive qualities, and admit that their capacity for patience is larger than it used to be. Nevertheless, they berate themselves for not having more patience.

The attitude that she was not a spectacular housekeeper was a common part of the self-image. For example:

> I guess I sometimes think that if I did organize my housework a little better, I'd probably be a better homemaker, but I do it in fits and starts. Some days we're quite well-organized . . . that's a hard one, because I know what my shortcomings are, but I'm not sure that it affects our [husband-wife] relationship an awful lot, again because he's so accepting.

Another woman's husband was not so forgiving:

> I'm not that good of a housekeeper and I think that's been our biggest contention--is my poor housekeeping. . . . When my husband really thinks about it he realizes that I'm not as bad as a lot of people, but I think his biggest problem with my housekeeping is that he worries I'll end up like my mother. Because to me, my mother was the worst housekeeper I had ever seen. I've seen people just as bad, but nobody any worse. And he always worries about that, and maybe that's one of my biggest faults.

I really don't take pride in my house as much as I
should. I like it to be generally clean but not
spotless, because it's so discouraging to clean the
same thing over and over and over again. I mean, I
can get my walls spotless one day and the next day
they look the same way they did before. I'd like it
to be cleaner, but I guess my biggest problem is that
I don't take care of it so it's totally clean all the
time.

Although the mothers may wish that they were better
organizers than they are, most of them claim at least moderate
skill at maintaining a sufficient level of planning and
performance to keep their families functioning. In a word,
"being organized helps":

I try to be organized because I find being organized
helps a lot. I'm not organized all the time but I am,
I think, organized or at least I am always trying to
be organizing and I am always working. You very
seldom see me sitting around doing nothing. I'll sit
down and read the newspaper for a few minutes but I
never just sit. I never watch T.V. unless perhaps to
be ironing and the T.V. happens to be on. I'd say I'm
an organizer and a worker and always trying to do
better. I'm not all that spiritual I'd say, but I try
to be that way but I'm not.

The mothers rarely considered themselves less organized
than their husbands, and often said they were better
organized than their husbands were. Take for example the
wife who described her husband as the type who would never
have high blood pressure or an ulcer because life was fun to
him. He tended to put things off and not worry about them.
She was the organizer and to some degree the worrier. "I'm
more organized than he is," she said, "he's a perfectionist in
what he does, and [when] he does . . . [something] he does
it perfectly, but if he doesn't think it is important . . . he
doesn't [do it]."

I'm just the opposite, I like my house neat and picked
up and clean all of the time. John could live with
garbage, anything, as long as everybody's happy,
that's fine. That's [happiness is] the most important
thing, but to me, my home is a reflection of myself.
I see myself in my home. I try to tell him that it
doesn't reflect on him because nobody sees that as
John's job--this is my job. This is my part of the
marriage. His is making the money to pay for the home

and mine is running the home and keeping it the way it should be. I tend to be more organized. I know that when we are going on a trip we should get the tickets, instead of the night before, when he just says "Why can't you just call the travel agent and tell them you want to leave for tomorrow," even though it is the busy season. Or, once we get the tickets, he's the type on the last night who changes it from Western to United because he likes the movie on United. These are the things that are important in his life, and I'm embarrassed to go to the ticket counter and say "We want to change because we like your movie better." It's just silly things like that I think that's where I add stability to the family because my husband, if I had to pick a person that my husband was like, it would be Peter Pan. He's a child at heart and he's never going to grow up. . . . So I think I bring more organization and stability into the family.

She said that she was more of a disciplinarian than her husband because he wasn't home with the children as often as he liked, and he hated to play the "heavy" when he was home. Consequently, she said she took major responsibility for child discipline. She also was more impatient than her husband:

I tend to get more upset than John over little things, over anything that I think needs to be upset about. I really wish I could do something about that, but I tend to get upset more before I think about it, to figure out what I'm going to do about it, where John doesn't . . . I suppose I have a lot [of shortcomings]; if you asked him we'd probably have a whole list. I'm more impatient sometimes, but I think that comes with getting upset faster than he does.

The characteristic of procrastination seems to be one exhibited by many of the fathers of large families. One mother said that although her husband was a hard worker, he also procrastinated, and his putting off doing the little things sometimes caused friction between them. Her own strengths were managing and organizing:

Well, I'm a good routine person. I like to keep a schedule, and it's easy for me to serve meals at the same time every day and to keep something that needs to be done pretty much on a schedule done. For example, laundry, that has to be done regularly. That's easy for me to do. I can usually remember things that other people might need to do at different times in which they're involved. In fact, I do better when things are running smoothly on a schedule than when something upsets the schedule and throws it all off.

She went on to say that she enjoyed being supportive to her husband and actually enjoyed doing many of the tasks that went along with being a homemaker.

The high value the mothers place on being organized and having patience showed up again and again in the interviews. Often they were mentioned together:

> For instance, being able to file and physically organize things is an ability of strength. An ability to make a particular job efficient although I can be terribly inefficient. I can do a job and acquire new skills and ways to make it go faster or easier. I think, I'd say I probably acquired a great deal of patience, that things upset me nearly as easily as they did years ago. The same kinds of things don't affect me anyway.

One mother said that in her family her husband brought a greater capacity to love to the marriage than she did and that he had a calming effect on everyone. Asked what she had contributed to the marriage, she said: "organization, to a degree":

> I can see if I am organized, then my family is. My testimony of the gospel, because I feel like that, has been a strength not only for him but for my children. I like to work hard. My husband isn't a physical worker a lot. . . . I can work hard so I kinda do more of that physical [work].

Myself as He Sees Me

Other clues to the mothers' self-perceptions were provoked by the question, "How would your husband describe you?" The typical answer was a list of positive traits. Recurring themes were: dependable, diligent, competent, attractive, hard-working, ambitious, and patient. Most of the mothers are confident that their husbands think they are good wives and good mothers.

An unanticipated finding in the answers to this question was the high percentage of women--almost one in three--who said they really didn't know how their husband would describe them. The interviewer probed by asking, "If he were telling someone about you, what sorts of things do you think he would mention?" but even this probe elicited very little from about one-fourth of the women. We suspect the women who said they didn't know may receive less clear-cut messages from their husbands, or perhaps more negative feedback, than do the other two-thirds to three-fourths among whom the dominant perception is that their husbands love and appreciate them.

Feedback from husbands is a major source of psychological support. It reinforces the conviction that the things the mothers do are important. It is hard to imagine that wives who could sincerely report positive feedback like that described below could have much difficulty with self-image:

> He has a lot more faith in me most of the time than I have in myself. He seems to think I am extremely competent and confident and capable. He is very flattering.

> He just thinks I am wonderful, which is just grand. At least that is what he tells me, I don't know what he tells other people. He thinks I am pretty. . . . He thinks I am really a good homemaker and mother and wife and he is proud of the things that I do. He is wonderful about asking my ideas and opinions and acting like I really helped him.

One mother gave us the usual response that her husband viewed her positively, but then explained that it was partly because of impression management on her part. She said she hid aspects of herself or the home situation from him:

> I think he would see me up here, where I see all my faults, and I think he would rate me much higher than I would myself. He sees my homemaking skills and working with the children and things like that as definite assets. He doesn't see all of the times when I am interacting with the kids, and he doesn't get all of the bad sides. When he's home I try to keep things at an even keel, and if there is a problem, unless it is a major problem that he needs to be involved in, if it's something like saying, "Make your bed this morning," I try to do that when Daddy is not home so

that there is a more peaceful atmosphere when Daddy is home. So he sees more of the positive things.

Several mothers did mention specifically their husbands' impact on their self-esteem.

It's hard to say good things about yourself, I mean it's like you're bragging, but then if you've heard your husband say this, whether it's true or not, that's what you would probably say. He must know deep down in his heart that I'm not the best mother in the world, but if he feels that way that's important enough.

Other highly positive perceptions of husbands' attitudes:

He sees me as someone who loves children. He often comments that if there is a baby in the room, inside of three minutes I've got it. I think he's right, and I think he loves this. I know he loves that in me. He would probably describe me as being very supportive of him.

He thinks I am nice, he thinks I am smart. He says I am smarter than he is, but I am not. My version is the true version, because he is much smarter than I am. It is funny because you really don't describe each other too much. He would probably say that I am a good mother. That is what he would say to you. This is not necessarily accurate or true. He would probably also say that he thinks I play the piano well and I don't . . . I really don't. It really frustrates me, so I say to him "don't say that." What else, he thinks I am tall and beautiful, bless him.

From what he's told me, he thinks that I have more ability than I do. He says, like I have ability to do pretty much anything that I want if I want to. I think he would describe me as a shy person, too, a quiet person. He also would probably say that I am good-natured most of the time. I think he has more confidence in me than I have in myself.

Well, he would call me a fat old lady right now. [She was pregnant]. No, let's see, how would he? I think he thinks I'm competent. I want to say warm, I think he feels I'm warm, although I'm not this warm with everybody as I am with him. I just think he thinks of me as a comfortable person. He thinks I'm prettier

than I am, because pretty I'm not and never have been.
But he has an appreciation for me as a physical person
that I find really satisfying. It's amazing to me. I
can't imagine that myself, but he finds it. So, I'm
not going to question it, I'm going to accept it. I
think he feels I'm a good mother. I think he has a
lot of trust in my decisions as a parent but then
mostly because we kind of share the same thing. We
feel the same way about parenting, about what we want
our children to do, and have developed it together
over the years, so it's no surprise that it would be
the same and that he would accept it. I think he's
proud of me. He's told me; he said that sometimes
when we've been in a group and we've participated in
conversation that he's never afraid of what I'm going
to say--which I think is an interesting
comment--because he said he knows some men who worry
about what their wives will say. And yet, he has that
kind of support, that he feels comfortable that I can
handle myself socially.

I don't know what he would say. I have had some of
these people come up and say that he is proud of me.
He tells me I am beautiful. He tells me that he loves
me often. He does tell me that he is proud of me.
I'm sure there are times when I get mad that he would
rather I didn't.

Most of the answers given by the mothers referred to
both positive and negative personal traits. The mothers
admitted that they and their husbands have strengths and
weaknesses, and that they have to deal with them. For
example, when asked how her husband would describe her, a
wife laughed and replied, "Good days or bad days?" Then
she continued:

Some days he just has nothing good to say about me,
and sometimes he has everything good to say . . . and
nothing bad about me. As a general rule he thinks I'm
a terrific mother . . . . He thinks I'm not so great
of a teacher. In Family Home Evening he sometimes
gets impatient with the way I'm putting across the
point . . . . Sometimes he's very pleased with the
way I'm handling the children. Most of the time he
is. Sometimes he'll say, "You're handling that wrong,
let me take over this discussion." He won't really do
that, but in my mind I know that's what he's thinking,
so I'll just say, I'll just kind of back off and then
he'll come in and finish off the thing that he feels

is important to tell the child, especially the older
ones . . . . He'd say that I am in a rut or that I've
got my old thinking pattern still working and I need
to learn that things have changed now.

The dominant feedback from husbands, as filtered
through their wives' perceptions, is that the wives are busy,
hard workers, stable, competent, and good with children.
Said one mother:

I think he would describe me as a hard worker . . . as
honest . . . as being fun at times. I think he would
describe me as being maybe too strict or too not
willing to bend . . . maybe not willing to let the
house go, not willing to let things go in order to do
something else, maybe too set in my ways in a lot of
areas. He would describe me, I think, as
capable . . . . Stable maybe. He would describe me
as being very stable apart from the "fun at times."

Another woman, whose initial answer to the question
about how her husband would describe her was a "don't
know," finally answered the question in a way that illustrates
both negative and positive perceptions:

He always sees me busy. I think especially now, he
would like to see me relaxed a little bit. I really
don't know. It would be very positive, I know,
especially if he were talking to someone else. I
don't know if he would ever voice a negative feeling
because I have never heard him. The only negative
feelings I've got are the things that I bring upon
myself. For instance, if I haven't managed to do the
dishes or follow through on the children to get them
done and I see him out in the kitchen sink he may be
giving a message of "What has happened today that this
isn't done?" But he would never say anything like
"You're lazy," he would just go do it and I would read
other things into it, "You're telling me this and
really. . . ." And sometimes if I really should have
done it, then I feel guilty, but I would never get a
vocal message of negative, but once in a while I get a
few action signals that tell me that "I'm not
especially happy." He hates me to be on the phone,
involved with someone else if it's at a time that he
needs me and is unscheduled. Now, like you're [the
interviewer is] coming on a schedule, that wouldn't
bother him, but if we were needing to go somewhere, or
if he just had an hour block of time and I was busy I

would get the feeling, "I'm not first in your life--I'm somewhere else." He would never say it but I would get those messages.

Not too many of these mothers said that their husbands would view them as companions who were fun to be with. Being fun was mentioned by only one woman in six. Here is one example:

He would describe me as a good sport. He likes it that I go skiing with him and that. He really likes that. Probably the first thing he would say is that I am slender. That's very important to him. That's probably why I am.

When fun was mentioned it was often in conjunction with many other adjectives:

[He would say] "she is a steam roller." I think that he would say that I am very self-assured, very determined. I know what I want in life, and I usually go after it. I am trying to learn good methods of doing that, however, I tend to be rather determined, a good mother and a good wife, fun to be with, but occasionally grouchy and sometimes wishy-washy.

Oh, he probably sees me as very ambitious, well-motivated, determined. He laughs about how I overplan every day. He thinks I am a good sport.

As one would expect, there were also some replies from wives who were less positive about the way their husbands see them. In response to the "How would he describe you?" question, these mothers replied as follows:

As his workhorse, I guess, I don't know. Once over the phone he was talking to somebody and he said, "My wife" and I criticized him afterwards. I said, "How come you called me, 'My wife', that sounds like you kind of don't know me or something." He said, "Well, I think that sounds very possessive." So I don't know.

I don't know. I can't answer that, I don't know. It always comes out nicer [when he's talking to someone else about me] than when he's around me. It makes me mad. I get these rude remarks about burning cookies.

That's difficult to say. In the negative aspect, my husband sees me as selfish, thinking of myself. I think that's about the most negative point but he, too, feels that I'm a good mother in dealing fairly as I can with the children. He appreciates the fact that I am diligent in being with the children. . . . He once called me intelligent. I don't know if he would agree anymore. . . . It's hard to judge what he might think because sometimes he surprises me. I feel negative about myself most of the time because I don't feel I'm hitting the level I should, so when I try to decide what my husband might say to me, I'm really kind of saying what I think he may think of me, and I'm not fulfilling the goal that I should have.

I don't know. Usually fat; I'm usually pregnant. I'm not right now but usually that's part of me.

Unfinished Business: Negative Characteristics

Negative descriptions of self, when they occurred, usually reflected one or more of three main themes: shyness or discomfort in social groups; having negative self-attitudes, such as being discouraged or feeling inferior, along with a feeling that such negative attitudes were wrong; and not being sufficiently patient and tolerant.

Shyness and introversion. That a fair number of the mothers of large families say they are uncomfortable in social situations may be a partial consequence of their usual preoccupation with children and children's problems. Many of them do not feel they have frequent enough opportunities for in-depth conversation at an adult level. To some degree, unless they consciously work to avoid it, family responsibilities may crowd out other friendships, and a mother one day realizes that she has almost forgotten how to talk to adults.

However, several of the mothers said that hesitancy in social gatherings or non-assertiveness was a long-standing personal characteristic, sometimes predating marriage and motherhood. Also we should emphasize that an image of self as shy or introverted was not typical among the mothers. Many were assertive and outgoing, some even overbearing. We take the time to consider it specifically only because it did show up fairly often among the negative characteristics the women mentioned in describing themselves.

Several of the mothers who said they wished that they were more outgoing also said that they were improving, that they could handle most social situations better than they used to. Here are some examples of the shyness syndrome:

I used to think of myself as very shy. When I was in high school I used to think of myself as a little turtle, if anything would happen I would crawl inside so I wouldn't have to face it. I think I'm still on that side. I'm not an extrovert by any means, but I'm not quite the extreme that I used to be. At least I hope I'm not. I'm generally happy.

Sometimes I am bashful and sometimes I am friendly. It depends on the situation. If it is a ward situation I can probably be friendly, but if I am surrounded with a big group of strangers I am more prone to be bashful.

I tend to be a little nervous and am probably too eager to please. I am terrified of offending people, I want to keep their good [will], actually the adjective for that is "chicken." I would almost rather do anything to avoid offending people.

[I am] kind of a mouse sometimes. [I need to] speak up. Sometimes I tend to let people walk over me, I think that is why I am always president of things. I never get mad and tell people off, but I am a not a mouse at home, though.

This last woman echoed a fairly general concern with her weight. She said, "I used to be pretty. When I get my weight off, I might be again. I am not as outgoing as I wish I were. I sometimes get stuck with the small talk in a group of people."

Another shy mother revealed the following self-perception:

I'm quite shy in new situations. . . . Sometimes social situations make me uncomfortable. Sometimes I would just as soon stay home as go to a really involved social thing. Like a party if there are lots of games and things, I would just as soon skip it. Not that I don't like being with people, I don't always like the games that might be involved and that kind of stuff. I like talking to people but I don't always like to do other kinds of things with them.

Sometimes I don't have very much self-confidence when it's something new but that's mostly in new situations, because in some things I feel like I do have pretty good self-confidence. When I think about what things it is, it's things I've done a lot.

This mother went on to say that, "Probably I'd be a little happier with myself if I weren't quite so shy in new situations," but she qualified her concern about shyness with a statement of general acceptance of self: "I don't know that I'd change too much about myself really. Like I say, most of the time I'm pretty happy, I really am."

Maintaining the Self-image

Our major strength is that we [my husband and I] feel good about ourselves. We don't have any hang-ups about who we are, what we are; we know what our role is. I see so much of that of people around wondering who they are, what they're doing. That's a really important [strength]. . . . Each of us have a good self-image and consequently we can work through most anything because we are not wondering what we are.

As this quotation suggests, an appropriate self-image was defined by many of the mothers as an essential characteristic. Several women said they had self-image problems and were consciously working to improve their self-conceptions. When a mother, apparently very capable, listed an inferiority complex as one of her major weaknesses the interviewer said, "Whatever for? Inferior to whom?" The mother answered "To my husband, because he is so good, and so talented and I start going nutty and he's the one that comes and gets me feeling better. He's just so good that I feel really bad." There apparently are problems in self-image that may come from being married to someone that you think is better than you are, and this mother was experiencing those problems.

One respondent said she thought she saw herself quite clearly, both her positive and negative traits, and said, referring to herself, "that she needs to grow a little bit stronger in self-esteem but that she is willing to change and wants to change and wants to be better." Another woman who said that she was important to a lot of people was asked by the interviewer if she was important to herself. Her answer conveyed some dissatisfaction with her self-image. "Probably least of all to myself, and that isn't how it should

be. That's something that is maybe one of my weaknesses
that I need to work on."

Another who initially answered the "Who am I?" question
with one word "tired"--later settled for another
word--"trying" and said that she wasn't happy with her
identity, that she wanted to improve it; "to improve . . . the
impatience and things like this."

These mothers of large families are very busy women.
One of the areas which they sometimes save time on is
personal grooming, and the feeling that one does not look her
best undoubtedly has some negative impact on self-esteem.
Some mothers in our sample spoke disparagingly about their
weight, others said they didn't have time to maintain
themselves at a desired level of attractiveness.

I don't spend an awful lot of time on my personal
self. I'm not vain. I probably ought to be a little
more, care a little more maybe about clothes and
things like that. If I put something on my back,
that's enough. As my teenage daughters come along
they'll push me that way though, wondering about my
lipstick and things, this kind of thing. That partly
comes from not having a lot of time. I like to be
neat and tidy, but I don't spend an awful lot of time
on my personal self."

Sometimes a woman in jest would offer a negative
description of how she felt about herself, then withdraw it.
These initial, joking responses are clues to negative
self-perceptions that the mothers may not feel are appropriate
to voice seriously. For example, asked what adjectives she
would use to describe herself, a mother's first response was
"Oh, lazy, dumb, stupid," then she laughed and said, "no,
oh, sometimes I feel like those. I don't know." Then she
said:

I feel like I've not progressed as quickly as I want
to, and that I let inadequate feelings sometimes not
let me do the things that I could or should do, you
know. I feel happy, most of the time. I feel
sometimes that I wished that my brain worked better.
I really do. Sometimes I think, how could I forget
that? or how come I can't think through all those deep
things that I would like to be able to? How come I'm
not interested in some of those grander great things
that would make me a better person? I was walking
with my daughter one day and we were talking about

being expected to do a lot of things and she said, "What's wrong with being [simple], with simplicity?" I said, "Yeah what's wrong with simplicity?" So sometimes it can get too much and you want to be more than you are. I think that I could push out and stretch out more.

Here is another comment illustrating the pervasive theme of consciously having to work at maintaining a positive self-image. "I have a great deal of potential which maybe I don't always live up to, but I have it. I can some day become as great or greater than any woman in the world." This mother also qualified her description of how she looked: "When I spend the proper time, I'm not bad looking."

The sense of divine mission discussed earlier, while motivating, may also contribute to discouragement. The mothers compare themselves to their ideal selves, their potential achievements, and of course they come up short.

It frustrates me sometimes because I don't live up to who I am—that is my biggest frustration. Other than that I am fine. I get frustrated when I feel like I am not doing what I should be doing. Then sometimes you get frustrated and you take it out on the youngsters, the poor little scapegoats, but I am trying not to do that. It's just living up to my blessings, responsibilities.

The interviewer asked where the frustration came from and the woman continued: "Oh, just knowing that you aren't keeping the commandments like you should. It is probably my own expectations. Oh, let me think, like being patient, things like this."

Here is another illustration of the interplay between potential self and the present, mundane self:

If I think about it in that line [as a potential goddess], then I would act a lot different than I do, but sometimes I get to thinking "Who am I? I'm just a doormat, a servant, a nosewiper, anything, just somebody to blame everything on when something doesn't go right, someone to be expected to do everything." Sometimes I get to feeling that way but when I really think about it I think that I am pretty blessed. O.K., I'm a mother and a secretary and a telephone answerer and a wife and a housekeeper, but I'm also a child of God and so I'm a lot of things.

Asked if she were happy with her identity she said, "Generally I am. I get discouraged but generally I'm happy. I'm happy I've got a lot of kids, but it's just so hard because they're so demanding."

One way to deal with feelings of discouragement and dissatisfaction is to attribute them to body chemistry (usually a menstrual cycle) rather than one's performance as wife, mother, and potential goddess. Then the "flaw" is in one's physiological make-up, not one's psyche.

> Oh, about once a month I feel real negative and just nothing goes right . . . I used to worry about it more than I do, I mean now at least I recognize it as something that will go away—these negative feelings—so I try to not make any permanent decisions during that week and it helps to know that I will feel better . . . in fact, I can almost time it. I'm just going along feeling fine and so I sometimes wonder how much of our whole personality is controlled by chemical things in our bodies. If this one monthly thing can happen to me, what other things are happening that we don't realize?

Another way to explain problems of low self-esteem is to see negativism about self as part of the struggle of life, an unchangeable part of mortality.

> I am struggling with life and trying to meet my needs as well as my family's at this point in my life. I am meeting many of my needs through my service to my family. . . .

> Generally the last year, I have asked myself that question, "Who am I?" I felt like I was nothing, I felt like I was not accomplishing anything and maybe I am not, I am still struggling with the events in my life. I feel more at peace within myself than I have, so I must be getting some of the fulfillment that I need. How long I will feel satisfied I don't know. I am sure it will only be for a short time because then I will have to struggle and grow in another area. Whenever I have felt too comfortable, then is when I have to worry about something coming around the corner: it's time to grow. You can't be too comfortable in some things, then you don't grow for too long. I enjoy being involved with my family, I really do. I am proud to be a mother of eight children. I guess my greatest enjoyment and

association is with my family right now. I haven't always felt that way but that's how I feel now. With this realization and with this feeling, I have found peace and contentment.

A third method of maintaining a positive self-image mentioned in the interviews is an emphasis upon the positive qualities one has, rather than on the ones that are lacking. A mother lamented,

I feel a little bad because I don't have any talents, like my husband is so musical and other ladies are so creative and that and do all those kinds of things and I don't particularly have those kinds of talents. I don't sing or dance or play a musical instrument or paint or that kind of thing.

The interviewer told this woman that she seemed to have a real talent with her children, that she was very effective in relating to them and the mother answered: "Yeah, I feel good about that. I do like to spend time with my children. It really doesn't bother me too much, but every once in a while I kind of feel dumb, not talented."

The pursuit of patience. No other quality was mentioned as either asset or liability, as often as patience. It was cited as a personal strength, as a trait in short supply, as something to be nourished and expanded, as an attribute that had increased over the years. When mothers listed their weaknesses, impatience and its synonyms, such as irritability, or having a short temper, were high on the list of things being "worked on." Sometimes patience was cited as both strength and liability by the same mother: she was pleased to have as much patience as she had, and today's supply was generally greater than last year's, but she found that she needed still more.

The families where one spouse is much more patient than the other may have an advantage over some of the families where both parents find themselves lacking the necessary patience. A mother listed as the first shortcoming she could think of the fact that both she and her husband were impatient. She said they were working on it and trying to improve. Her own strengths, she thought, were that she loved the children, and loved to have them around. She liked to cook and she liked building and furnishing their home.

We had fun building it and choosing things for it and things like this, but I can't think of anything profound. It is fun to help the children with their things when you're not harried with their music lessons and things like this, and to watch them learn and grow.

Asked for other positive characteristics, she said she was supportive of both husband and children, that she didn't want to take her husband for granted and sometimes she did; that made her feel bad, and she was trying to work on it. In concluding her answer she returned to what she saw as her major flaw, "Now I'm impatient just like he is. I am, darn it. Sometimes I tend to be overly critical of myself too much, and sometimes I don't have enough self-confidence. There are some things that I really have a lot of self-confidence about and other things I don't."

The first thing that another mother said when asked about her husband's strengths was a compliment to his patience.

He has a lot of patience to the children. I see that in him because sometimes I lack that quality, and he's very forgiving. If somebody errs or I do something that was a mistake or misjudgment or one of the children does something, a minute or two minutes later he doesn't remember it. I mean on purpose. I'm sure he's learned to do that, but he does not carry a grudge.

The quest for patience takes several forms. For some it is a matter of trying to avoid a negative role-model. One mother mentioned it in the context of not wanting to be like her mother, who was hypertensive. Her goal was not to be nervous, or easily frustrated or upset. Even so, she said, "You get under a certain amount of pressure, and [then comes] the straw that breaks the camel's back, and you lose your fuse or whatever over something that isn't at all the cause of your problems, but it's that finally you've had too much. You can't do any more, and you get upset. I do."

Referring to her own shortcoming, another mother said,

There's so many, this is like a confession. I'm short-tempered sometimes. I think I've improved through the years, but I can get really short-tempered with my children and my husband too. I tend to not wait and see; [I need to] be patient, wait and see what happened before I get upset. I get discouraged more easily than my husband does. I have this stereotype of how things should be and when everything doesn't fit I get discouraged sometimes, whereas he doesn't. He's the optimist and I'm the pessimist. We're opposites. He's an extrovert and I'm an introvert, that kind of thing, which is probably good because . . . it kind of helps you to be rounded out a little bit.

Several mothers are described below. They mention a variety of positive and negative attributes, but notice how often they refer to patience or the lack of it as they catalog their own, and sometimes their husbands' strong and weak points.

First, take the mother who identified one of her husband's weaknesses as having a hard time keeping appointments because he loved to talk to people and let the time get away. She said her strengths were teaching the kids to do little things, from model-making to sewing, plus she was the one who pushed the children in their education. "And I guess punctuality is probably something I am trying to teach them. Those types of things probably are where my strengths would be, but the better qualities like control of temper and things like this are my husband's contribution. I take care of the mundane." She then described her own weaknesses in a way that revealed some self-image problems. Her weaknesses, she said, were

Just about everything. I have a quick tongue, a bad temper when it flares, lack of patience, and I yell sometimes. I told my husband that was a good reason for us to move out here [to the country]. I could go out and yell at the cows and they couldn't hear me. At least they wouldn't talk back. No, I work at controlling those things, but if I didn't they would really and could get out of hand quite easily.

Another mother said that "being able to cope as a mother" was her strong point, "and I'm really not sure what I contribute to the marriage, other than as a mother and wife." Identifying other strengths in response to further questions she said, "I'm fairly patient. I don't get upset over spilt milk or something like this. You just go spill it and you clean it up. I find with a large family that you can either get upset and shook up over a lot of things [or not], so probably patience might be one of the biggest attributes."

As to weaknesses, she listed one for herself that she had already listed for her husband, procrastination.

Another mother said that probably her most important strength was her special gift of understanding children. Second, she talked about her talent for promoting spiritual harmony in the home. Then turning to her weaknesses she said,

> Temper would be the biggest one for both of us, especially when we are tired. We get irritated at little things that really aren't that important over all . . . probably one of my biggest faults is that I get too emotionally involved in things. I go to the bathroom and close the door and cry it out. When Jeffery gets angry at me, usually it's for something I haven't done more than something I have done. He gets angry at the kids and then I get angry at the kids, and then I get angry at me for being angry at them. You know, it is kind of a chain reaction more than any specific kind of thing.

Faith and flexibility were mentioned by another mother. She said her major strength was her faith in God and her activity in the Church. Second only to her faith and its expression in religious activity was patience, "There's no real trauma in my life." Yet despite her possession of one kind of patience, she said her main weakness was the shortage of another kind of patience:

> Too quick of a temper. That would be my greatest weakness I am sure. I haven't controlled that well enough, and I fly off the handle, particularly when I am tired, and that seems to be a lot of the time lately. I am too sharp with the children on occasions, and I regret it. They accept my apologies when I do. I wish I didn't have to apologize for those things. I feel that I'm falling down in certain ways of teaching the children responsibility. I have let it go myself. We have become lax, so I see my greatest weakness is not following through with the commitments I've made.

She said that this weakness in herself was not helped by the fact that her husband also had a temper, was quick to judge, was stern, demanding, and expected a lot of the children.

Sometimes a wife's positive view of herself is associated with the qualities that she brings to the marriage which she feels combine with those of her husband to make a viable whole. For example, there is the woman who said that the nicest thing her husband brought to their marriage was discipline, the ability to keep to a schedule. "If we say we are going to read the scriptures in the morning," she said, "my husband gets up and reads the scriptures to the children in the morning. It isn't something he does today, and tomorrow he is too busy." Her contribution, she thought, was drive. She did not see drive as more or less important than discipline.

> Now I attribute his contentedness to his home [while growing up]. He was just happy, and was very content with his life. He was not looking for a brighter day. In other words, he was very content to just go on living the way he was living. Now I brought to the marriage drive. I pushed him beyond his contentedness. See, I said, "Oh, Harold, you can go on to school." After he got his bachelor's degree I said, "I just know you can get your master's." Not that I was forcing him—I didn't force him, I encouraged him. I brought encouragement to our marriage, and he just went ahead and did it, and he is very glad that he went and got his master's degree, so I contributed some good things to the marriage.

The drive she contributed was contrasted by another mother to her husband's characteristics of procrastination.

> I wish he would set more goals to accomplish things. I almost feel like everyday you can get something done or even once a week you should have a list of what you want to get done. He's tired when he comes home and he just likes to read the paper, kick up his feet, and even turn on the TV and just completely relax. I am probably the opposite of that. I'd rather not relax. I'd rather keep doing things and getting things done, so that's my biggest problem right there.

Another mother emphasized her stick-to-itiveness, her stubborness in continuing to try, but said that she was not as good a housekeeper as she ought to be, and that she was impatient. Everybody, it seems, needs more patience:

> Sometimes I'm too impatient, too impatient with myself and too impatient with my children, and also sometimes I have a tendency to notice—I really try to work on this—I sometimes notice, especially when I'm upset, notice too much of a negative in myself and kids and

in things that are going on, and I try to work on
that. I think that that would be the biggest thing.

Sometimes patience in middle-age is harder to achieve
than it once was. True, there has been a chance to learn
patience over the years, but there are now new demands and
more children. It seems there is less time and energy than
there used to be:

That would always be a good quality to have and not
expect your child to be so perfect. You've got to
realize that they are children and have patience. I
often wish I had a better ability to get them to want
to enjoy doing certain things more, that it doesn't
seem a drudgery to them. Some people just know how to
make it seem so fun, anything. I often wish I had
better ideas to make things more exciting, although I
used to play more games, like I had more time. When
we played games on certain jobs they would want to do
it more. We called it "Jungle Cleanup" or something
and each little task was like their picking up snakes
or the Indians are coming. I find if you use your
imagination and play games like that, they will really
respond better, so maybe it's my laziness. There's so
much to do now and I just want to get it done--that I
lost that--what do you call it--zip that I used to
have when I had just one or two or three children.

A wife described her husband's main strengths as being
organized, consistent, and disciplined. As for herself, while
she did not think she was as organized as her husband,
organization was one of her better qualities. She said she
was not as consistent as she ought to be. "My husband can't
understand why, if you decide you are going to do something
in a certain way, why you can't forever do it that way,
because he's consistent."

Most of the mothers see themselves as better with their
children than their husbands are, at least in the matter of
following through and disciplining with patience. For
example, when the interviewer commented to one mother that
she seemed incredibly patient with her children, the mother
responded:

I am probably too much so, to let them run around like
I do. I am really not as patient as I should be.
Maybe that is one of the good things, because my
husband would be the opposite. He would have no
patience at all. In fact, I don't like him to

babysit. I don't like the way he takes over and tells
the kids to do this and he . . . puts them in the
corner to keep them quiet if he has to.

A comment on another husband:

He has the tendency not to take time to straighten the
problem out. He'll just say "stop it," and not give
the children the chance to explain what they are doing
and why. The problem's just very minor, mostly he's
really super with the kids. And like I said, if the
kids are really getting on my nerves I'll yell at
them, and I don't think this is the best discipline.

Time and again, patience and being slow to anger were
mentioned as the virtues that strengthen the self-image. An
example:

I think I'm quite even-tempered. I don't think
there's an awful lot that bothers me about him [her
husband] and what he does. I'm not easily annoyed. I
think we're both pretty even-tempered. I think for
some women their homemaking skills would be more
important than they seem to be in our home. We like
to take care of things, but it isn't a major product.

Most of the mothers saw themselves as balanced and
practical. Said one, "I think I contribute a fairly good sense
of balance as well as judgment and so does he." However,
this woman who said that her balance and good judgment were
positive attributes also said that she needed even more
balance and patience in her perspective:

I still need to work on patience. I still need to
learn to see a proper balance to make the right
choices as to how to use my time during the day. I
need to take myself less seriously sometimes . . .
sometimes I get bogged down thinking that everything
is depending on me instead of seeing each day for what
it's worth.

One of the few mothers who explicitly linked formal
education to ability as a mother was one who had had some
child development training in college. She felt that it helped
her to understand her children better and that contributed to
keeping their marriage happy. Questioned further about
possible weaknesses, she said--in harmony with most of the
mothers--that she needed to be more patient:

Sometimes I get a little uptight I think, when things don't go exactly right, and then I have to stop and think, "Is this something I need to slow down on and have more patience with the kids and give them more time to accomplish their jobs or am I nagging too much?" . . . At night I'll think back on the handling of the children and have I really handled them the right way. Children can take a lot out of you. I'm always kind of concerned about how I handle them . . . I think when it comes right down to it, you don't always know the answer to everything. Sometimes you look back if you've handled everything just right, how you could do better."

Other self-characterizations treating patience:

I think I'm quite a satisfied person. I don't think that there's an awful lot that I want. There's not an awful lot that I need to keep me happy in terms of that. I think that sometimes I'm not as patient as I should be with my children, although for the most part I think we manage pretty well. It's just that I can get pushed a little bit. I'd like to be more patient with them sometimes.

I'm kind of impatient. I like to think of myself as tolerant but a lot of times I find I'm not. That's a [good] quality to be. I like other people to be tolerant of me, but sometimes it's hard to be tolerant of other people. I have strong opinions about things, usually about what I think are important things like raising the kids and how kids ought to be and stuff like that.

Sometimes I get impatient. I want to go off and do other things that I can't do and I think I should be more satisfied to just go on. I think sometimes that gets me down a little bit, because I would like to go off and do some of my old interests that I can't do right now . . . I wish I were more consistent. I wish that when I set goals and that I wanted to accomplish them that I would stick with them and do them. I feel that I am awfully wishy-washy . . . I wish I were more, that when I said I was going to do something that I would do it.

Reviewing all the responses to the questions on personal strengths and weaknesses, we find dominant themes appearing repeatedly. The mothers see themselves as too impatient, as quicker to anger than they would like to be. On the other hand, many see themselves as more patient than they used to be, more patient than their husbands, even more patient than other parents. And if some said they were less organized than they would like to be, others pointed to family organizational skills as their strong points. More mothers stressed "being organized" as a strength than as a weakness.

While the mothers' self-perceptions have some intrinsic interest, they are also useful for what they convey that may be generalized beyond these 41 families. That is, we may look at the self-images and ask "What is there in these mothers' feelings about themselves that has relevance to other mothers?" or "What lessons are imbedded in these self-conceptions?"

One of the Christian Fathers, Gregory of Nyssa, wrote that "To find God is to seek Him without cease. For seeking is not one thing and finding another; the profit of the quest is the quest itself." Gregory's approach to personal piety seems to us to apply to the quest for patience, and organization, and ultimate success in parenthood. A synthesis of the mothers' perceptions of who they are, what they are about and how well they are succeeding suggests that "To find successful motherhood is to seek it without cease." Continuing to try is the whole task; none has "arrived." Some of the mothers who might be judged as most competent, from an objective point of view, are beset by self-doubt, frustrated by their weaknesses, lament their impatience and wish they were better organized. At the same time, they can see improvement when they compare their present and past selves. Some of the attributes they desired in the past they now possess.

With regard to relationships with one's spouse it seems puzzling to us that some wives could not give a ready answer to a question on how their husbands would describe them. Of course, some of the women who answered "don't know" may have been hiding from themselves, or from the interviewer, negative definitions held by their husbands. But for many of the women who said they didn't know, it was apparent in other contexts that their marriages were reasonably happy, and that the wives' struggles to maintain positive self-concepts would be greatly aided by conscious, specific communication from husbands which conveyed the positive attributes they saw in their respective wives. That many of the mothers genuinely didn't think they knew how their husbands would describe them is apparent from their responses to follow-up questions and interest in what the husband's answers might be:

Q. How does your husband see you? How would he describe you?
A. Just a good-hearted person.
Q. What else would he tell me about you?
A. He'd probably say, "Oh, she's too modest" or something dumb like that.
Q. I'd believe him . . . What other things would he tell me about you?
A. Oh, I don't know. He'll be home in two weeks. You want to talk to him then?

Q. How would your husband describe you?
A. I don't know. I would have to ask him. He always has favorable comments. I feel like he feels good about me.
Q. If I were to ask him, what would he tell me about you?
A. I don't know.

Q. Well, how does Andrew see you? Does he agree with your perception of yourself? . . . How would he describe you?
A. I don't know. I have never really asked him. No, we are in total agreement with what we are doing. We are both very close.

Q. How does you husband see you? Or how would he describe you?
A. He thinks I'm a homemaker. I think he thinks I'm . . . I don't know, probably kind, loving.
Q. If I were to ask him what would he tell me?
A. I don't know. You're not going to, are you? If you were to ask him what would he tell you? I don't know. I'd be interested to know.

Q. What other things would he say about you?
A. I don't know. I'd be interested to hear.
Q. Ask him.
A. All right. I'll ask him.

In telling contrast to the above illustrations of limited communication between spouses, at least in regard to the quest "to see ourselves as others see us," are the comments of wives who found it strange that the question would be difficult for many women:

Q.   What would he tell me about you?

A.   He would probably say that I'm thoughtful. I could just tell you what I've heard him say before. He would tell you that I'm sensitive to people, spiritual. Is that enough?

Q.   That's good. That's interesting, because a lot of women have no idea how their husbands would describe them.

A.   <u>Haven't they ever heard their husband say anything about them?</u> . . . It's hard to say good things about yourself, I mean, it's like you're bragging, but then if you've heard your husband say this, whether it's true or not, that's what you would probably say. [emphasis added]

Q.   How would your husband describe you? How does he see you?

A.   He thinks I am great. Probably a lot of the same ways that I have described myself.

Q.   Has he ever said anything?

A.   Always, everyday. Every time that I do anything, he will go out of his way to congratulate. When we go someplace he tells me how nice I looked or what a great conversation that I held. Everybody likes being around me. He is very, very positive in building me and helping me to appreciate me more.

A final reflection on the self-images is revealed in this chapter. Certain characteristics seem "normal" among mothers, at least among these mothers of large families. Other mothers generally may take heart in the findings that:

1)   Most of the mothers have periods of discouragement and low morale. Many have at least occasional feelings of low self-image, or have to work at being optimistic and feeling good about themselves.

2)   Most feel that their problems are their own fault. That is, there seem to be guilt-producing mechanisms in operation, such that when things don't go as well as a mother thinks they should, she blames herself, saying something like, "If only I were better organized. . . ." In fact, as will be shown later in this book, many of the situations for which mothers blame themselves are due to countervailing pressures or external constraints over which the mother has little if any control. Too often, it seems, mothers have been taught to blame themselves when they do not react to impossible role demands in ways that might daunt superhuman beings.

3) Most of the mothers have difficulty meeting the various demands of the wife and mother role. In resolving conflicts and deciding priorities, many have consciously decided that having a spotless house, while desirable, clearly has lower priority than other family attributes. Furthermore, it is extraordinarily difficult to keep oneself well-groomed and well-versed while responsible for the grooming and versing of many children.

4) Most mothers feel they have many faults and personal weaknesses that need improvement. They seem to share the virtue of dogged determination, and there is evidence that just "keeping on trying" has worked for many of them.

5) Self-doubts and self-disparagement are very common as the mothers review the ways they have organized, disciplined, and motivated their children.

6) Despite the continuing struggle--for self improvement, better organization, better control, more patience, better financial management, better child discipline, and better relationships with husband--in which all were engaged, there was the clear collective perception, on balance, that the rewards of the struggle were worth the costs. The mothers are basically positive about their abilities as teachers of children and of their abilities to create homes that are loving and supportive. They see themselves as moderately organized, hard-working, persistent, committed women who love and are loved, and who will eventually prevail.

CHAPTER V

FINDING TIME FOR EACH OTHER

* * * * *

To every thing there is a season, and a time to
every purpose under heaven . . .

Ecclesiastes 3:1

There are several commonly held assumptions about the
effects of children upon the husband-wife bond. One
argument is that children stabilize a marriage. If that is so,
perhaps several children make it even more stable, at least in
the sense that parents are less likely to divorce. There is a
countervailing view that children, especially young children,
consume an inordinate amount of parental energy. When a
new baby arrives, the conventional wisdom has it, the
husband may feel neglected. A mother may not have the
energy to care for both children and husband, and the
conjugal relationship may suffer. This competition for the
attention and time of a wife and mother may be heightened
with several children.

Similar to the wife's need to devote her primary attention
to her young children is the increased economic strain that
having many children may place on a marriage, and this
strain usually falls heaviest upon the father. The larger the
family, the greater the economic demands, and the more likely
it is that the father will be forced to look for ways to
augment the family income. This combination of parental
responsibilities and increased economic demands upon one or
both parents is likely to leave them less time for each other.

Rearing a large family does not necessarily weaken the
conjugal tie. Having many children may bring a couple closer
together, in that they are engaged in a common enterprise
requiring cooperation and sacrifice and mutual concern. Many
wives do not participate much in their husbands' occupational

life. However, if they have many children the parenting demands are likely to be such that the father must help out in home maintenance and child care, and this common activity may build marital solidarity.

If having many children is not to be divisive to husband-wife relations, it is essential that the couple continue to have some time together. The mothers we interviewed emphasized their own need for such one-to-one time with their husbands.

The interview schedule contained several questions on time spent with husband. Among the most direct were: "How much time do you and your mate spend alone together?"; "How many hours did you spend last week?"; and "How do you feel about that time?". Reactions to these and other questions about the marital relationship, especially those on shared recreational interests and conversational topics, provide some clues about how mothers prioritize the demands on their time and how they ensure that there is some time for maintaining and enriching the marital relationship despite intense, competitive pressures from children and from organizations outside the family.

To the question about how much time the respondent and her husband spent "alone together," the typical answer was that they did not spend much time together, not as much as the wife would like or thought they needed. That the direct competition between couple time and parent-child time is usually to be resolved in favor of parenting is evidenced by the following representative remarks:

Well, even when we go to sleep at night we're not even alone. It seems like we always have a kid crawling in or I'm in bed with them. He says to me one night, "Where were you last night?" and he says that several times, and I say, "Well, I think I was in bed with you for about five minutes," because sometimes I'll lay down with our little girl to get her to sleep and I sing her a song. I can sing loud enough that the other kids can hear too in the other bedroom, and I fall asleep sometimes. Then I'll get up and I'll crawl in bed with him and then she'll come and crawl in and it gets so crowded that I'll crawl out and get on the floor or he'll crawl out and get on the floor. It's really a riot. Let's see, time [with husband] to sit and talk together? Not very much.

[We do not go out alone together] as often as we
should. The kids get mad every time we're going to go
out. And they go, "Oh, no!" We should get out more
than we do, alone. Probably once a week we go
somewhere. Not once a week, maybe once every two
weeks.

A mother who was unable to estimate how much time she spent
with her husband said they had very little time together
because they now had teen-aged children competing for
late-night time as well as young children demanding close
supervision during daytimes:

We used to have evenings free. Now with older
children, there's usually someone still up as long as
we are, at least, although they may not be physically
right in the same place with us.

An impressive number of mothers affirmed that time alone
with their husbands was essential to their own
well-being--"it's the break in the week that keeps my
sanity"--and to the stability of their marriage. Yet when
asked precisely how many minutes or hours of such time they
had shared in the recent past, many were unable to account
for much time together. Some women blamed their shortage of
time with their husbands on the lack of available space. Said
one, "That's almost impossible around this house because it's
so small; you can't just find the time other than when you go
to bed." Others said that they presently faced unusual
circumstances which limited their time together, but that
these circumstances were exceptional and temporary.
Occasionally a mother, chagrined to find when she actually
began counting it up, that she spent less time with her
husband than she had thought, remarked that even though
she and her husband didn't do much together, they had more
time together than most of their friends and neighbors.

Sometimes it hardly seems like any [time that we spend
together]. We usually try to do something together
once a week or so. But sometimes two or three weeks
go by and we suddenly realize we haven't been out for
a date or done anything where we've really been
together and talked. And yet I think compared to many
of our friends and those that we know well, we
probably spend more time together than any of them.

A mother of eight described her brief encounters with
her husband, added up the minutes, and concluded that at
most she had half an hour a day with him, composed of a few

minutes early in the morning and a few more at night when he came home from work. A mother of eleven who said she didn't have enough time alone with her husband said, "I need that time, I really do, and I miss it when we aren't able to have it." Another who thought it critical to have time with husband told how sometimes her friends didn't see their husbands alone for days at a time:

> I was talking to a friend the other day and she was saying, "Well, I haven't seen him for two days, but we're going to talk tonight when we get home from this thing," and I know how that goes too. That's real easy to have happen. Especially when I'm morning sick, I go to bed just as soon as things are calming down at all and then we miss that time. And I think that's part of the reason that I get feeling more frustrated in that time [when pregnant] with everything, because I physically cannot stay awake any longer or feel like being up or anything like that. So that cuts out time [with husband] if I'm going to bed at the same time the kids are.

Some mothers seemed to have minimized the stress from competition between couple time and parenting time by a conscious lowering of the priority of time with husband. Note the sense of loss that shows through this woman's account of her decision to abandon sharing family-farm activities with her husband:

> If I wanted to go down like I used to before we got a family, I'd go down and drive a truck while he was harvesting the corn or go down and watch him milk or something like this. I could spend more time with him that way, but after we had about our fourth child, I just decided, well, if I'm going to get anything accomplished, I've got to quit doing that.

Another revealing illustration of the conscious downplaying of the need for time together as a couple was the revelation of a "time together that almost was." One mother admitted neglect of their husband-wife relationship, but said she felt that during the present "hard years" it was the right thing to do:

> Like Saturday night after the kids' performance and everything, he [her husband] said, "Listen, after we get the kids down, we will take the truck and get some gas and get a milkshake." Then we didn't do it. He at least thought of it. He wanted to, but we didn't

do it. So, I am saying, true, we may have neglected
our social side of our marriage as far as getting out
and going to movies and time alone. Justly taken, we
really have neglected that part of it. But on the
other hand, I feel such a team, I feel like such a
team to my husband. Through these hard years right
now, through these building years, I don't know,
maybe we are foolish, I couldn't tell you. Maybe the
day will come, and I will come back and say we took
the wrong path. But right now I feel really good
about it.

Another mother who had had serious difficulties in her
marriage explained how the lack of time together had been
one of their problems:

We really did not have a lot of alone time. Now that
is one thing I did wrong. Mike was the type that
liked to go out to dinner or something. Sometimes it
was such a hassle to go out that it wasn't worth it to
me; then he would be mad. I would say, "If it is
worth it to you then help me to call the baby tender,
and get the kids ready," and yet he didn't. It really
isn't his role to do those things. So he was more
willing to go out than I was, and I probably should
have made more of an effort. Looking back, I'm
probably a better mother than a wife. I was more
sensitive to the kids than I was to him.

Although the mothers were virtually unanimous that time
with their husbands, away from the children, was essential to
their marriage and their own mental health, the foregoing
comments suggest that a few have decided to postpone such
enrichment until a future time when they face fewer demands
from their children. Others revealed a philosophic,
short-term procrastination which does not seem to reflect a
conscious reduction in the priority of time with husband, but
may have the same effect as the family pressures continue to
compete successfully with couple needs. Statements like these
are not reassuring:

We usually try to have it [time alone together], but
we've also found out that we can live without it if we
need to for awhile.

[How important is time alone together?] It's
important when we get it. We don't necessarily, and
perhaps regretfully, we don't plan. We don't say,
"now we're going to go out. We're going to go out

once a week." We said that once, but it never happened and it became too stressful to try and make it. And so we decided, "Well, when the time comes, we'll go." It really hasn't been that important to us because we've been able to deal with one another without having to take that time.

Comments like "we can live without it if we need to" and "when the time comes, we'll go" may be danger signals. If these interviews reveal anything it is that mothers of large families continue to be pressed for time. Even those couples who have made a conscious commitment to find time for each other have great difficulty doing so. Those willing to wait until "the time comes" may find that it never does.

Most women said they weren't having enough time alone with husband, even though they gave it high priority. The key to having such time, many said, was "taking it" or "making it," no matter what. A mother who continued to find the time, despite her growing family, said:

You have to make the time. Often times I'll just go and sit on the bathroom step while he's shaving and we talk before he's going to work or something like that. Even if you had 15 kids [she had seven] there's got to be time, you've got to make the time.

Her message to harried parents is a positive one: "If you don't have sufficient time with spouse to maintain sanity and stability, it is your fault for not 'making' the time somehow; it must be given a higher priority." The same woman described the quality of her time alone with her husband:

Oh, it's precious. It's really very special time. You need it, it's the only thing that's going to keep you together [and] keep you talking. The things that you want to tell him sometimes won't wait until the next day, or the next weekend off, and things he wants to tell you, the same.

Strategies for Time Together

The strategies mentioned by the mothers for finding time alone with husband may be grouped into six categories: working together, leaving the household and its responsibilities to others, the conscious adjustment of personal schedules, having a regular "date night," catching a moment, and clustering available time. There were numerous comments that if some such conscious, planned technique for "stealing" time together was not followed, couples would have no time to themselves.

Working together. We refer here not only to working together for pay, as in a family business, but to joint activity away from children in family production such as gardening. Those wives who played a major role in a family business often spent many hours in their husbands' company. In fact, judging from the interviews, couples who shared an economic responsibility--who must cooperate to some extent in providing for the family--seemed to have an easier time maintaining communication. Perhaps this occurs because the work responsibility requires that they communicate and that the time in communication be given high priority. Working together in voluntary action or church assignments also fits in this category. One of the mothers said that she was a Den Mother and her husband was Cub Master, and that they had fun working together in scouting activities. There were instances where gardening or canning served as a focus for joint activity and mutual sharing:

> [On planting garden together:] That was really kind of neat, because even walking up and down the rows we were talking about something, and it's a chance that I get to visit with him.

> He's always willing to help with the dishes or whatever there is to do and he'll can more fruit than I do. We have our best conversations while we're canning fruit together. He's really good to help and he never minds it, because he knows that's the time we have together, and we have more conversations while we're working together. A lot of couples would have to be going out to dinner or something like that.

Gardening or home production do not always lead to increased time together. Many times husbands and wives divide up the additional work rather than sharing it. In some of the families that had orchards or large gardens, the mothers said that during the summer they found it hard to have time together, although they might plan to make up for the missed summer sharing by spending extra time together in the fall and winter. Said one mother, "From now until after the crops are taken care of we won't spend much time together, as far as just he and I. But then [after the crops are in] he could be around here just about all day long."

In other families summer was a time when couples had little time together because the husbands were busy with breadwinning, often taking on supplemental summer work, "moonlighting" at seasonal trades such as raising bees, caring for orchards, landscaping or construction.

Leaving, or the liberal use of babysitters. By the time they have seven or more children, many families have one or more teenagers capable of sitting with the other children, at least for short periods of time. Other families have relatives nearby who can be called on for help. Several mothers said that the way they found time was to use babysitters, whether for evenings out, brief vacations together, or for a wife to accompany her husband on a business trip.

Even those mothers committed to getting away periodically sometimes find it hard to leave children whom they feel need them. Getting away may be necessary to their own health and growth, but they feel guilty about going:

> I am a doting mother and it is really difficult for me to leave the children. For instance, for those trips, or even for an evening, to leave a new baby or a young child that is not feeling very well. But it's been well worth it to do that, and I think it has been good for the kids, too.

One way to deal with the feelings of guilt is to emphasize to oneself that getting away makes one a better parent. A mother who estimated that she and her husband spent five or six hours a week together said that when they didn't average that much, they became harder to live with:

> When we don't [have time alone together] we can tell by the way we treat the children. We say, "Hey, we've got to be more diligent and keep this time aside." So then we conscientiously go about allowing more time and making more time for each other.

Another way to have time alone is to send the children outside or to friends or relatives. Under this "clearing the household" strategy, the couple doesn't leave--the children do. A mother who used this approach said, "There are times when we'll just say 'everyone out of the kitchen after dinner.' We may sit there and talk for an hour or two."

Here is another affirmation of the benefits of getting away for a time by the mother of eleven children who takes fairly frequent trips with her husband. Asked how she felt about that time, she said:

> I love it. I love it when we're away, but it's so hard to get away from the kids . . . because it's hard to set up the whole thing and get a babysitter and know that everything will be okay when you get back. I think it will be easier when the kids get a little bigger. See, we've had to do it when I've been nursing, when I've been pregnant, when the children were just teeny. Our youngest now is two, so I think it's going to get easier to get away. . . . When we're away, it's exciting. We read, and we usually go to some recreational place where we can do something fun, and discuss issues and ideas and things without being interrupted.

Even a "local vacation"--getting out of the house and going to a local motel--can serve as an inexpensive way to maintain one's perspective and provide strength to continual coping:

> We do take a week off every year and we do go three or four days, just the two of us. This has helped . . . . Some nights when I couldn't cope with things or things were just too much for me, we would just go to a nearby town to a motel and get away. And it is amazing, the perspective you have on things the next day . . . . When I was pregnant with my last child I went [away] once every other month, because it was so hard on me physically and emotionally . . . it was worth the expense to do that.

An energetic mother said that over the years she had managed to spend necessary time with her children and still get her other work done by doing two things at once. She said that most of the time when she sat down to visit with a child or to talk over some issue, she had needles and thread or was crocheting. Her time with her husband had similarly been "doubletime" with part of her attention to him and part to her work of the moment. But recently, she said, she had changed her priorities. Lately, her doing something else along with talking to her husband had begun to make him nervous, so she had decided that she would no longer divide her attention between him and the sewing. She said her family had entered another stage, a stage where there were no more little babies and now she felt that she ought to be more of a companion to her husband:

He's been really, really--very, very patient with me
all these years of having little babies and always
[my] doing something while he is with me . . . he's
never grumbled, never ever.   I know he doesn't like to
do things alone . . . now I find that we've come to a
point where we don't have little ones and I am free to
go . . . . For a lot of these years he'd just stop at
the grocery store or he'd just say "What do you need?"
and then he'd shop and bring it home. Well, now he
says, "Come and go with me," . . . and I think, "Why
waste the time with both of us at the grocery store
when one of us could accomplish the same thing?"   I
feel that he just wants me there, and so it's my place
to be there.

Adjusting personal schedules so that there is waking
time together, often after the children are in bed, is another
effective way to find time together.   To make this technique
work, one must "wait out" the children, which may be quite a
trick when they are teenagers: "Our kids don't like to go to
bed very early, so that's a problem to get everyone settled
down."   Thus, taking time for each other has its costs; the
moments must be taken from something, and sometimes they
replace sleep.   A mother of eight said that she really enjoyed
her time alone with her husband, but complained, "I just wish
it didn't cut into our sleep time; a lot of times it does, then
it's hard to get up in the morning."

A husband who held two jobs and also had to do a great
deal of studying at home was only able to find time alone with
his wife by staying up late after he came home from working
at his second job.   His wife explained that on the night
preceding the interview, "He got home at a quarter after
twelve, and we sat up until three last night visiting, and I
knew he had to get up early."

The regular "date night".   Some families have a
scheduled evening reserved for Mom and Dad to go out
together alone.   Often it is supposed to happen every week:

We have a Friday night date just for us two alone, and
that time we just save for ourselves.

We usually do something once a week.

We go out every Friday night. We set aside that
evening for ourselves.

At the time of the interviewing, the ideal of a night out once a week was being encouraged by Church leaders in the community.

> Here again, the Church says, go out on a Friday date. We really haven't done that and I am not saying we are wrong, and yet I just feel really close to Harold. Maybe I don't need Saturday night dates every Saturday . . . . We haven't always had our Saturday night date. Maybe we would have been happier if we had of. If I know what happier means . . . . Our marriage hasn't been built through Saturday night dates, our marriage has been built through support.

There was some reaction against the weekly scheduled date as being too programmed. A mother who favored taking time together whenever convenient explained:

> We don't have a definite date night every week as some people do and as is sometimes recommended. We feel like we can get ourselves into a situation where if we feel like we <u>have</u> to go out on a date every week, then if the time comes when we can't go out every week and we sit on the couch and we look at each other and wonder "What are we going to do?"

This mother said that she and her husband enjoyed talking together more than going out to movies or dinner, although they occasionally did go out. Going to weddings and wedding receptions or going grocery shopping together were opportunities to be together that they enjoyed, even though they sometimes took one of their children with them. She continued:

> So we really don't have closely programmed, set-up time for us to be alone. We just take advantage of everything. Like today, he came home and the children were in bed after their lunch, and I sat down at the table with him and we were together forty-five minutes. We discussed things that were bothering us.

Catching the moment. This approach to finding time together fits the description just quoted, "we just take advantage of everything." It involves taking time together whenever the couple has a few moments alone, perhaps between or after other assignments. A mother who practiced this method said that when her husband came home late at night from church activities, they would sit at the table and eat cheese and crackers and talk.

Another mother described how she and her husband "catch the moment":

When he gets home from work, we just sit down and talk for a few minutes, before we have supper or anything. And usually every evening before we go to bed, too, we usually sit down and visit and talk about our day.

One way to find time together is to apply technology in ways that allows one to take the children along and still be alone together:

As soon as he got the truck, he got those little sliding windows in the cab and the camper part, and then the kids ride in the back on the foam pad or a sleeping bag or whatever they want. If they need anything, then they can bang on the window and I can tell them "no." Then he and I can go places and do things--we can take the kids with us--and yet we are talking. We're together as a family, and yet he and I have time together.

An imaginative couple arranged to find some time alone and some time together alone at the end of the day by walking to meet each other:

Real often he walks home from school, which, by the way, is an excellent way for him to get rid of the stresses of school before I bombard him with the stresses of home. When he drives home his two worlds crash together. Suddenly here are all his school problems and all of his home problems. When he walks home, it gives him time to sort through and relax and clear his mind, and often I'll walk over and meet him half way. He'll call and say, "I'm leaving," and I say, "Okay, I'll meet you." I'll just walk over and then we'll walk home [together]. It's good for me. It clears my head and stresses I have.

Sometimes couples with very young children find church meeting time an opportunity to be together. Explained one:

During the last year we have not gone to Sunday School. Our [baby's] daily nap is at 10:00 and it's just absolutely horrible to spend it out in the foyer [of the chapel], and we have taken that time to be together. So the two of us stay home with the baby and this gives us time to just be together.

For husbands who must travel on their jobs or their
church assignments, time together is sometimes "stolen" by
wives riding along to assignments or commuting with the
husband to work. A mother admitted that although she and
her husband tried to have a weekly night out, they often
didn't manage to get away. So she "catches the moment":

> Yesterday morning I rode to work with him, just so we
> could visit. We try to go out once a week, but we
> can't always. Most of the time we do, even it if it
> just for a ride or if he has to go and do an errand
> with his business, I will ride with him.

Other couples manage time alone by combining their time
together with an exercise program such as jogging together.

A mother of ten described some of the variety in her
time "away from it all" with her husband. Asked how she
felt about their time together, she said:

> I think we both look forward to it. And sometimes
> it's nothing more than just going for a ride. In
> fact, one night we just sat in the car in the garage,
> and I said, "Look, there's a nicer view than this
> dirty garage." So we just drove up the canyon. But
> we don't particularly need to be doing anything, we
> just need to be together and be quiet. Neither one
> of us was really saying too much. It was just nice
> to be together. Other times it's more elaborate.

Clustering time together. People who have occupations
where the work load varies sometimes have periods of slack
time. Mothers whose husbands had such variation in job
demands said that they took time together several days in a
row during a slack time, and then they might go for long
periods with little time together. A mother who said that she
almost never had time alone with her husband, who was
taking classes and also helping to build the family home after
his regular work, said that, within the past year, they had
spent 10 days in Hawaii and a vacation in Florida, both
without any children along.

Unfortunately, most families couldn't afford such
elaborate vacations. Here is a more typical example of
clustering:

> When time allows we may get a whole bunch right at
> once--several nights, perhaps a movie or dinner or

something. But then it may go for a long period of time [before we can do that again].

We were impressed with the number of mothers who said that they _needed_ to "just get away from all of the children and to leave for a day or two." To be a good mother, it seems, does not mean that one must _perpetually_ mothering, constantly with children. Getting away is not easy. It takes planning, and a certain toughness of spirit to resist feelings of guilt and to trust the caretakers who have temporarily shouldered responsibility for the children.

Time alone with spouse was not related to the number of children in the home. Those women whose husbands were involved in a continual complementary relationship in helping with child-rearing and domestic duties were more likely to be able to "spring loose" than were mothers whose husbands were less involved. And husbands who helped their wives prepare to leave the family in the hands of relatives or babysitters for a few days were more successful in dislodging their wives on a second honeymoon than were chronically absent husbands who walked through the door with the announcement: "How'd you like to take off this weekend and go to California?"

Taking advantage of unexpected moments does not always require advance planning, but in most large families the "accidental" or semi-planned opportunities for time alone do not happen often enough.

Chapter VI

SOLITUDE AND LONELINESS

* * * * *

Woe unto them that join house to house, that lay field
to field, till there be no place, that they may be
placed alone in the midst of the earth!
Isaiah 5:8

Mothers of many children do not have much solitude,
especially when their children are young. Whether they
define their shortage of time as a problem depends on many
factors, including personal psychological makeup, family
background, and expectations about how successful mothers
ought to organize their lives.

Many family analysts claim that time for solitary
meditation and introspection is essential for the maintenance
of a balanced, healthy life. Here, for example, is an eminent
sociologist's paean to privacy:

> Privacy is the return to ourselves. In privacy
> we regain the perspective that makes us selves. In
> privacy we think as we are, freed from pressures, from
> inhibitions, from ulterior motives. Without the habit
> of privacy we lose the feel of our being, the sense of
> integrity. Without it we see and hear and act at
> second hand, creatures of the crowd, competitors in
> the market place, caterers to the values of others.
> The more organized we become, the more our
> society hems us in, the more we require preserves of

privacy. We need to guard our times of leisure in order to cultivate, now and then, the mood of meditation.[1]

If this view of restorative power of solitude is correct, then whether the mothers are aware of it or not, when demands of family and home crowd out personal solitary time, their capacity to cope successfully with family challenges may be diminished.

Time Alone and Mental Health

Most of the mothers were quite emphatic about the need for time alone:

It keeps your perspective, it keeps you relaxed enough so that you can cope with the rest of the time. I know one mother of nine children once said that suppertime was the witching hour. She turned into a witch because everybody was going great guns and kids were crabby and dinner was trying to get fixed and dad was coming home. You know, you just have to have a good-sized family to appreciate that.

This mother described herself as relaxed. She said she didn't insist that her children go to bed at a certain time, but that if she doesn't get evening time alone at night because they stay up late, she expects that they will sleep in the next morning. She didn't schedule any specific time for herself. Instead, she said, "I take it when I can get it. I spend a lot of time on the bed thinking and doing what I darn please."

To some, what is important in time alone is not the nature of the activity but its effect on one's morale. A mother explained,

What's important to me is doing something that makes me feel good. It might be creating a dress for a daughter, or it might be doing an extra special meal. Sometimes to me, that's more creatively fulfilling than going out and spending an hour in the library or

---

[1]Robert M. MacIver, The Pursuit of Happiness, New York: Simon and Schuster, 1955, p. 47.

painting a picture or something like that because that's just me. Or it might be involvement in crafts or anything, but I would say it averages to an hour to an hour and a half in a day.

Another mother said that the only time that she felt overwhelmed by her responsibilities was when she wanted some quiet time and all the children were running around needing attention. Then she was likely to withdraw for a time and rest, or have some quiet time to herself. She said she needed it every day:

I feel like I've got to take a half an hour to an hour every day. Sometimes it's more when the kids are in school, my other children are playing and we kind of switch off with the neighbors . . . mine will go over to their house so I have an hour in the afternoon to read or to sew or something or just to rest, to look at a score and listen to the music I enjoy, or practicing.

She went on to explain that she felt this time alone was essential to her well-being:

I think everyone does, whether you've got children or not, you still need a little time to yourself. When we were first married before our first child was born, we were married over a year and he was going to school and I still needed it. I was teaching full time but when I came home I had about two hours before my husband got home . . . and that was time when I made dinner or sat and looked at a magazine or read a book or practiced. Everybody can use that quiet time any way they want. Sometime I get more nervous than others and I need to use my hands. I've got needlepoint and I can do that and relax, but I never do any handwork like that when my husband's around because he thinks that's a waste of time.

Several of the mothers thought that the ability to organize, so that they could have time alone away from their responsibilities, was a critical challenge. One mother said that she had perhaps half an hour a week of such time. She said she rested in the afternoon sometimes, and that was time alone in a sense, but it wasn't the same kind of renewal as doing something that she wanted to do. She went on to explain how important her solitary time was: "If I don't have things working well inside of me then I can be part of the family problem and not part of the solution. I become irritable. I don't roll with the punches, I get witchy and so it is in the best interest of the family that we take good care of mother." She said that her usual activities for solitary renewal were reading and going alone to the mountains.

> The best thing I do to refresh myself is to be alone in the mountains, and I love wild flowers. I love to identify them. I love to be able to name them. I love the sound of the creek, I love the sound of the wind. You can hear it coming far before you ever feel it. You can tune yourself into these kinds of nature things, and that's very refreshing to me. You sharpen up your ability to see. It's interesting as I say to people, "Look at all those shades of green outside my kitchen window," and everybody sees green, but very few notice the different shades of green. When you start counting you can see a half a dozen shades of green outside. These kinds of things are the kinds of things that fill my cup and help me to face life, just a few minutes doing those kinds of things. That sounds dumb to say, "Go look, see how many shades of green." . . . there is a certain amount of joy in observing things that the Lord has created.

Most of the mothers indicated that they had less time to themselves than they would like. Some justified the little time they had by defining their present life style as a necessary but temporary stage when the demands upon them were especially pressing. Others rationalized an inadequate share of solitude by saying that if they ever really needed to, they could take time for themselves. These mothers were getting by with little time for self, because the priority they placed on time alone was lower than that for a variety of other activities and services for family members. Most seemed to feel that the time they had alone was sufficient even if it was not as much as they would like. Some of the mothers--we were impressed that they were a distinct minority--have consciously defined time for self as important enough that they take it consistently and without waiting to feel that they are going to "explode" or break down before personal privacy achieves top priority.

Surrounded as they are by many children, imbedded in complicated and often conflicting schedules and subject to more demands on personal time and energy that they can possibly meet, most of the mothers still manage to spend some time alone. About half said they had at least an hour a day they could call their own; the others had less than that. This is not to say that most indicated that they had too little time; only about one in four said she really needed more time alone than she had. The others may have defined their "need" for time differently, or distinguished between their "need" and their preferences. Most did say that they would like more time to themselves.

That the mothers probably do not have as much solitary time as they need is suggested in the way they initially reacted to the question. Asked how much time she spent alone, one mother responded, "Just totally to myself? Oh gosh, not very much." She went on to say that such time was not planned:

> Well, it usually just happens. I was just thinking that I take the kids on their early morning paper route on Sunday morning. I just love that. Nobody's up when we get home and I have about an hour all to myself and it's so nice to read and do the things I want to do. I'll say an hour a day, I guess in the evenings, I have to myself.

Generally, the typical response, regardless of the number of hours reported when we actually had them add up solitary time, was some kind of "not much" perception. The main solitary time for many mothers happens when the children take their naps. However, during nap time, the mothers were often involved in homemaking activities, so their "time alone" was not recreational or without responsibility.

The half hour to an hour a day that the majority of mothers mentioned when questioned in detail about time alone is often not quality time for them. In fact, as the response of this mother of eight reveals, in an average day there may be no time at all:

> Ha! More like zero, very, very little. Very little time and it's very hard for me to accept that I never have any time to myself. I sat down, I think it was Saturday night, and it was ten o'clock and I hadn't done my practicing. I sat down to do my practicing and the doorbell rang and all my kids came in. I had four kids in five minutes asking questions and finally I just said, "Oh, forget it," and just said, "I'm going to bed, good night." I very rarely have any time to myself, maybe in the afternoon when I have maybe all the kids down to nap. . . . They're in and out and they play very good or they're playing outside, sometimes I'll have a little more time then. In the morning if I wake up at six o'clock before the

baby wakes up I may have a little bit of time. I
don't know, if I even get half an hour a day to myself
that would be something because . . . maybe a half an
hour a day. I can't say that I ever really have any
time to myself, a set time to myself during the day,
ever. I go shopping. When I go shopping, since I
have big kids, I try to always go shopping by myself.
I feel like I've got to have that hour, that time by
myself, so maybe the half an hour to an hour a day on
the average.

The interviewer went on, questioning her about any
other ways she used to "escape" temporarily from the
pressures of the household. Movies and dining out with her
husband were mentioned, but they seem to occur
infrequently:

He tries to get us out once a week, but it usually is
more like twice a month. We go out to dinner
together, not that we can afford it, but it is kind of
like you can't afford not to so we get together, so we
can just talk and that's usually all we do. He likes
to go to a show sometimes too, but, shoot, I think
maybe I've been to two shows in the past year.

A mother of seven said, "I don't need too much to get
me going again, which is a good thing. I would usually take
a bath at night and read maybe 15-20 minutes. Lots of days
that's all I get." In the summer time, she said, her children
stay up late at night and so she loses that time, but they
sleep later in the morning and if she gets up she can have an
hour or so of privacy. "I usually try to read scriptures, but
it's alone time. It's usually doing things in the home, but it
is alone time."

Some of the mothers blame their own lack of organization
for their difficulties in finding solitude. "I should be able to
plan better," the message goes, and thus a mother has an
additional sense of guilt or inferiority. Mothers who don't
find private time by rising early in the morning may wonder
why they can't do better about rising early, or scheduling
their daytime better. This wistful comment by a mother of
seven, who said she presently had no time alone, illustrates
the "I should do better" attitude:

I should plan things when they are in Primary
[children's meeting at church]. That's what I should
do, because everything's peaceful then. They don't
always lay down. What I'm doing when the baby's

115

asleep, that's when I'm working with school so I really haven't had any time. Not really. I just feel pressured, there has been something to do, so here lately I haven't " [had any time alone]. When I send them off to swim I can have some time. They went swimming yesterday and it was kind of quiet and peaceful. . . . When school starts Greg goes a full day, last year he was home a half a day, but this year he is a first grader and he goes the whole day long, wow, I'll have a lot of time next year . . . it's been hectic this summer. If I wasn't having school with them after lunch, I'd probably have a couple of hours I could do something. Or, if I could get up really early. . . .

Mothers who don't plan time alone rarely have much of it. Explained one:

Just myself? I don't have a definite time. . . . I certainly take a bath by myself. I sew or I'll cook. There's lots of times that your children are around but they're not right with you.

Asked how many hours of privacy she had each day, she continued:

Well, that would be pretty minimal. Probably late at night when I'm writing in my journal or reading is really the only time that I have definitely alone. When I get up even early like I did this morning, I woke up quite early because I had to get my daughter off by 7 but even then my husband was up and she was up. I sure wasn't alone. At the most, one hour--if I get that.

This mother went on to say that she didn't feel abused or exploited because she didn't have time alone:

It doesn't really bother me. I don't even worry about it. I guess it's just not a big wish of mine. I don't make any plans to be alone. I don't want to be alone I guess. I guess you have to read alone but many times there are little kids, I'll sit on the couch and read but they're still around, I mean the television will even be on; is that alone?

Approximations to Solitude

Some of the restorative benefits of time alone may be obtained in time spent under decreased responsibility for usual tasks, even if one is not technically alone. We hope that this optimistic assumption is actually so, for even those mothers who said they had sufficient "time alone" often redefined the meaning of time alone in their answers. The redefinitions made it possible for mothers to affirm that they had some time to themselves even if they were rarely away from their families. Such redefinitions were very common, suggesting that for these women quality time alone is a rare experience.

Among the redefinitions, which we may call approximations to solitude, was the notion that "time alone" was time in which mothers could do what they wanted to do, even if others were present. Frequently this reference to doing what they wanted to do did not refer to recreational time, but rather to performing housekeeping tasks without interruption. Such approximations to solitude often happened at nap time. With the small children asleep, mothers could concentrate on getting the work done. One mother who said "not much," when asked how much time she spent alone, said that her time alone was not scheduled. What she did when she had such time, she said, depended on the demands of the day:

> Sometimes I'll take a nap, sometimes I'll do a project that I can't do with the kids up, sometimes it will be a fun project and sometimes it will be a house project like cleaning that I just can't do with the kids involved, or maybe I'll be working out in the garden. Sometimes it will be talking to a friend, catching up on letters, or working on a lesson.

Here is another explanation following a "not much" initial response, showing how mothers' "solitary time" is often just another kind of work time:

> During good weather there is time when the kids are playing, when I'm alone as far as being in the house alone. But I still have the responsibility of checking and making sure that the kids are still where I think they are. But to be alone without responsibility [happens] very, very seldom.

The quality of some of these mothers' time "alone" is such that its utility for renewal is questionable. If time alone is when children are napping, or when family members are in another part of the house, the mother is still responsible for supervision, to answer questions, or to deal with interruptions. For example, one mother told us that her time alone was when her baby was asleep, her five-year-old was playing with friends, and she herself was working. Apart from that, she said, she had "almost none." By counting this "almost alone" time, she could report as much as ten hours a week. Another mother in her "almost alone" time said she pulled weeds, sewed, played the piano, or read.

If one's solitary time is composed of momentary fragments or is vulnerable to constant interruption, it is at best an approximation to solitude. A description of time alone as having to be "squeaked in" or caught in snatches illustrates the problem. One woman said she averaged between one and two hours a day, but then explained, "it's never one or two hours all together." Instead, it was in brief segments:

> I just have to catch a little bit here and a little bit there. I'll go in to start sewing and one of the children will come running and need something and so I'll have five minutes and the telephone will ring. So I just never can count on having an hour that I can spend by myself because I just have to know that there are going to be interruptions.

Note the references to interruptions in this statement by a mother who said that she had "very little" time by herself and that what she does have, she gets by rising early:

> I swear, even at night time I have one child that comes and crawls in bed by me almost every night. If he didn't wiggle so much I wouldn't mind. I told you I get up early in the morning, and I can go out and work out in my garden and I have been doing that more. . . . It is so nice, I can just be up there alone talking to my little plants and not be bombarded.

In addition to gardening, in her private time this woman fixes breakfast, gets dressed and does "just mundane things," so even her morning alone time is mostly devoted to family tasks.

Following the usual "not very much" response, a mother of six explained that on Sundays there was no time that she had alone, and went on to say, "In fact, on most days I'm not alone, but maybe I'm doing something without someone else being involved." Pressed for an estimate she said perhaps between a half an hour and an hour a day. She said she often had time in the evening when she wasn't alone, but when she was doing what she wanted to do and her husband was doing what he wanted to do. "But as far as being alone, that's really rare for me."

Another mother said that she had defined nap time as her time, even though her motherly responsibilities continued: "When the kids are napping, I consider it's my time although I have to be in the house; if you consider nap time [as time alone, I have] maybe an hour a day." As with many mothers, her activity during that hour reflects the opportunities and demands at the moment: "I read sometimes, and watch MASH on T.V. If it's after lunch I take a shower, have a bath. I usually don't have time for baths."

Another approximation to solitude is the relative peace that occurs when a mother who usually must watch five or six children is only responsible for one or two. A mother of seven, after saying that she spent no time completely alone, commented that "I do spend quiet time with just one or two others in my family." Her answer manifests an interesting redefinition of time for self: to the mother continually surrounded by many children, time with a few may seem like time alone.

Only a few interruptions may seem like solitude to a mother beset by continual interruptions: "Sometimes I feel like I'm alone even if people are running around; if I'm doing something I want to do and they're not coming constantly--just once or twice--I still feel like I'm alone whether I am or not."

A third approximation to solitude is achieved by psychological withdrawal. Operating on less than an hour a day of solitary self-renewing time, some mothers adapt by closing out the noise and activity around them. Mothers who temporarily concentrate on their own thoughts and needs--or, rather, who choose not to pay attention to what is happening around them--may reap some of the benefits of time alone. A mother who had children at all ages from tiny babies through the upper teens commented that the only time she had to herself was acquired via the "shutting out technique":

If you mean completely alone, not any time, I guess, but I can close everything out and be by myself with the kids around. In the mornings, I let the kids play around here and I don't pay attention to them as I should. And I act like I'm here by myself and I can go ahead and talk to myself. Sometimes I do that.

Here is another mother who uses the same technique:

Sometimes I'm alone when I'm with everybody, do you know what I mean? I tune out everything. I think that's one of the things that causes me to be able to withstand everything that's going on. The myriads of things that happen and the bombardment of children and the phone and everything, the neighbors and all the things that are expected of me. Sometimes I'll just sit at the table and look up at Timpanogos [mountain] and people will be talking and coming in and saying, "Mom, I need this," and "What about this," and I won't even hear them.

Psychological withdrawal has its disadvantages. Adults may think one is behaving strangely, and children may adapt by becoming obnoxious. The mother last quoted commented: "It causes screamers. He's [her son] learned how to scream to get what he wants because sometimes I don't pay enough attention to him."

Finding Solitude

It is our impression that most mothers sometimes tune out their children's comments, queries, and demands. That is, they develop the capacity to concentrate on a task, or a thought, despite potential distractions at every hand. To be selective about which statements deserve response is, after all, a form of concentration. However, the approximation to solitude achieved by attempts to tune out the nonessential is not a very good substitute for time alone. Neither is the fragmentary solitude composed of a few minutes alone every now and then during a busy day. And real solitude--a substantial slice of time to oneself--must be planned. Indeed, the single most important prerequisite for maternal solitude is that the mother must consciously seek it, arrange for it, "take it."

How do busy mothers arrange things so that they can sometimes be alone? If we consider only real solitude and not approximations to it, the techniques mostly involve literally getting away, sending other family members away, or erecting barriers within the home.

"Hiding out"--solitude at home. Among the successful techniques for finding solitude within the home are these five.

--Impose a real barrier between self and other family members, by closing doors or locking oneself away.

--Impose a psychological barrier by creating family rules, complete with stiff negative sanctions, to the effect that when mother is having her quiet time, she is not to be interrupted.

--Send the children away temporarily, out into the yard, or to a neighbor's, or to some activity away from the home.

--Remain at home on occasions when the rest of the family leaves to participate in some activity.

--Get up in the morning before anyone else is awake, or stay up at night after all have gone to bed.

A mother of nine said that she had at least an hour per day alone, but that was achieved by rising at 5 in the morning:

It's just time you have to have, and you have to do it, but it starts the day better for me if I get up and do those things. Otherwise there's no privacy in the family, I mean you have other problems coming through. But I can have the [bath] water as hot as I want it, and I can sit there as long as I want to, within reason, or I can jump in and out, and nobody's going to care and nobody knows what I'm doing. Then I read, or I sew, or I do whatever.

One who averaged two hours of privacy each day said of her time:

That has to be either before everyone gets up or after [they go to bed]. . . . When I put the children down, then that's the time when I am by myself and I usually use that time to think, to plan . . . . I use that time, that quiet time, for those things that require quiet. Like I can't really read and concentrate like I'd like to when they're asking me questions or there's conversation going on, because I feel too much interruption. So I take this quiet time when they are asleep to read and study. Then if I want to play the organ or do something else I do it before they're up,

or after they're in bed. Or this exercise [on T.V.].
I must do it at that hour because that is the only
time I can have that direction, so it must be done
[then] and they understand that.

One woman remarked that the only time she ever had
alone was when she stayed up later than everyone else. If
her husband was up at the same time, she said, that was
comparable to solitary time "because he might be doing
something on his own and it is more just a peaceful
companionship," but she said she needed such time, "when
there's not all the commotion, just thinking time." She said
she had perhaps an hour or an hour and a half of such time
each day during the summer, and maybe two hours during
the school year. When the interviewer rephrased the answer,
"an hour and a half a day," the lady emphasized "At night!
My day is in the night."

One of the mothers who said she created as much time
alone as she needed characterized her time alone as times
when the children could take care of each other. However,
the possibility of interruption and her continuing
responsibility was understood: "Anytime I want, I can just
go in and read and the kids take care of each other, they
have their assignment and what not; if they run into some
kind of problem, they simply come and ask me." This
mother's way of gaining high quality time alone was to get up
early. "I'm also great at getting up at about 3 or 4 in the
morning and sewing, when I can get it done fast with no
interruptions. And writing, that's when I write." During
the day, she said, she is not afraid to tell the children,
"This is my time, leave me alone now."

Another who said that her time alone generally depended
on how early she got up commented that while there wasn't
much time when she was entirely alone, "when I'm ironing or
something like that, the kids aren't usually around and I can
think and plan." She said that when she felt she needed
time, she was not shy about explaining that she was working
on something and that the children had to find something else
to do.

An imaginative mother had three techniques for getting
time alone. She stayed up late, or she locked herself in the
bathroom and spent quiet time in there, or she arranged for
a babysitter and took off for half a day. A technique she
had used earlier in her marriage was to set aside one
afternoon a week that was defined as her own: "I would just
have one of the girls babysit all afternoon and they just knew

that was Mom's day. Lots of times I went shopping for the family, but sometimes I just did some of the things that I wanted to do." Her "hide in the bathroom" technique is innovative. She said:

> I have a library in the bathroom and sometimes I spend
> longer in there, sometimes I just go in and lock the
> door, and I say to the children, "I have to be alone
> right now, so please don't bother me unless it is an
> emergency. I'll be about twenty minutes, maybe a half
> an hour; just go out and play or do your job," or
> maybe I outline something [for them to do]. It's a
> time that I just need to be alone, so I'll just say
> "I've got to have this time."

She manages to have her older children care for the younger ones by assigning one older child to take care of the baby and nothing else, and some other child to be in charge of general babysitting.

Here is another version of the "hiding out" approach:

> I spend an hour in the bathtub at night and everybody
> knows they're not allowed to knock on that door unless
> it is life and death because Mom is taking a bath with
> bubbles.

A mother of nine said that she averaged perhaps ten hours per week of time by herself, getting it late in the evening. However, her solitude at night was bought at a price: If she had time to herself late at night, then she had to sacrifice time with her husband. This kind of trade-off, where time with spouse is exchanged for time with self, was exemplified by the mother who said that lately she was frustrated because she had no time alone. Then she revised her answer to say that she jogged every morning, and that 45 minutes was her time alone. She said her husband sometimes came to run and talk with her, but she usually did not encourage him to come along: "He feels a little bad that I don't welcome his company, but I really do like to be by myself during that time."

The method of staying home while the others leave was described this way:

> Sometimes it's just when he [her husband] and the
> children are gone. If they're going somewhere, I'll
> stay home on purpose to be by myself. It's usually
> when I've been feeling a lot of stress or I'm tired of

so many people around or something. If some of the children have somewhere to go, or maybe he'll go to the store and take some of them with him. I've been known to stay home from Sunday School so I could be all alone. It's really hard to find time to be all by yourself without any other person around too right now, because you don't walk out and leave your one-year-old in the house alone and things like that. Sometimes I go for a walk in the evening, now that's when the weather is nice. When it's cold that doesn't appeal to me at all, but when the weather's nice sometimes I'll just go for a walk by myself, so that's more a summertime thing for me. Usually if I can do something I want, I don't have to be totally alone to find it relaxing and calming.

"Getting Out"--Solitude away from home. There are two basic rules for getting private times away from the household. They are (1) Leave, and (2) Leave the children at home. Some of the mothers combine solitary time with necessary chores by doing errands in the car alone. A mother who said she did not have very much time alone said that she took it when she needed it, and that sometimes it might be as little as five minutes in a day. She said there had been times in her life when running an errand alone in the car was "my big desire." This mother recalled a time after one of her children was born when her husband offered her a day to do with as she wanted. She took a book, went up into the canyon, and spent the day reading by a stream. She remembered that day because it had happened sometime within the past seven years, but she couldn't remember precisely when. Nowadays when she needs time alone, she said, she waits until the children are home from school, has the older ones watch the younger ones, and goes for a ride in the car.

Then there is the mother of nine who said that she was lucky to get an hour a week alone. The only time she was away from her responsibilities and free to do what she wanted to do, she said, was when she went to the beauty shop:

> Just to sit down and read a book--I guess about the most time I get to do that, is whenever I go to the beauty shop. I try and get there once a week. I find that is really about the only time, unless I take a child with me, where I can just sit down and be undisturbed and really read for a half an hour or study something underneath the hairdryer.

As with many of the mothers, she saw her lack of time alone as a necessary consequence of this stage of life: "I really don't get very much time in this period, which are the busy years. And I expect that, although I'd like a little bit more time to myself, it just isn't possible."

Another mother said that whenever she felt the need to be alone, she could usually manage it. "If I want some time alone I'm generally able to take it. If nothing else, I go up to the library and browse through the books or go window shopping or whatever."

The problem of time alone becomes worse in some respects as one's children grow up. Mothers who had teenagers as well as young children remarked that their teenagers stayed up later than they did, and so evening time was no longer solitary time. Some parents adapt by leaving the household and taking their private time outside the home. Said one woman facing this situation:

Oh, I think that is one of the changes that you have to make. When your children are small, you put them in bed by eight o'clock and then the evening is ours, then they get so all of a sudden you have teenagers that stay up later than we do and that is hard to learn to live with. I think that is really frustrating. "Won't we ever be alone?" And this is when my husband and I started going away for weekends and overnight, so we could have that, because it was hard to adjust to that, it is very hard. If I find that things get difficult for me, I will go up in my room. We have a lock on our door and I will just lock the door and read and be by myself. We have very little time unless we take it. There have been times that I have felt like I just have to be alone, and I'll just go in the car, drive into town, and do some things that maybe I have to do, but I will do it by myself. I will do these errands [alone] instead of taking the children.

LIFE IN LARGE FAMILIES

Loneliness

National surveys show that about one-fourth of the adult population answers "yes" to the question, "During the past few weeks did you ever feel very lonely or remote from other people?"[2]

In view of their struggle to achieve even a little time for themselves, we might think that mothers of large families enjoy being alone and that loneliness is not one of their problems. However, as anyone who has been lonely in the city can attest, loneliness is not merely the yearning to have other people around. Instead, it is the absence of certain kinds of people or attention.

Our question was framed this way: "I know it is hard to imagine a mother of several children being lonely, but are there times when you feel you are a lonely person?" About half of the mothers said that they were lonely some of the time. Many of the others who said they weren't lonely went on to explain techniques they used to avoid loneliness. Among those who said they were lonely, the most frequent response was an expressed need for the friendship of an adult, for someone other than the children. Although several other reasons were given, the only response that appeared very often was that they missed having adult friendships. This finding fits well with the stereotype of the mother of many children as someone who often doesn't take time for friendships or activities with adults because of the press of family responsibilities.

We identified three major types of loneliness: loneliness for adult companionship, loneliness for family members or relatives, and loneliness as an aspect of melancholy or depression.

Loneliness for friendship. For many women the attrition of their friendship ties seems to have happened gradually as activities with husband and children demanded more and more time. Some moved to their present neighborhood leaving close friends in other cities or across town, and have simply not established deep friendships in their new setting. Some have an image of other women as imbedded in warm relationships with close friends, and feel a sense of relative deprivation.

---

[2]Norman M. Bradburn, The Structure of Psychological Well-Being, Chicago: Aldine, 1969.

One mother noted that a difference of ages between herself and other adults in her neighborhood had prevented her from having close friendships, but then explained that she had never formed close friendships with people her own age either:

Well, at the other ward [church congregation], there was no one really our age, so a lot of the time I kind of felt like I didn't have much social companionship with other women my age. There's not an awful lot of time right now for it anyway. . . . I'm not really used to having a lot of close friends my own age anyway because I never did have. I find it somewhat difficult to get on a really close personal basis with women my age."

Others felt a need for more friendship ties but didn't find much opportunity for developing them.

There are times when I will be feeling sorry for myself, like I don't have any friends and who would I call when I needed help, but I don't think generally I would be [lonely].

I don't associate with anyone on a friendly basis very much. We don't have much of a social life as far as going out with other couples and doing things like that. Once in a while I'll chat with my neighbor. That is kind of fun to me, but as far as going out with the girls and going to club or something like that, I don't do that. I don't even go to Relief Society [women's church meeting] anymore . . . . I might feel like that [lonely] once in a while, but usually I enjoy being with myself.

Sometimes I have felt that way. I don't really think of a time, but like I say, most women I assume, have friends that they kind of chum up with--really good buddies. A lot of people here in town are related to each other. They are sisters or sisters-in-law and they are all just one big happy family, and I don't have any relatives here, so I've felt lonely sometimes like that, because I don't have anyone close to me. My folks are living in Salt Lake and I don't have a close girl friend anywhere. It isn't a thing that has bothered me, but I have felt like it would be nice to have someone to call up and go shopping with or something. . . . I guess that's been the only time

127

> I've ever noticed it [when I thought], "It would be nice to have someone to go to that sale with."

The sense of something missing includes not only adult companionship but intellectual stimulation:

> Yes, just sometimes when I am working [at home]. I don't [feel lonely] during the summertimes when all of the kids are here. But in the wintertime, sometimes when everybody is gone and I am here with the three little ones, I miss adult conversations about all kinds of things. I would love to be able to be in a discussion group. In fact, I have been thinking I would probably join a book discussion group, but I didn't realize this about myself until [recently]- . . . . Sometimes I just really miss being able to sit down and have some good discussions. Relief Society doesn't do that for me. I really would like to be able to discuss a lot of things with people.

> Sometimes you just like to talk to a grown-up and so if somebody just happens to stop by that is grown-up it is fun. You just like to talk to someone who speaks your language.

Another woman said that she was lonely when her husband had been gone for a time, when she hadn't had much adult conversation, or when she hadn't had someone she could talk to about feeling depressed:

> Sometimes I do [feel lonely] when I haven't seen my husband for a long time or when I haven't had any adult conversation or something; when it's been all children for hours on end, days on end, or something like that. I feel that I just wish I had someone close I could talk with. Or if I'm depressed I'll feel real lonely and I've had a few problems with that. I'd say to myself, "I wish there was somebody I could call and talk to and they'd understand without my having to go into all the details, and things like that, and be sympathetic and understanding."

Asked if there was someone that she could talk to when she felt like that, she said there was, but "sometimes when you're depressed, you just don't want to bother anyone. I'd like to be able to talk to my husband. . . . I have one friend in Arizona who I feel like I can talk to who doesn't judge me for being depressed."

If one has only a few close friends--and most of these mothers of large families don't have a wide circle of confidants--loss of one friend can make a great difference. One of the mothers said that she felt bad because her good friend just moved far away. "I always felt real close and I could call her, and now she's not here."

This woman did have lots of acquaintances: "I sure have a lot of good friends, not real close friends, but any of them I could call up and start visiting with. In fact, I'm one that feels that it's a waste of time to visit. Maybe that's one of my problems, I need to do that more. Like I don't neighbor a whole lot." This woman's ambivalence about "visiting" is not uncommon. For the mother of a large family, time is precious, and often there is a sense that "I don't have time for friends anyway."

Loneliness for family members. If her emotional life is almost entirely bound up in her family, then if the husband is away or the children go visiting, the mother may feel abandoned or alone. At first she may welcome the solitude, but for a few of our informants, having husband and children gone for an extended period was a trying experience.

> If my husband takes my children somewhere and they're gone too long, I can't stand it. I go bananas! He used to take them, when we lived in our other house . . . for three or four hours and I'd think that was just really great. I could whip through my housework in an hour, but after a few hours I get really lonely. When my husband takes the boys on the fathers and sons stuff or goes fishing with them, or something, overnight, I feel like it's really not very many people if there are just a couple of kids here. I feel like it's really weird. . . . I feel lonely sometimes when my husband's gone, even though all the kids are here.

There are also expressions of loneliness for the attentions of a family member--typically the husband--who is too busy when the wife wants to talk.

> I have always liked to be alone. I have never been one to have a lot of people around like some people have, and I've never felt lonely. Well, sometimes I've felt like at times I wish my husband wasn't so busy so I could talk to him, really sit down and talk. I guess I've felt a little alone in that way, but that hasn't lasted very long.

Sometimes you can feel alone in a crowd. To me it is a feeling of nonemotional support. It is a feeling of loneliness. Yes, I have felt lonely, but it's rare. I find a need for friendship that is not always fulfilled in my life--friendships with other women as well as friendship with my husband. If my husband has more hours away from home, then there is so much more of a need for companionship with another adult. In this case it would be another woman. I find those [needs] increasingly filled by my children themselves as they grow older. I used to tell my children, "If I'm talking like a two year-old it's because I've been around two year-olds all day," but I can't say that anymore. I've been around older children. I used to feel like I could babble like one at night sometimes. I don't feel that way so much anymore, and I think it's because this feeling of companionship with daughters and sons has become a more important part of life.

Fo others, loneliness is when their needs are not being met:

Oh yes, the aspects of having another adult to talk to sometimes makes you lonely, when you don't have someone immediately to express your feelings to. Perhaps your moods are such that you are lonely. You may have them [children] all around you and up and down on your lap, but you can still be lonely. I guess that time when you are feeling most lonely is when you feel your needs aren't being met. Yes, there are times, definitely.

Yes, in the sense that no one is quite with me in whatever I am doing. The children are not really friends or companions [to me], and if my husband is really busy or away on a trip, yes I do [feel lonely].

Loneliness as melancholy or depression. Loneliness is a part of the "cabin fever" syndrome that some of the mothers described. It also is related to dissatisfaction with self, feelings of inadequacy or lack of preparation for what she was doing. One mother said she felt lonely when she was faced with raising children and feeling that she didn't know how:

I think the only time I probably did [feel lonely] in my marriage was maybe when we had our first two children. Sometimes, maybe I felt that way a little bit. I wasn't used to small children when I got married, and sometimes two seems like quite a bit, because I had really no practical skills at taking care of small children.

Here are two situations where frustration and dissatisfaction with parenting are interpreted as loneliness:

I think most often [I am lonely] when I haven't done something that I was supposed to or when I lost my temper and got angry at one of the kids--it's when I'm disappointed in me. It's not the outsiders. They are involved in it, but it's because of me that I feel, "What am I here for? Why am I doing this?" And there have been times when I've been pregnant and felt, "Do I want another one? I can't handle what I've got."

There isn't really a time when I get lonely, but I would say more times out of--nine out of ten times--if I were going to have those feelings it's in the evening time just when the sun's going down. Well, that to me is just a kind of melancholy period of the day anyway, when things are just starting to go to rest, and your activities of the day are slowing down or should be slowing down, and that's actually when I have more time for reflection. If I were to allow myself to do it, I could become very depressed, if that's the word. I don't have a word to describe it, but you're just down sort of, and that's when it would come to me, in the evening time . . . if I would allow myself, I could have one every night sort of thing. You can just sit and think of things that are depressing you or are bothering you.

Recipes for loneliness. Most of the women who said they weren't lonely referred to former periods of loneliness or activities that prevented loneliness. Typical responses were "not lately," "there have been times," "not generally," "not right now, particularly at this time in my life," "I can't really think of a time but . . . ."

As one's children mature, they become potential companions. They may not be such good conversationalists or confidants when they are young, but in many families other family members are the primary cure for loneliness. Here is one mother's depiction of this principle in her life:

One time we were hiking and I got a cramp in my foot, and so my husband sent all of the kids and the kids' friends we were hiking with, he took them and went to

the top, and I went a different way and I tried to
remember what it was like to be lonely, like before I
got married (because I spent a lot of time in the
mountains just all alone and felt that real
loneliness). And so I was trying to think what it
felt like to be really lonely, and just as I was
getting that feeling, when all of a sudden from the
top of the cliff, "Hi, Mom," and it was echoing all
around, and I thought, "There is no way I could be
lonely."

Having a good relationship with one's husband, and
finding a friend that one can talk to without fear of
disapproval or rejection were mentioned as ways to prevent
loneliness. For some, the solution is keeping busy enough
that one doesn't have time to be insecure. But even the
busy, well-organized mother sometimes has her lonely times,
and has to have some ways to lift herself out of it:

I don't even know why I am talking about it [being
lonely]. It really doesn't [happen]. Honestly it
doesn't, but it does happen and I think it surely has
got to happen to somebody besides me. The big winter
snowstorm and the lane is completely full of snow, and
you think, "Oh, what am I doing out here all alone."
That's when you have to work on your own system of not
feeling blue. I wrote a poem once about it. I
slipped it in between a book that I was reading.
Every once in a while I get it out and look at it and
smile because it is still quite a help to me when I
read it. . . . Sometimes you feel like you need a
friend, or I've forgotten how it was, but it is just
you yourself. All you've got to do is employ some
techniques and you can get yourself out of it. I
don't stay depressed very long. I might feel bad.
Like all day long I haven't seen anybody, or heard
anybody or been anywhere but with my children, and the
typical word is "cabin fever." Well, I don't want it
to last, so I get busy and change it.

It is important for people to recognize that they are not
unusual if they sometimes feel alone. Even people who have
no apparent reason to be lonely say they sometimes feel that
way. And those who say they are never lonely can tell you
what they do when feelings of loneliness come:

I'm not a lonely person. I'm happy alone. I'm happy
with people. No, I don't ever feel lonely. I haven't
hit that phase of life yet. I've always had people

around me. If there isn't anybody here I can find somebody. I mean, I've got a list right now of people that I need to do something for or give something to, and if I just had a minute I would do it. . . , so if I am lonely, I go find somebody, because I have health to do it.

Finally, if one must choose between the search for solitude and sense of loneliness as problems affecting mothers of large families, the need for solitude seems the more pressing problem. In fact, some of the mothers thought they would find a little loneliness a welcome change:

I wish sometimes I was lonely, then I would go do something I wanted to do. I like to write in my diary, for instance, and my diary hasn't been written in for months and months.

Do I ever feel lonesome? No, I think I look forward to that time, when I have so much time that I feel lonesome. I'm not saying that time will ever come.

I haven't had the time to find any time to be lonely.

I like to be alone, because I can read when I'm alone. I think people that read never feel alone.

* * * * *

In the past few chapters we have characterized the women in our study as generally thoughtful and purposeful in dealing with religious beliefs and social pressures about child bearing. We have described some of the mothers' perceptions of themselves and suggested that more feel the need for solitude than feel lonely.

So far, we have concerned ourselves with who the mothers are and how they feel about or cope with intangibles--beliefs, pressures, emotions. In the next chapters we would like to turn our attention to the more concrete, "how-to" aspects of mothering, a description of what the mothers in these large families actually do.

Chapter VII

MANAGING A CONJUGAL CORPORATION

* * * * *

Organize yourselves; prepare every needful thing; and
establish a house of order . . . .
                              Doctrine and Covenants 88:119

Many of the women in our study were married to
professional men or business executives, men who presumably
are skilled in effective administration, whose professional
success depends, in part, on their abilities to motivate others
and delegate responsibilities. Although mothers of large
families may not view themselves in these terms, they, too,
are top-level administrators in rather impressive conjugal
corporations. Unlike their decision-making husbands,
however, who at sundown can often look back on the solid
accomplishments of a day well-spent, many of the women
lamented the redundancy of their daily activities.

This attitude was perhaps best expressed by the account
of a mother whose friend was married to a bricklayer. Her
friend's husband, she told us, came home one evening to hear
his wife complaining of the never-ending task of washing,
cleaning and cooking. He replied: "Well, that's true honey,
but I do the same thing" [lay bricks day-in-day-out]. The
harried housewife quickly responded: "Yeah, but then
nobody comes and knocks down your wall at the end of the
day!"

Henry David Thoreau observed that "the mass of men
lead lives of quiet desperation. What is called resignation is

134

confirmed desperation."[1] Mothers of large families are often stereotyped in two ways. Sometimes cast as "supermoms," their domestic life is pictured as a heavenly haven of happiness. The other stereotype, in line with Thoreau's commentary, depicts the mother of a large family as trapped in a twilight zone between resignation and desperation. The accounts from our interviews suggest that neither stereotype is accurate; the most organized mothers have their moments of desperation, and the most resigned have their interludes of success, order and satisfaction.

Each large family is like other large families in many respects. For example, washing dishes for ten or twelve people is a considerably more complicated operation than doing dishes for a "typical" family of four. At the same time, each large family differs from all other large families. Some families operate on tight schedules and a finely-honed division of labor, while others "hang loose" when it comes to housework. Some homes have fathers and husbands who play the role of "chairman of the board," or who assist their wives as operational officers of the organization. A few husbands assume the role of executive emeritus, and are content to merely observe domestic life from the distance.

A Day in the Life of an Everyday Housewife

When asked to describe the activities she squeezed into a typical day, Shirley, who often starts her day with a brisk game of tennis at 5:30 a.m., referred to her personal journal for an account of the previous day:

> Dashed to get dressed and get the little boys dressed. Then I drove to [another city] where I had my hair curled, cut and blow-dried--felt like a new woman.

> Dashed home to fix lunch for [my husband] and the children. Dashed to the laundry room to begin the first of four loads of laundry.

---

[1]Henry David Thoreau, Walden. N.Y.: Walt Black, Inc., 1942, p. 34.

Dashed to [a sick friend's] house, to bring her a calendar. I love to visit with her. She possesses the most pleasing personality. Dashed home to begin dinner preparation. B. is home sick with a sore throat. I promised J. I would take her shopping for a pair of pants, so we dashed downtown. She bought some pants, then we dashed to the paint store to pick up some wallpaper for the bathroom and phonebooth.

Dashed into the house to finish making dinner and set the table. Dashed into the living room to skim the evening paper and then [my husband] walked in. Dashed into the kitchen to get the water and milk poured and the food dished. Ate dinner and then dashed out of the door to pick up K. from dance class. Dashed into the house where I bathed three children, helped K. with the dishes, grabbed my journal and dashed into the living room where I'm listening to J. practice.

She concluded that her journal account described a very typical day in her life.

Caroline described the perils of combining housework with the demands of raising a very large garden which requires weekly irrigation. The family sells much of their produce to supplement their family income. Her "typical" day consisted of the following:

I got up at 6:00. Normally I would get up at 5:30 during the school year. Fixed breakfast. Today we had our water turn until 11:00, so that meant we had to go out and get busy. We had some ditches we had to clear, so yesterday I was out there pulling weeds, cleaning ditches.
[I had to] go pick up my husband at the job site. At 11:00 I came in and changed [the two babies]. They both had wet diapers.
More water came in the ditch, so I got a shovel and my old shoes and went out and tromped in the mud and got in the water. I worked until 12:30 and was exhausted. Took my husband back to work. Didn't pick up the kitchen at the time because breakfast dishes were still sitting in the sink.
I took my husband to the job site and when I got home I was wet from the knees down and was barefoot from being out in the muck and the water. And so I decided "Why not wash the cars while I'm this way?, 'cause I just have a few minutes before I go in and

get cleaned up for C. Then I have to take C. to baseball practice."

She then related how, after a very hectic day of playing chauffeur and farmer, she had picked her husband up at work, and brought him home. He walked into the house and said "I appreciate the fact that you washed the cars, but I came in the house and it's upside down!" Caroline described her reaction: "You just have to say that to me once, and I get livid, which I shouldn't do, but I do. In a sense it's best, because I don't have ulcers, ever."

Stella's day with her nine children may not have been typical, but it _was_ somewhat eventful:

> I met K. in the hall with a glass of water, and I looked in his room and there was water leaking from the ceiling, and he had taken a bowl of chocolate pudding and had given it a toss. And he had two friends in there and they had taken two pounds of dates and had thrown them all over the floor. Then they were walking in the dates and the chocolate pudding and were taking glasses of water and just going like this up to the ceiling.
> That night we had planned to take the children to a Walt Disney show. That was their special time with the family. We were all going out. I was so upset with him, he's a very brilliant child, and he's always one step ahead of me, so I always have to keep him channeled. And I had been busy and had expected him to busy himself with his friends--which he had! But I was unhappy with his choice, and so I let him know that I was, and told him that he needed to help me clean it up, and I sent his two friends home. And so he helped me pick up the dates, and I mopped the pudding off and it took the floor two days to dry . . .

Mothers as managers. Our initial characterization of mothers as "administrators in conjugal corporations" was not intended to be entirely whimsical. The economic worth of a mother's labor has been computed by a number of alternative means, and assessments range from $25,000 to $47,000 a year. Such calculations consider the costs which would be involved if the mother were absent from the home and the laundry were sent out, a professional cook were paid to feed the family, baby sitters were hired on a continuous basis, a live-in housekeeper were employed, etc. What such economic-equivalent accounting often ignores is the worth of a mother as a manager. She controls a sizeable economic budget, supervises a number of individuals, and produces products of inestimable worth.

The list of duties which salaried administrators are expected to perform within organizations is a lengthy one. Among the more important duties performed by successful managers are recruitment, training, delegation and allocation of tasks, motivation, job enrichment, and quality control. Mothers of large families are also responsible for these management tasks. Let's consider each of them separately.

Recruitment

Although maternal-managers may be somewhat limited by their pool of potential helpers, the degree and type of help they receive largely depends on their own initiative. This is especially true with regard to the age at which they introduce their young children to the wonderful world of work.

Age of beginning helpers. The philosophical orientations regarding the age at which children should start assuming responsibilities varied a great deal among the mothers. At one end of the continuum was a mother who said that children are only small once, and so they should be allowed to enjoy it. Two other mothers, however, said that it was more important to teach their children to work than it was for the mothers to receive any useful help from the children.

The ages for a child's assuming specific responsibilities ranged from around 20 months to about age six. One mother said that any child over a year-and-a-half should be taught to mop up spilled beverages. Another mother said that one of her boys has been shoveling snow since the age of three. Several mothers said they encouraged their pre-schoolers to make their own beds, even though it was sometimes necessary for the mother to straighten out the beds later in the day, especially if company was expected.

In other families three- and four-year-olds help to wash and dry the dishes. Many two-year-olds are expected to pick up their own toys, and it was not unusual for a mother to expect her five-year-old to vacuum his or her own bedroom. Some of the women felt that assuming regular household tasks should roughly coincide with a child's beginning school.

Help from hubby. In terms of how successful they were in recruiting housework help from their husbands, the wives' descriptions ranged, in our terminology, from husband as super-spouse to husband as domestic-drone. There were at least seven husbands whose wives described their performance of housekeeping chores in the most glowing terms. For example:

He's a good house-husband. Right now he's finishing the bread I started a few minutes ago. There's nothing he won't do from changing stinky diapers to putting in air conditioners, and all the things in between. Because he does housework our boys do it.

He's really, really good. . . . He scrubs the floor better than I do. He'll do a little cooking, he can clean the bathroom better than I can. . . . He pretty well takes care of the outside.

If necessary, he does all the cooking and washing and everything. He makes the bed every morning. He helps the kids with the dishes now and then. Mows the lawn and does gardening and grocery shopping 99% of the time.

Oh, he's just super. He is really good! I mean he requires no upkeep for himself because he takes care of himself completely. I mean I don't ever have to pick up after my husband. He puts everything away; he's a very tidy person, and yet he understands that since we have put priority into this music and into the paper routes that I can't be expected to keep everything that way.

Harold is as much like his father. . . . His father worked on the farm and his mother went out and helped the father when he needed her and he would come in the house and help her when she needed him. I never go to Harold's parents' home but when after the meal his father doesn't pick up a towel and dry dishes. Now that their children are gone, their marriage is a cooperative marriage where the father is always there supporting the woman in the household.

(My husband) would mop the floor, wax, dry the dishes, he'd wash the dishes, he'd iron his shirts if he had to, he'd make the bed in the morning.

He's very supportive. He always jokes about it, that he has to go back to work on Monday to get his dishpan hands healed up. He's not wild about changing diapers, but he'll vacuum. He's not great on the laundry, but he can do it if he has to. He's always fixed the washer and dryer, whatever, when I have an appliance breakdown. And he takes care of the cars and all that kind of stuff. We sort of share the yardwork such as we do it.

At the other end of the helping continuum, four of the women indicated that their husbands' housework help was extremely limited. In none of these instances, however, did a wife seem to be upset about a husband not doing "his share."

A mother of seven said that her husband would help if they expected company, otherwise he wasn't inclined to help at all. "He feels that I have it organized enough so the children should do it. I don't feel he should do it." Another mother of seven asserted that her husband would "pitch in once in a while to help me," but then she rather self-consciously confessed that "whenever he does, I feel guilty about it." The wife of a busy church leader said that her husband had helped when their eight children were smaller, but that now "he doesn't do it, and I don't expect him to." The last of these mothers, who received almost no help in maintaining the house for their ten children, excused her husband's lack of involvement "simply because he doesn't have time."

Toward the super-spouse end of the continuum were five other husbands whose help didn't quite deserve a four-star rating, but whose contributions were, nevertheless, very helpful and greatly appreciated. Here are samples of comments by their wives:

> On Saturday he vacuums and does general pickup and invites the children to help clean, which is very helpful. [He] sees to the yardwork and garage. He'll help make beds once a week when we're changing beds.

> He'll put in wash . . . doesn't enjoy cooking . . . does yardwork.

> Helps around [the] house . . . helps get kids ready for bed. Tells the kids stories.

> He's a number one handy man fixing things . . . gets the kids ready for bed.

> [His contributions are] mostly organizational . . . He
> makes lists every morning, "Okay, now who's going to
> do this and who's going to do that. . . ." He'll make
> the bed, straighten the bathroom.

A mother of eleven also described her husband as an
"organizational man" whose housekeeping contributions were
primarily of an administrative nature:

> My husband works really hard. When he comes home he's
> usually extremely tired. He rarely helps around the
> house. He's good at talking with the children and
> helping them with their homework. As far as helping
> with vacuuming and doing the dishes or anything like
> that, mowing the lawns or anything, he'll help by
> saying "The lawn needs to be mowed" and the boys will
> get it done, something like that.

Toward the domestic-drone end of the continuum were
about one-third of all husbands. Nearly all of them helped
somewhat, but generally only after considerable prodding.
Their wives hoped for more sustained help than their
husbands seemed inclined to render:

> He helps whenever I'm pregnant . . . does everything
> whem I'm sick.

> He used to help when the kids were little. . . . He
> doesn't always notice everything I would notice, but
> if I say "This needs to be done" he'll help.

> He's not really great with helping with the housework.
> He's more inclined to help with the children than he
> is the housework. He's good about doing the yard. He
> plays ball with the kids . . . and takes them places.
> He'll do things if I ask him.

> My husband is a very neat person. Personally I don't
> have to pick up after him at all, except I kind of
> have the feeling that if he were doing [more] things
> the rest of the house would be just as neat as his
> drawers, which is a little frustrating. But he
> doesn't do housework unless I'm working or at the
> hospital having a baby.

> He's very sympathetic. I don't know that he really
> does a lot. But if he could see that I was really in
> a pinch he would chip in. But he really doesn't do

141

much at all. . . . He maintains the yard, cars, [he's] a good fix-it man.

A number of mothers appreciated their husband's efforts in spending time with the children. Sometimes this involved a daily ritual of reading bedtime stories, and other times fathers took one or all of the children along shopping or running errands.

The wife of a professional man described her husband's involvement with the children:

> My husband is using his noon hours to take one of the children for a special time, so I take them down when he calls me and tells me he's ready. I take them down to his office and they have lunch and a special time with him until it's time for him to start [work]. . . . Then he calls and I go back and pick up the kids.

Training

Regardless of the age at which children are recruited into the "labor force," a certain amount of training is required for all but the simplest tasks. In these families, much of the necessary training is provided by older children who have been previously trained by their mother.

One of every ten families had enacted a buddy system, in which older children shared housework assignments with younger children. Stella explained her rationale for matching children to jobs in this way: "The bathrooms have to be cleaned, and so I can't have someone in there who's just learning unless I've got someone that can show them how, because they have to be clean." In the other families the older children usually had the responsibility of assuring that the younger ones learned how to work and that the assigned tasks were accomplished.

Lana assigns her children various tasks with a different kind of older-younger arrangement. She assigns a task to a younger child one week and then the same task to an older child the following week "so that in rotation, if I don't get around to it, the next week it will get a real deep cleaning by somebody who would do it real well." A mother of six said that she also had no rigid schedule of assigned activities; she merely depends upon whomever happens to be home at the time.

142

Allocation of Tasks

Many mothers gave elaborate descriptions of their method of allocating housework among their children. There were a number of variations on job charts, rosters, calendars, job jars, and so on. One mother constructed an elaborate job chart, with dimensions of nearly two feet by three feet. On it were listed all the names of the children, the days of the week and the specific tasks to be performed by each child on a given day. The value of such a chart, or an equivalent method, is attested to by Linda: "We worked out a chart a few years ago . . . [My eight children] have got the pattern established so they know which one we're doing, so all I've got to say is 'Whose turn is it to do the dishes?'"

The physical description of charts included the "wall street" model cited previously, a wooden chart where tasks are posted on little cards in slots which facilitate weekly rotation of duties. There's also the rotating circle chart, with the children's names on the inner circle which rotates within an outer circle upon which are written all the jobs to be done. Another mother developed a chart with pockets for cards; she distributes "job cards" among the pockets, thus specifying which children are to do which jobs on a given day.

At least two of the mothers held to the notion that children should be allowed to choose their own assignments around the house. One said that she received pretty good help from her seven children by merely telling them what needed to be done and then letting them choose what they wanted to do. Another family, which had tried both the laissez-faire approach and the rigid job chart, concluded that the more flexible approach was better for them.

There were nearly as many ways of getting the housework done with the help of child-power as there were families in the study. Just as expectations differed considerably, so did the methods of assigning the jobs that had to be done.

Emily, mother of ten, described her family's division of labor as "organized loosely." Generally speaking, the older children had well-established tasks to do. However, beyond a certain age--perhaps 12--the older they were, the less was expected of them because of their increased involvement in church and school activities.

LIFE IN LARGE FAMILIES

After reviewing the variety of ways that housekeeping tasks were divided among family members, we decided a detailed account of who does what would probably not generate as much insight as describing the differences in the range of activities delegated to children in these families. We were struck by the differences among the mothers in what they expected children of various ages to do. For example, two mothers complained that picking up after their children was one of the most distressing aspects of being a homemaker. Laura, a mother of eight, observed: "As all mothers know, you have to spend hours putting things away the kids get out." On the other hand, many other homemakers considered picking up to be one of the first jobs their children learned. In a majority of the homes picking up children's clothes and toys was not mentioned as a major problem.

Another almost universally expected children's contribution to family maintenance was the bedmaking. The expectation that a child older than five or six makes his or her own bed is almost universal in these large families. Most mothers confessed that the smaller children, and sometimes lackadaisical teen-age sons, did a suboptimal job of it, but the "bottom line" was that mothers didn't have to make eight or ten beds each morning. Associated with this almost universally assigned chore was the changing of one's own sheets on a more-or-less weekly basis.

Just as mothers assume the larger burden for "inside" jobs and fathers often carry the burden of the "outside" jobs, many families have divided their work assignments into yardwork and garbage for the boys, and cooking, dusting and vacuuming for the girls. However, this was by no means a hard and fast rule. Families with older girls and younger boys may require the girls to do more yardwork, for example. Connie, a mother of eight, proudly extolled the accomplishments of her teen-age son, who has ironed as many as twenty shirts a day.

Vacuuming was another task commonly delegated to children. A few mothers said they reserved cleaning of the living room for themselves but delegated the cleaning of all other rooms, including the bathrooms, to their children.

Setting the table, clearing the dinner table and washing dishes was a task which the children in all of the families shared. However, the degree and frequency of involvement varied from one household to the next. Many mothers did the breakfast dishes themselves so as not to delay the arrival of their children at school. Other mothers served breakfast early to assure that their children would be able to do their assigned duties before they had to leave for school.

With regard to doing dishes, it might appear to an outside observer that the daily delegation of dish-doing to alternating children would be preferable to a whole household having a hand in the dishpan. Nonetheless, two of our 41 families did just that, if not daily, two or three times a week. Jenny, mother of ten, described her family's procedure for doing the dishes as follows:

> At night it's hard to assign a child to do the dishes for 12, 10, 11, people. So we just decided that the whole family would have to do the evening dishes, and nobody leaves the kitchen until they're done. We just say, "Nobody leaves the kitchen," and if they do, then they get extra duties, and they don't like it. They didn't like it at first, but we can get it done in pretty short order and that's all the frustration.
> We don't assign any one thing. They just know what needs to be done, and they just keep working until it gets done. The girls usually put the food away because they know more about the fridge. I'm the only one that's excused. Usually I'm taking care of [the baby]. That's the time to give him a bath.

Jean's family of eleven children share a similar arrangement, with the exception that the family as a whole does the dishes only on Sunday and Monday evenings. On the other nights the children rotate their kitchen assignments.

Many other necessary tasks were performed by children in the 41 homes. These duties included dusting, mopping and sweeping floors, doing the washing, folding clothes, preparing certain meals and baking. However, the expectations and performance of the children varied greatly from one family to the next. In some families the children were given very challenging tasks to perform, and the mothers said the children generally did what was expected of them.

An example of the kind of help youngsters can provide, if given an opportunity, encouragement and a little training, was a mother's account of how her teen-age daughter not only picked their strawberries, but also made them into jam without any help from mother. Another mother found it easier to care for her nine children because her oldest daughters cook dinner and her oldest son cooks an occasional breakfast. And a mother of ten said she had several bakers among her children who furnished desserts and often baked bread for the family. One enterprising nine-year-old boy was able to bake bread with "remote control" instructions from his mother.

In addition to making assignments for getting the housework done, most of the mothers perceived the need for one-on-one contact with each of their children. For example, Patricia discovered that a broken dishwasher was a mixed blessing in facilitating her spending time alone with each of her nine children. She explained it this way: "I found that [doing dishes] is one time that I can converse with the children, so if I'm available I most frequently will wash the dishes and then call whoever I need to talk to and whoever is available to wipe and assist me in the kitchen.

Motivation

Carrots instead of sticks. Motivational strategies varied widely among the mothers, although a majority used some kind of point system as an incentive to get their children to help with housework. After the accumulation of so many points per task the family goes to a movie, a restaurant, or recreational resort as a reward. One mother said that attitudes toward the job were as important as completing the job itself. In order to encourage an attitude of "whistling while they work" she awarded children one point if the task was accomplished, and two points if it was completed without complaining. After so many points are accumulated the children receive a long-anticipated treat.

Betty uses a more immediate reward system in working with her seven children. She pays them a token amount of money for each little task. She explained her system of cupboard-cleaning this way: "If they needed a dime I'd give them a dime, for a drawer. If it's a difficult cupboard, I'd give them maybe a quarter."

Lavish praise. One of Lawrence Peter's well-known Peter Principles is the the so-called placebo effect, i.e. "an ounce of image is worth a pound of performance."[2] "Kathy's

---

[2]Lawrence J. Peter and Raymond Hull, The Peter Principle, N.Y.: William Morrow, 1969.

corollary" to that principle is that an ounce of <u>praise</u> is also worth a pound of performance with younger <u>children</u>. She contends that once you have successfully labeled children as "good workers" and then you continually reinforce that label with praise, most of the children will meet your expectations most of the time.

<u>Picking up after children</u>. One mother of nine described the common problem of children not picking up after themselves and then gave her imaginative solution:

> We have children who just kind of drop their clothes wherever they are and get undressed, and it takes me a long time to pick up after them, and it's not my job to pick up after them.
> They need to be responsible, so I got a big garbage bag that I keep in my bedroom, and when they go to school I just go around the house and pick up all the clothes, and it goes in the "mad bag." Then, in order to get the clothes out, they have to pay a dime for everything that's in there.

Linda suggested another method of encouraging her eight children to pick up their toys:

> If a toy was put away, then nobody can play with it without having permission to use it. If other children leave the toy out, then it's up for grabs, and if it's a good toy and the kids ruin them, they have no one to complain to but themselves for not picking it up and putting it away.

<u>Work games</u>. Many of the mothers have not forgotten Tom Sawyer's technique for getting his friends to whitewash the fence. Making games of work is especially effective for teaching younger children to enjoy work. Here is one mother's system:

> "We'll see if you can have your bed made while I make my bed." The idea [is] that if mother is working too then they are willing to do what they are supposed to. "See if you can have these spoons on the table while I cut up the lettuce for the salad." That kind of thing.

A mother of ten combines work games with teaching her preschooler:

> The best thing you can do to develop the visual discrimination is to have the child set the table, put

things in the right place or unload the dishwasher and put the forks in with the forks and the knives with knives and match shapes. So, that's the kind of thing that I have her do because it's developmental for her. To sort socks, for example, to match the socks is a really good exercise for a kid her age, and so she does that.

Job Enrichment: Tricks of the Trade

An outgrowth of the human relations approach to management is the enrichment of a person's job which enhances his or her feeling of self-esteem. This may be accomplished through giving individuals a variety of tasks to perform, increasing their level of responsibility, etc.

Rotation of tasks. Most mothers generally agreed that a rotation of tasks among children helped alleviate the boredom of routine housework. Over half favored a weekly rotation of jobs; roughly one in five preferred daily rotational schedules, especially with the dishes, and about the same proportion said they preferred to have the children assigned to various duties for a month at a time. With a bit of an understatement, Charlotte defended her system of yearly rotation of tasks among her seven children on the grounds that "changing jobs adds confusion."

Despite her well-intentioned plan of constructing a roster with specific assignments, Sherrie admitted that the system sometimes breaks down. "I ran into so many problems with the girls taking turns doing the dishes, so they had to work together the last month. All three of them have been out there doing dishes at night. It's been pleasant, too. They have a long talk; it takes them a long time because they talk."

Stella avoided all rotation problems by declaring that "the assigned chore is their room." By implication, if the children assume responsibility for their own rooms, her task in maintaining the remaining rooms in the house is lightened considerably.

One enterprising domestic administrator adds a touch of enrichment by delegating housework tasks through the luck-of-the-draw. All of the household duties are listed on slips of paper, and the children draw out a more-or-less equal number of tasks and then do them as fate has prescribed. She mixes in the "good" jobs with the "bad," so that theoretically everyone will have at least one enjoyable job.

A few mothers were involved in self-enrichment through aesthetic activities which could be combined with housework and make it more bearable, either by providing variety during the day or by "doubling up" a chore with a fun activity. For example, three of the mothers were taking vocal or piano lessons, a fourth was a professional musician who often played her instrument for fun and profit, a fifth took art classes at the University, and a sixth took dancing lessons. The aspiring singer said that she sang as she vacuumed and often recorded and replayed tapes while washing dishes, folding clothes, etc.

Many of the mothers had "solved" housework problems ingeniously. Some of these creative management techniques are described below in the hope that other homemakers may find them useful.

Summer kitchen traffic. When one has eight children, many of whom are playing hard all day long in the hot summer sun, the number of trips to the refrigerator for a cool drink can boggle the mind. And the number of glasses used can produce an empty cupboard by dinner time. Arlene solved the problem in this way:

> You see those little cups? We really have a problem because everybody comes in and runs the water to get it cold and if I put a big container in the fridge, it's used up. The fridge is open all day. So I put ice water in that jug every morning and everybody just uses their own cup, and then I don't have dirty glasses all over.

Each of her children has a cup marked with the first letter of his or her name, so there is no conflict or confusion over which glass to use.

Dirty fingers on the walls. Several mothers complained about the continual soiling of doors and walls because children walked through the house with dirty hands and touched things. One mother makes spot checks on the children's hands throughout the day. If they're not reasonably clean before they have entered the house, the children must forego a dessert, a movie or some other reward.

Cooking. We mentioned earlier in the chapter that several mothers delegate a substantial portion of their cooking to husbands and older children. For those mothers less inclined to delegate culinary chores, Emily's solution to feeding her ten children may be helpful:

> Often before I get breakfast cleared up, I'll have a casserole assembled and ready. This helps get the pressure off the dinner hour, because if I'm tired of cooking dinner, then I'm not free to meet children's needs.
>
> The slow pot is a lovely way to manage, and we eat a lot of soup and lots of things that you can just prepare ahead and just stick in the oven, and all you have to do is last minute preparations.

To reduce summertime cooking by a third, two of the mothers prepared only two meals a day. Breakfast was served around nine a.m. for the children still at home, and then another meal was served around two-thirty in the afternoon. The children then fended for themselves during the rest of the day, usually having a snack before bedtime. This arrangement assured the family of two nutritious meals a day, and no one seemed to mind preparing a supplementary supper as needed. This arrangement was said to free up considerable blocks of summer time.

Reducing elephants to bite size. In response to the question, How do you eat an elephant?, the appropriate response is: one bite at a time. At least two families have found that dividing extremely large tasks into bite-size units has been very helpful in preventing children from becoming too discouraged as they face big jobs. For example, one mother divides her very large kitchen into sections so that, instead of strapping one unwary youth with scrubbing the whole kitchen floor, each child is responsible for one manageable section which can be done in short order.

Sarah explained her family's division of labor for outside work:

> This year everybody has his own garden. They got to choose what they wanted to plant and then that person has a certain area to do. He can do anything he wants, but he has to keep it good, weed-free. So far it's working really good.

Rewards of Housework

The 41 mothers were asked a series of questions relating to housework. We began with very general questions and then zeroed in on the specifics of who does what around the house. The reactions to housework generally ranged from "I like it, I like a clean house" to "I hate it; it's the pits."

The seeming insensitivity of children and husbands to many a mother's ongoing task of maintaining the home was expressed well by one mother: "My kids think I love it, but actually I've never enjoyed housework. I can't think of anything rewarding [about it]."

Even if they do not enjoy it, the mothers indicated that their housework provided some sense of fulfillment. Almost two thirds of the 41 mothers had a positive attitude about some aspect of housework, or could identify a few repetitive tasks which they liked. A very common reaction to housework was that the mother felt rewarded when her house was clean. It may be burdensome to arrive at that point, and some women confessed that they never do, but when the house is clean, even for a fleeting moment, she experiences a feeling of triumph.

Specific tasks which the women liked varied considerably. One woman's drudgery is another woman's diversion. Two different mothers used identical words to describe the most rewarding aspect of homemaking: "When I cook a meal and everyone enjoys it." Several others agreed that cooking was a creative outlet for them.

Some homemakers who read this book may think that women were being facetious when they said that mopping the floor was the most rewarding of their household duties, but two mothers, in all seriousness, said just that. Three other women expressed a certain fondness for vacuuming, others said they enjoyed sewing. One mother confessed that, although doing the laundry was not a popular chore with most of her friends, for her it was enjoyable.

Mary, mother of eight, couched her response to housework in poetic terms:

I think it's very challenging, housework and
mothering . . .
To set a goal and accomplish that within the time
limit I've
set.

> To watch my children at their play or work
> and see them achieving in areas that I've tried to direct
> them.
> To look out the window that's clean and sparking
> and see the world looking clean because my window's
> clean.
> To provide a meal to satisfy a tired husband and family;
> that's good,
> and it refreshes them and makes them ready for the
> evening.
> To awaken early and provide breakfast
> for our family that's going out to work;
> those are really the rewarding things.

Another mother expressed similar sentiments in focusing upon the managerial by-products of housework rather than the work itself. It was rewarding to her, she said, to "watch the children work together and assume responsibility to learn how to do things."

The beauty or bondage of housework is largely in the eye of the beholder. Each individual homemaker defines the situation for herself. Marilyn, in reviewing her experiences caring for eight children, shared the observation that "you can feel like [household duties] are drudgery or worthwhile. You can feel sorry for yourself when you have to do dishes all the time, or you can realize that there's accomplishment, and I feel that way about it."

Mary echoed these feelings: "Maybe doing the dishes with your hands in the water isn't always enjoyable, but having the counters clean and the dishes ready and sparkling [that's rewarding]. The reward then comes after the task."

One mother, momentarily overlooking the less rewarding aspects of housework shared her feelings that household duties "ought to be enjoyed, and usually I do. . . . Housework is rewarding because my husband likes a clean house." Another mother exercising the power of positive thinking observed that "If I look at it from the perspective of 'I'm cleaning Cindy's room' instead of 'I'm cleaning a bedroom'--if I'm doing it for a person--then it makes the work easier to do."

Jenny, a mother of ten, shared a healthy yet realistic attitude toward housekeeping:

I don't keep house very well, plus the fact that
we have a philosophy that the home belongs to our
family and the kids are just as responsible as I am
for cleaning up and so on. Some of the things I do
are mostly food preparation, laundry, and just keep
things altogether and managing. Many mothers say they
feel trapped. I don't feel that at all. <u>I don't feel
trapped here</u>. <u>I just am glad that I can be home</u>. I'm
glad I don't have to go away to do what I do.

One mother of nine, when asked what aspect of
housework was most rewarding to her summarized the feelings
of many homemakers with the pithy reply: "FINISHING IT!"

Dealing with Drudgery

At least half of the housewives answered the query on
the <u>least</u> rewarding aspects of household duties with a
variation on the repetition theme. It is the "doing it over
and over" rather than the task itself that bothers them.
Many of them lumped all the housework into a collective
bundle to which they reacted in terms such as:

"I can work all day long and look around me and
see twice as much to be done as I've accomplished."

"It's always there—always dirty again."

"Just the sameness—a complete continual round."

"You do the same thing over and over and over."

"It's just something that you do and you do and
you do and you do."

Levels of frustration varied considerably among our
respondents, but the frustrations themselves are nearly
universal:

"There's never enough time."

"It doesn't stay done, and it's boring."

"It's never a job that is completed."

"I get it done and in three hours it falls apart
again."

"I can never remember totally having a clean house."

Although most of the women were able to identify a task or two which they felt to be somewhat rewarding, virtually all of these mothers found many aspects of the domestic life unrewarding. And the emotional intensity revealed in the responses leaned largely toward the demanding aspects of homemaking rather than its rewards.

Ideas about which activities were most demanding varied from one mother to the next, as did the identification of most rewarding duties. Although one mother sincerely claimed that she loved to do ironing, pressing clothes was at the top of the "hit list" for several other mothers, many of whom eulogized the inventors of permanently-pressed clothing. At least three mothers said that their greatest discontent was having to continually pick up after their husbands and children.

Doing the laundry also headed the list of unpopular tasks. A mother of seven described her children with a mixture of pride and frustration: "They're great at taking showers, I've never seen cleaner kids in my life. They use a towel once and it goes in the wash. . . . I'm used to washing umpteen dozen loads of towels."

Television commercials notwithstanding, cleaning ovens also ranked high among the categories of unfavorite things. Scrubbing floors, cleaning walls, refrigerators and bathrooms also deserve honorable mention among most disliked tasks. With the aid of the sometimes elaborate schemes of delegation, many of the mothers of large families have greatly reduced their responsibilities for the disliked chore of dishwashing.

One mother joked about the continual challenge of managing a household for eleven people, saying that she was afraid that someday she would pass away and then everyone would discover that room where all the unmended and unironed clothes had been stashed away.

Quality Control: Living with Imperfection

An attitude shared by several of the mothers was that they were "cleaner of last resort." With respect to housework, the mother's motto is "the buck stops here." Said one:

> If I ask them to do something, generally they do. If it doesn't get done I will do it for them. If it gets too tacky and I have someone coming over, I'm not going to be embarrassed because they are tacky. [emphasis added]

Here is another illustration of a mother's commitment to a clean house, and how she ensures a "quality product":

> Well, my children would say, "How come it has to look just right?", but I don't know, I like to be clean and I like the rooms cleaned. I've gone to get my fourteen-year-old out of school and have her come home and make the bed. We've done it twice to her and this has been five years ago and because of that we've never had to say again "Make your bed."

There is a certain price one must pay for the "curse of respectability" in the quixotic quest for the "Immaculate Homemaker of the Year Award." And while few, if any, of the mothers interviewed view themselves as trying to keep pace with that mythic award winner, they do have an image of how a well-kept home should appear. Most of them described a process of adjustment, a scaling down of personal expectations about housework which had accompanied the growth of their families. Thus, while many of the mothers expressed a sense of frustration in never being able to have a perfectly clean house, nevertheless, they had learned to adapt to this stressful challenge by striking an effective compromise with reality. Said one:

> I used to not go to bed until my house was absolutely straight. But [now] come ten o'clock, if everything isn't straight it will keep until tomorrow. I mean you really don't have to vacuum your house every day, the floors will stay there--unfortunately they do. I like to have a [clean] living room. I told the children to please leave me one [clean] room so that when people come I don't have to be embarrassed.

A mother of eleven objectively summarized her own capabilities as a homemaker in the following terms:

> I like to work. I'm really a pretty good worker. I find that I'm not an immaculate housekeeper. It doesn't really matter to me if every bit of the house is clean. I find if I try and keep the house too clean, then I'm uptight trying to keep it that way, because there's so many people walking in and getting it dirty, and it's just difficult to keep the bathroom in perfect order.

Another mother explained her managerial philosophy this way:

> There are only so many hours in a day, and though I would love to have everything spotless and everything in their place I simply cannot do that and keep a happy home. In terms of time with kids, I feel that it's easier to keep things organized if things are clean and straight.
>
> Sometimes it's more important to sit down and practice with one of my children or sit down and read a book.

A compatriot of hers echoed an attitude of healthy compromise:

> "We're not spotless people; we'd rather be happy than spotless!"

Chapter VIII

DEALING WITH STRESS

* * * * *

The reward of one duty done is the power to fulfill
another.

--George Eliot

In addition to responding to several general questions
about life in large families, the 41 mothers in our sample were
also asked to respond to a structured questionnaire. This
instrument included a series of statements describing various
reactions to stress. Mothers were asked to indicate the
extent to which they either agreed or disagreed with each
descriptive statement. Responses ranged from "strongly
agree" to "strongly disagree" with a provision for those who
were uncertain in their feelings. For reasons of sheer
efficiency, we have collapsed the strongly agree and agree
responses and reported these below.

Reactions to the Stresses of Large Families
(N = 41)

	Percent in Agreement
I'd sooner have too much to do than not enough	88
I end each day with a sense of accomplishment	59
There are too many demands on me	39
I often feel overwhelmed	34
Sometimes I just want to give up	24
At the end of the day I'm exhausted	20
I always feel "on top" of my duties	12
I experience a great amount of nervous strain	10
I am usually tense or nervous	5
Sometimes I wish I'd go to sleep and not wake up	0

I'd sooner be busy. The research in organizational behavior indicates that role overload is only one kind of stress experienced by workers in large organizations.[1] The other side of the coin is boredom and under-utilization.[2] It is an understatement to say that none of the 41 mothers we interviewed suffered from either boredom or from a lack of things to do. In fact, 88 percent of them agreed that it was better to have too much than not enough to do.

Sense of accomplishment. A few mothers indicated that the recurrent routine of housework and caring for a large family sometimes robbed them of a real sense of accomplishment. One of them said:

> A month seems like quite a long while. If you can look back over that long a time and think, "Gosh, I have done this and this and that all this month, and I haven't done all I wanted to do," then you can start feeling depressed.

Notwithstanding the fact that many women shared similar frustrations with the fact that "a woman's work is never done," a slight majority of them (59 percent) concurred that the end of each day brings with it a sense of accomplishment.

Overwhelming opportunities. Sixteen of the mothers (39 percent) indicated that too many demands were made on them, and one third (34 percent) said they frequently felt overwhelmed by all they had to do. When asked how often she felt overwhelmed, Arlene, a mother of eight, replied: "About once a day, absolutely!"

Interviewer: What do you do when you feel like that?

Arlene: Oh, a good cry is a good help. It helps for me to unload it on my

---

[1]Robert L. Kahn and Robert P. Quinn, "Role Stress: A Framework for Analysis," in Alan McLean (Ed.) Mental Health and Work Organizations. Chicago: Rand McNally, 1970, pp. 50-115.

[2]Robert D. Caplan, Sidney Cobb, John R. P. French, Jr., R. Van Harrison, and S. R. Pinneau, Jr., Job Demands and Worker Health. Washington, D.C.: U.S. Department of Health, Education and Welfare, 1975.

husband, and he is very, very understanding and positive. He never scolds me or says I have it better than most people, or anything like that.

Interviewer: What doesn't get done when you get overwhelmed?

Arlene: I let the housework go. I should spend more time with these babies reading stories to them. Little Becky has gotten . . . four or five books under her arm and walks through the house and says, "Story time, story." Poor thing comes to me first, and then goes to her brothers and sisters. She usually finds someone to sit down with her, but I'm afraid that it hasn't been me very often.

Stella contended that she seldom feels overwhelmed.

I've got lots of people to do the work that overwhelms [me]. . . . It would mostly be when I have something come up with my church responsibilities, . . . If I haven't prepared well and have a lesson to give, plus everything else to do, then I feel overwhelmed.

Feelings of exhaustion. In his modern classic, The Stress of Life, Hans Selye describes the process of stress resistance in terms of three stages: (1) the initial alarm reaction where the body prepares to face a threat or challenge; (2) the resistance stage, wherein one continues to cope with continual challenges; and (3) the exhaustion stage, when the mind and body ask for a "time out" through symptoms of illness.[3] It is one thing to become ill and ask one's employer to be temporarily relieved of one's obligations. It is quite another matter to be the mother of half a dozen or more small children and ask to be relieved of one's duties. Judy described the problem (and her solution) this way:

Mothers aren't allowed to get sick. That's what William says, "You're not allowed to get sick. It's all right for me to get sick, but you can't get sick, because everybody will fall apart if you are sick."

---

[3]Hans Selye, The Stress of Life. N.Y.: McGraw-Hill Book Co., 1976.

William has taken time off work before and stayed home
if I have been sick. Or, if it has been on the
weekend, he will fix the meals, etc. A lot of times I
count on the kids to help out.

There may be a rather wide-spread perception that
women who bear several children are somehow immune to
illness, especially to the ravages of morning sickness and
miscarriages. Although many of the mothers in our sample
enjoyed very robust health and sustained energy levels, this
was definitely not the case with all of them.

A case in point is Norma, the mother of eleven who was
pregnant at the time of the interview. She remembered that
she had been so sick with her first child that she was barely
able to get out of bed for several months. Subsequent
pregnancies weren't any better, but her increasing
responsibilities wouldn't allow her to slow down for morning
sickness. For this mother, the birth of a new baby was
almost like a vacation. Her husband's insurance had good
maternity coverage and she took advantage of a quiet week in
the hospital after the newest baby arrived.

June, the mother of ten, said that she had "morning
sickness really bad with the kids until Mark was born. I was
really sick, and I figured if vitamins are supposed to be the
answer, then there's got to be some kind of problem." She
explained that her physician gave her a series of Vitamin B_{12}
shots which solved the problem.

Lana, a mother of eight, replied that most of her
physical illness had been related to pregnancies.

Other than that, I can't say that I've really suffered
any great difficulties after the three miscarriages.
Then with the three boys I did have problems. I had
to be cared for for the first five months, and then
after that things were generally fine.

Colleen, mother of seven children, described her most
serious bout of illness shortly after the birth of one of her
children:

I was in the hospital and the baby was about three
months old. They didn't know what was wrong with me.
They thought I had had a heart attack. My mother was
teaching school, and so we couldn't really ask her to
come, and so we called his mother [who] flew out here

within a couple of days and spent about two-and-a-half weeks with us. Then she took the two older boys back with her on the plane, and they spent a month all together there, and [this] gave me a chance to rest.

The remaining mothers in the sample said their illnesses were confined to an occasional episode of the flu. Generally speaking, no illnesses requiring hospitalization and extended care were discussed by the mothers.

In our sample one of every five mothers said she ended each day with a feeling of exhaustion. Only five of the mothers expressed agreement with the notion that they always felt "on top" of their duties. Four of the mothers confided that managing their respective conjugal corporations induced a great amount of nervous strain. However, only two mothers characterized themselves as "usually tense or nervous."

Sleeping without waking. Although many of the mothers poignantly described their feelings of frustration and frequent exhaustion, none of them indicated that some days they'd "like to go to sleep and never wake up." The recuperative powers of a good night's sleep seemed to provide adequate regeneration for the entire sample. However, several mothers did state that it was a rare night when at least one of the children didn't wake up and need comforting.

Methods for Coping

The tricks-of-the-trade which people use to combat stress probably vary with the number of people one consults. In order to confine the range of possible coping strategies, we included a list of eight techniques commonly discussed in the research literature. The mothers were asked to indicate which of these techniques they used regularly.

Of course, several of the women used a combination of different techniques.

LIFE IN LARGE FAMILIES

Coping Techniques[4]
(N = 41)

Percent Used
Frequently

1.	Setting priorities	80
2.	Asking for help from others.	63
3.	Not taking on too much: saying "no"	59
4.	Postponing things when necessary	51
5.	Delegation of duties	49
6.	Sticking to a job until it's done.	49
7.	Resigning when "overloaded".	39
8.	Using my workload as an excuse	34

Setting priorities. It may appear to be easy to rely
upon the Savior's admonition to "Seek ye first the Kingdom of
God" (Matt. 6:33) in establishing one's priorities. But what
course of action does a mother of a large family take when
her domestic duties conflict with her lay calling in a Church
which involves every member as a Sunday School teacher,
Cub Scout den mother, etc.? Several of the women had had
to wrestle with this problem. One mother of seven described
her resolution of the dilemma:

> I feel like your family comes first. If you feel so
> pressured that you're not doing what you should do as
> a mother, that you're going when you should be home
> working with your children, you have to do something.
> So I did. That was hard, but I've been in (my Church
> position) two years. My baby was two weeks old when I
> went in. I worked hard and showed them it could be
> done and did the best I could. I felt I had served an
> ample time. I felt the Lord was happy with me, with
> what I had done.

---

[4]Those interested in pursuing the mechanisms for
reducing role strain should read the following: William J.
Goode, "A Theory of Role Strain," American Sociological
Review. Vol. 25, 1960, pp. 483-496; Stephen R. Marks,
"Multiple Roles and Role Strain: Some Notes on Human
Energy, Time and Commitment," American Sociological Review,
Vol. 42, 1977, pp. 921-296; Sam D. Sieber, "Toward a Theory
of Role Accumulation, "American Sociological Review, Vol. 39,
1974, pp. 467-478; Jackson Toby, "Some Variables in Role
Conflict Analysis," Social Forces, Vol. 30, 1952, pp. 323-327;
Robert Merton, "The Role-Set: Problems in Sociological
Theory," British Journal of Sociology, Vol. 8, 1956,
pp. 106-120.

> I need to spend more time with my children, and I . . . could do a job like that when I'm older . . . the bishop understood, and so I was released last Sunday from my job. It's hard because it's the most enjoyable job I've ever had, and my children enjoyed having me do it.

Four of every five mothers relied on the establishment of priorities as a favorite coping device. As mentioned in the chapter on "Managing a Conjugal Corporation," most of these mothers were experts at making lists and allocating tasks.

Asking for help. Nearly two-thirds of the women indicated that calling for help was an oft-used method of keeping their heads above water. One mother described such occasions as "SOS days."

> I tell my children "SOS, I need you. I don't care what you have to do tomorrow, it's SOS day." They usually don't complain too much.

Saying "no." Related to the notion of setting priorities is the ability to decline invitations to continually increase one's responsibilities and opportunities. Latter-day Saints are generally instructed to accept all Church callings and to never seek a release from a Church position. They are also expected to share the leadership burdens in civic and educational groups. Furthermore, they are taught that although people can be released from Church callings, they never can be released from the position of parent. One mother of seven responded to these cross-pressures this way:

> I'm getting much better at saying "No, I just can't do it, I'm sorry." I used to feel really obligated if someone asked me to do something, and I would try to do it. But through having [a child with medical problems] . . . and a lot of experiences at that time, and some discussions that . . . [my husband] and I had, I began to learn to say no. Whether other people realize it or not, it really doesn't matter. I'm beginning to be able to pace myself a little bit more.

Another mother of seven shared similar views: "I've learned that that's how you maintain your sanity is to learn to say no. It's really a problem with these gals that get themselves into real binds emotionally. Most of them haven't learned that, and they have a 'guilt thing'."

Postponing things. Fully half of all the mothers indicated a rather regular reliance upon postponement as a way of dealing with competing pressures. Jean, the mother of eleven, admitted that she occasionally felt overwhelmed by all her domestic duties. When asked how she coped on such occasions she replied laughingly, "I just put it off until tomorrow."

Another mother, who has ten children, adopts a similar attitude on occasion:

> You say, "I don't feel like doing that today. I'm going to baby myself." So you do it. Kids have come home to breakfast dishes, and I tell them I decided I didn't want to do that today. They say: "Watch out for Mother, she's 'on one.'"

Delegation of duties. Half of the women found that delegating various duties alleviated the stress in their lives. As Stella said earlier, they've "got lots of people to do the work. . . ." The chapter on "Managing a Conjugal Corporation" discussed in detail some of the specific tasks which mothers delegate and how they do it.

Sticking to the job. Again, half of the mothers indicated that, when confronted with a seemingly unsurmountable challenge, the only way to get from here to there is through. Thus, the consensual comment of one mother indicated that the most rewarding aspect of housework was "finishing it!"

Resigning. In keeping with the previous discussion about setting priorities and learning to say "no," 39 percent of the women indicated their occasional reliance upon resigning from the heat of battle when they felt overloaded.

Resignation can also include a temporary withdrawal from the domestic fray. This is precisely what one mother of ten does:

> I think that it's legal to do something you want to do. I think it's legal to take a day off. Now, I don't do that very often, not very often at all. But, in a crisis, I can say, "Hang it in your ear!"

A compatriot, with one less than a dozen, described her temporary flights from family fights:

Sometimes I need to get away . . . even if it's just in my bedroom. I'd say when everyone's being a grouch or everybody needs me.

Using my workload as an excuse. About one-third of the mothers occasionally plead for respite on the grounds that they already have too much to do. One mother described her use of special-pleading in the following account:

When I was moving I couldn't believe with all the pressure I had, all the people who wanted me to teach Primary and Sunday School, just right in the middle of everything. I just can't believe how they thought about that . . . . They must not have thought. But I was able to tell them what I was doing, and they could realize and say, "Oh, I am sorry; we understand."

At least one mother expressed an opposite kind of concern. She was upset about being left out of the "action" because of her large family. She once asked the ward Relief Society president why she, as the mother of seven, was never called upon to help cook meals for families with a mother in the hospital. She was informed that a ward policy indicated that mothers of large families were not to be given requests for preparing meals for the sick or bereaved. Undaunted, she and her family have a weekly project of preparing meals for others on their own initiative.

The "Supermom Syndrome"

A problem which bothered some women was the expectation of others that mothers of large families are somehow "superhuman." Living up to this idealistic image caused some of them no small degree of distress. Linda, the mother of nine, expressed it this way:

I think we do each other a great disservice by making blanket statements like, "Your children are always well-behaved," or "You are the best mother I've ever seen." Nobody should ever say that to anyone else. I think it is very important to give compliments whenever you can but to make them precise. For example, "You handled that situation beautifully," or "I bet you worked a long time on that, I really appreciated your efforts." . . . I don't want to do the supermom bit to other people because I know it can do nothing but make them uncomfortable. I don't think there's a person in the world who would feel like she

LIFE IN LARGE FAMILIES

was a supermom, so I don't want to burden her with
saying that she has to be for my sake because that is
the image I need.

Mother's Day madness. Barbara shared many of Linda's
perceptions of the supermom syndrome, for she, too, is the
mother of nine. Our interviewer asked if there were times
when she felt overwhelmed.

Barbara: I think dinner time is always a good
                time, and Mother's Day is always a good
                time to feel overwhelmed.

Interviewer: Why Mother's Day?

Barbara: Oh, Mother's Days are horrible.
                Haven't you heard about Mother's days?

Interviewer: I thought Mother's Days were wonderful.

Barbara: Oh no, Mother's Days are horrible!
                Everyone gets up and talks about their
                sainted mothers and how they never
                screamed and were always there with the
                right answers and all that, and you
                think, Ugh! And so you go home just
                depressed. . . . It seems there's too
                much to do and too little time to do it
                all, and the kids don't do what you
                expect them to do, and you're writing
                out the check to the piano teacher and
                nobody's practiced the piano, it seems,
                for the whole year.

Emily, a mother of ten and wife of a prominent church
official, didn't agree with the assessments of Linda and
Barbara, however. She was asked if she perceived other
people's putting pressure on her. Her reply:

I saw myself being me, doing what I had to do so he
could do his job. I refused to let other people's
image of what they think a Church official's wife
[should be] affect me. [Did they have expectations
for you that you didn't want to live up to, or that
you weren't able to?] Oh, I'm sure they did. But I
just cut that out of my thinking, and I refused to be
sucked into that kind of a situation. I'm sure there
are people who thought I was a horrible [Church
official's] wife, but I didn't visit the sick and I

didn't run the [Church organizations]. I wasn't all things to all people. I just took care of the home scene.

Still another mother refused to be cast into the supermom mold:

Well, that is not the case in my family. My children know me the way I am. I get into the chocolates, sometimes lose my temper, and some days don't get my hair combed. They know me as I am and I'm not putting a show on for them. So I'm not trying to be a supermom, and they know it and don't expect me to.

Child Care Burnout Syndrome

One of the techniques which behavioral scientists use to get at people's "real" feelings is to talk about someone else's situation which might be similar to the one in which the person in question finds herself. The assumption is that we all tend to project our own feelings and perceptions into other people's situations. With this in mind, the interviewer provided each of the mothers with the following situation:

Researchers recently have become concerned about what they call the "burnout syndrome" among professional child care workers.[5] After just a few years of working with children, they are literally burned out. Do you ever feel that way?

A mother of nine replied:

---

[5]For examples of research in this area see: W. David Harrison, "Role Strain and Burnout in Child-Protective Service Workers," Social Service Review, Vol. 53, 1980, pp. 31-44; Herbert J. Freudengerger, "Burn-out: Occupational Hazard of the Child Care Worker," Child Care Quarterly, Vol 6. 1977, pp. 90-99; Christina Maslach and Ayala Pines, "The Burn-Out Syndrome in the Day Care Setting," Child Care Quarterly, Vol. 6, 1977, pp. 100-113; Martha A. Mattingly, "Sources of Stress and Burn-Out in Professional Child Care Work," Child Care Quarterly, Vol. 6, 1977, pp. 127-137.

I think I get real tired of it, but I feel that there
are wells to which you can go to replenish your
supply. I think you do feel that way at times, but
you really do have a more long-term interest than they
do, and that's got to be the difference.

Some of the mothers empathized with the possibility of
being burned out from working with other people's children
and emphasized the difference of dealing with their own
family:

The only thing that keeps you going is that they are
yours. You work your tail off, work with this kid and
work with this kid and you think, "Oh, what am I
doing? I'll never get through this." And then they
come home and say they got a hundred on this, or they
got an A+, or they did perfect on a dance recital.
Or, someone comes up to you and says, "Your son is
really neat to have in my class," or "Your daughter is
a joy." And you think, "<u>That</u> is what I am working
for."

A mother of eight, when asked if she ever felt symptoms
of the "burnout syndrome" as a parent, replied:

I can understand the feeling because kids are just so
nerve-racking. But the thing of it is they are <u>my</u>
children, and I love them and they're special to me. I
can see that they're so special, and that makes a lot
of difference. I don't want to take care of other
people's kids, especially little kids.

Another mother of ten indicated that the thought of
being "burned out" had seldom even crossed her mind. She
elaborated:

I love my children, and they [the paid child care
workers] may not have that same feeling. There's a
difference for the child that is not your own, so I
can see that. I think a mother has a motherly feeling
with her children, so that alone will probably make
her be able to cope with more things than if she were
under a lot of stress with some other children and
maybe having problems and difficulties . . . maybe
it's my personality that's kind of easy going. I'm
not too easily upset. Most things don't make me
frustrated or flustered.

A mother of ten, in response to the burnout query, replied that she felt "burned out" . . .

. . . mostly with housework, but not ever with the children. With the children it hasn't been too bad. One nice thing about a good marriage is that I think I look forward to John coming home more than the kids [do]. I don't know why; he doesn't do anything or say anything, he's just there and I feel that I have a good feeling.

When she first heard of the "burnout syndrome," Helen, the mother of seven, asked the interviewer:

Is it because maybe they work with the same age children? It's really getting fun now that my daughter just turned twelve last week. That's really fun to have a twelve-year-old daughter. You can talk, and she's babysitting, and doing all these fun things, it's really different; it's a whole different feeling than having little children. [Do you think it's the variety that keeps you from getting "burned out?"] Well, if you have a three-year-old for your whole life every year, that same three-year-old who is always three, I don't think you could take it [laughter]. You just have to know that there are phases they go through, that they're going to come out of that. My husband and I were talking last night about our boy who is nine. He's really conscientious, a good kid, but he's really crabby lately. I don't know, if things don't go his way he just can't take it. [My husband] says, "Well, it's just a phase, can't you remember when so and so went through this?"

None of the mothers condemned professional child care workers who might experience the "burnout syndrome." However, each in turn protested the notion that they themselves felt "burned out" as mothers, at least for any extended period. Lindsay, the mother of eight, summarized the insights and perspectives of most of the mothers:

No, I don't feel that way [being "burned out"]. But I can see it, and the reason I don't, I think, is because when a person is doing it as a profession there's a synthetic type love there. When you're doing it because it's your children there's a real love situation. Just as we couldn't achieve eternal life without the sacrifice of the Son, we can't take care of our children without the love that is manifest within the parent-child relationship.

. . . You do not have the capacity to put forth the love to another person's child that you have for your own. You love them, but it's a different type love. Just like I don't love my husband the same way I love my children. I don't love my children the same way I love my parents and my brothers and sisters.

Dispensing Discipline

Reasoning together. The various means of disciplining children in large families ranged from "sparing the rod" to "reproving betimes with sharpness." Connie explained that her husband is the major disciplinarian in their large family, and she described his "technique" as follows:

[He] operates quite a bit on sitting and just talking it over. He spends a lot of time reasoning with the older kids. . . . His is the more of a kind, gentle persuasion. So, through his example I try to be [like him].

When asked what she does to discipline her children, Connie replied:

I don't do one set thing. It depends a lot on your patience level. If you've had a bad day and everything's gone wrong and that child is just continually being an annoyance in some form or other . . . then your punishment will be more severe than if it is just the same thing under a different set of circumstances.

Withholding privileges. Carol recounted the disciplinary strategies used in her home where there is a wide range in the ages of her children:

Sometimes they get spanked when they're younger. Sometimes a privilege has to be taken away for a short time . . . a meal or something like that. . . . I don't like to say "Okay, you can't play outside for a week." That, to me, is ridiculous because to a child a week is almost like a year. I might say, "You need to come in the house for an hour, and after you've had some rest . . . you can go back outside."

She also shared the observations of many of the other mothers in the study that "it's hard to spank a fourteen year old; that isn't quite the thing when you're fourteen."

Tethering tiny tots.   Charlotte confessed that new babies "are nothing but total fun. The loving and the cuddling and the cute things they say, and the achievements that come. . . ."

> The hardest thing about mothering is keeping the lid on . . . like manners at the table. . . . The child will naturally push, so you're all the time having to bring them back. "You don't do that, you don't do that. . . ." That's the hardest part.

Combating conflict.   A mother of eight described her disciplinary approach to sibling rivalry:

> Like even yesterday, my older son was picking on my younger. Well, my younger son threw something, some lemonade, so my older son is a bigger boy, so he really had to get even.
> I felt like he had gone too far, so I said, "John, you can't do that. Why don't you go and apologize to Bob and go get him a treat. You'd better be friends." He was on his motorbike, and I was holding him, and he said, "What are you going to do about it?" And I said, "I guess I can't do anything about it." And so he rode off on his motorbike . . . looking like he was going to work, and came all the way around, bought Bobby a treat, and came back home.
> Then, when he walked through the door, I said, "Now, say you're sorry." "I'm sorry." "Now do it loud." He laughed and he did [say he was sorry]. Now that was a joy to see this happen!

Preventive discipline.   One mother of ten is a firm believer in what she calls "preventive discipline" in the form of keeping children busy "so they don't have time to get into mischief." She continued in a humorous vein:

> The only discipline I can think of is once when two boys were young, someone said somebody did something and the other one said that he was lying. As I remember, my husband said, "Okay, I'll have to pray about it and decide who's not telling the truth." So, the poor little guy who was at fault said, "Daddy, Daddy, I did it. I don't want Heavenly Father to have to come and tell you that I did it."

171

LIFE IN LARGE FAMILIES

She confided that the little ones are disciplined by a
light "swat on the bottom" while the older ones are generally
disciplined through reasoning.

Another mother used an alternate version of "preventive
discipline" in the form of anticipating problems and making
decisions well in advance:

> One thing I do to cope is to solve problems before I'm
> faced with them. For example, it's going to be a
> problem with my teenage girls to decide whether or not
> they're going to wait until they're sixteen to date.
> When they're fifteen and the most popular boy in the
> whole school has invited them to the dance, is not the
> time to make that decision. That decision needs to be
> made ahead of time. And so you start when they're
> fourteen, thirteen, twelve, and ten and nine, and say,
> "How are you going to handle that problem when you get
> to it?" You plan ahead, and you solve it before it
> comes.

Still another version of preventive discipline involved
reliance upon family prayer, scripture study and singing some
songs in the home in order to cultivate a pervasive spirit of
love and harmony among family members. One mother shared
the following:

> There have been times when we have knelt to pray and
> we have sung one of our favorite songs, "The Circle of
> Our Love," from Saturday's Warrior. That particular
> music and the scriptures did more changing within our
> home life than anything.
> When I start having difficulties with a child I
> can bet you two-to-one they are not saying their
> prayers and they are not reading their scriptures. I
> will be right every time. When they get back doing
> that, it is completely different.
> When we sing "As I Have Loved You" together, we
> can have a day that was just awful, and when you kneel
> down and have one of those songs sung, the whole
> feeling changes within the family.

Dealing with Depression

There has been considerable discussion recently dealing
with the problems of Mormon women and depression. It is
our view that, while Mormon women do suffer depression on

172

occasion, depression is no more frequent among them than in the general population of American women. In fact, our observations tend to confirm the notion that clinical cases of depression (involving visits to psychiatrists and/or receiving medication for depression) are rather rare.

Victor Frankl, author of Man's Search for Meaning, contends that people in industrialized societies often experience a so-called Sunday neurosis or existential vacuum when their lives are totally devoid of meaning.[6] It seems safe to assume that mothers of large families are not as likely to experience this absence of meaning as are childless mothers or mothers whose children have left home.

Another preliminary observation is that, at least with regard to the 41 mothers in our sample, moments of depression may occur, but they are not sustained for extended periods of time. Our interviewer asked all of the mothers how often they experienced feelings of depression. Kathy, a mother of seven, responded that she felt down in the dumps. . .

. . .when your physical body isn't responding like it should. That's really discouraging. I'd say that's probably the biggest problem. And then, too, if you feel like you haven't had your time out of the home, even just to go window shopping. I think a woman needs to get out, even if she's not going to buy anything, just to feel like you're up on things.

"Cabin fever" was identified as a cause of depression by several mothers:

I tend to feel like I need to get out and look at clothes and walk in the mall, or even buy a new pair of hose, just to feel like you have freedom. I think that's the thing [that's depressing] when you feel like you don't have any freedom.
It might be the psychological problem of just not having the car, but I think that if a woman feels that kind of pressure she needs to get out. I think I need to do more where I just take the one day of the week, just one afternoon and just do your own thing; that's

---

[6]Viktor E. Frankl, Man's Search for Meaning, N.Y.: Simon and Schuster, Inc., 1963.

your time to paint or sew. I don't do that as often as I should. But I have been so overwhelmed by everything and just keeping up, and if you aren't accomplishing something every week then you feel like you are not progressing, and that is when I get depressed.

Judy, the mother of eight, identified the causes of depression as the accumulation of "a series of events:"

Like last week, with this new job [in the Church], my period and the kids. I didn't feel like I was meeting their needs very well at that particular time. I was just kind of ushering them in and ushering them out and to bed and to meals and I wasn't spending the time with them that I should. . . .

There were just a lot of pressures at the same time. Instead of getting in there and doing something about it, you kind of throw up your hands in the air and say, "I am never going to make it, I can't do anything anyway. I failed again. I am never going to make it in this world." This is something I am learning how to cope with slowly. It is a learning process. I am getting out and doing something different. Yesterday, I told you that I read instead of doing what I was supposed to do so I went up and took a shower and got all fixed up. That made me feel a little better. It was the night of my class and that made me feel better to get out. So a change of pace sometimes does it. Doing something sometime for someone else (also helps).

Like they said on the TV program, people think they are very well-meaning, but actually they do more harm than good sometimes rather than just being understanding. I got to the point where it ended up being more of a spiritual struggle toward the end and I think that is kind of what got me out of it. I kind of had a confrontation with the Lord so to speak. I poured out my soul to Him, which I hadn't been able to do while depressed, and that helped. I think that was kind of when I started to get over it. What makes me angry with myself is that there has got to be a way to handle it. Then I think there is something wrong with me if I can't find out how to handle it. I am not adequate or something. Again, that makes me more depressed. What is the matter with me? I can't figure out how to handle it and I get depressed.

174

Several mothers shared feelings about being depressed at the time of their periods. Judy was one of them:

> I have this about a week before my period. I get this uptight feeling or this depressed feeling. It is a tired feeling sometimes and a "I can't do it" type feeling. That is about all usually. And then a few months ago, I had a depression that lasted about a month.
>
> As part of pregnancy sometimes I get depressed. Other than that I haven't been too bad, especially if I am doing something, I don't usually get depressed. I find that if I sit around when I start feeling guilty it goes in a cycle, then I get depressed. I feel more guilty and angry with myself and then more depressed. It's a simple thing that feeds on itself.

Asked if she ever felt down in the dumps or depressed, Eva, the mother of nine, responded: "Well as the term 'depressed' goes, real honest depression, no. I think some people misuse that term." When asked how often she felt down in the dumps, she replied: "Maybe three times a year or something like that." She indicated that occasionally following the birth of a child she had experienced post-partum blues. She continued: "My husband [now] sees that I get help to come in, and that way I get to sleep and just take care of the baby. This last pregnancy I had someone come in and I didn't have post-partum blues because of that."

Ellen, mother of seven, said she was depressed "maybe once a month at most." Asked about the things that discouraged her, she replied:

> It is mostly myself. I make myself depressed by not handling things well. You do something, and after you look and say, "I really blew that one, I really didn't do that one right." Usually I don't get depressed over it, it's a lot of things at once or one of those schedules when things are really hectic, everything kind of comes down on you. Sometimes you do get a little depressed. It's not really depression as much as it is discouragement.

Dolores is the mother of seven. When she was asked how often she felt down in the dumps, she replied:

> I don't think very often. . . . Well, the times I am mostly down is if I am under a lot of stress, for

175

instance, if there is company coming and the kids aren't cooperating. That is what gets me down more than anything. I wouldn't say very often. I would say every two months or something like that. . . . Usually if I can talk it over with somebody I feel better about it. I have fasted and prayed often, that is what I usually do.

When Lana, the mother of eight, was questioned about depression in her life she explained:

I don't think I usually feel very much depression. Sometimes it takes me a while to recognize it. You know how it is when you get emotionally depressed; you don't even know why or what's causing it. [You] can't step away from it enough to realize what you're in. You find that your feelings are hurt easily and you're on the verge of tears all day and don't know why. I step back and say, "Now the rest of the family hasn't changed, it isn't everybody else that's out of step."

She said she solves the problem of occasional depression by going to bed early, taking a nap the next day, and getting back on a regular schedule of sleep.

Christin, the mother of seven, replied that she feels down in the dumps "whenever father is gone. When he goes on a convention it is an emotional type of thing in me. I am fine until five o'clock comes and you know that Daddy should be coming home to take some of this pressure off."

What does one do for depression? Here is one middle-aged mother's response:

Well, I have to take estrogen, and that makes a big difference. As soon as [my husband] does everything wrong, or as soon as the children do everything wrong, then I know it is time for me to have a shot. With this shot comes enough energy so I can do things. There are days when you feel you're hopeless and helpless. I can remember crying many nights and saying the 23rd Psalm; "Though I walk through the valley of the shadow of death, I fear no evil." Some people have to go through these things to better appreciate life.

Barbara, the mother of nine, answered the same question this way:

I cry and then start over. I start over and make me
another chart for another week. I think that the one
thing we forget is that this life is a very real thing
and there is going to be some struggle in it, too, and
a lot of it is going to be mental. . . . If I feel
that way for a day that would be all. It wouldn't
last longer than that usually. . . . I guess I don't
really have a real valid experience of what you are
talking about when you are talking about clinical
depression.

When Betty, the mother of seven, described her
solutions for depression:

Oh, I haven't done it for a long time. . . . There
are some things I have found that help: getting
[things] out of books, reading the scriptures. I stay
up and even write a piece of poetry once in a while,
or of course prayer. You have got to get out and do
something, go somewhere, go visit somebody else who
needs help a lot more than I do.

Summary

The general impression from these interviews is that,
with rare exceptions, depression and feelings of overwhelming
discouragement are experienced by nearly all of the mothers,
but that these episodes tend to be brief. The causes of
"feeling blue" include being overwhelmed by a combination of
church and family obligations, a feeling of "cabin fever" from
not getting a chance to leave the house, the extended
absence of one's husband, occasional post-partum blues
following the birth of a child, and a few days of discomfort
related to the normal menstrual cycle.

The frequency of feeling down in the dumps was most
often expressed in terms of once or twice a month, although
some women indicated feelings of depression only a few days
during an entire year. The duration was limited to only a
day or two for most women; however, in at least two cases,
bouts of depression had lasted for a period of several weeks.

The "common cures" for depression included a very
diversified arsenal of techniques: estrogen shots, reading
the scriptures, fasting and prayer, "psyching oneself up to
the task," getting out of the house to go shopping, visiting
the hairdresser, crying, and talking over problems with a
husband or a friend.

Chapter IX

ECONOMIC REALITIES: CHEAPER BY THE DOZEN?

* * * * *

Two can live as cheaply as one:
Eat half as much and have twice the fun!
                    --Greeting Card Congratulations
                      on Becoming Married

Although definite savings from large-scale purchasing are possible, our interviews provided little evidence that the expenses associated with family life reflect the "cheaper by the dozen" principle. It will be recalled that the families selected constituted a "stacked deck" in terms of high parental educational achievement. Thus, by design, these families were generally far better off economically than families in which the parents have marginal educational attainment or occupational skills.

As one might expect in families with many small children, the brunt of the breadwinning responsibility in these families was borne by the father. However, in one-fourth of the families the mother had worked for pay during the past year, at least on a part-time basis, and two of the ten mothers who had worked had been employed full-time.

The median family income for the 41 families was $22,666. One wife had contributed nearly $20,000 to the family's income. In all of the other families the financial contribution of the wives fell below $6,000 per year.

Although an annual family income of more than $22,666 places the "average" family in our study near the top fourth of all American families, when that sum is divided among ten or twelve persons, the per capita income can drop to crisis level. To illustrate this point, note that in 1979 the average U.S. per capita income was $8,706. The 1979 per capita income for the eight Mountain States was somewhat lower at $8,254, and Utah's per capita income of $7,185 ranked 45th among the states.[1] But among the 41 families in our sample, the per capita income was approximately $2,313, or about one-fourth the national average.

Managing the Money

The interviews included several questions on the management of family resources. The mothers' comments suggested that in many families financial survival was due to the fact that one spouse invariably puts the brakes on the spending inclinations of the other. One matriarch with ten children confided that "money is always a crisis." She found it necessary to be the family accountant because her husband, she said, "would spend everything if I didn't say, 'Hey, hey.' On the other hand, we would never have anything nice if he weren't willing to spend." Another wife revealed that it was her husband--not she--who initiated most purchases: "He's always telling me about this bargain and that bargain that he's found. He's quite a shopper. . . . That's kind of a problem. I don't like him to do that."

One motherly money manager told of a genuine financial crisis her family had endured successfully. "We've had a few financial stress periods. He had a deal where he got involved with an organization that went bankrupt. My husband's the type of fellow that wasn't content to [just] take the legal way out, so we paid off all the debts of the bankruptcy that he was involved with personally."

Several mothers said that financial worries were among the greatest sources of stress in their lives. And even in those instances where the wife went to work to ease the pecuniary pains, the stress did not immediately dissipate. Sometimes there was conflict over how the extra earnings were to be spent.

This is the first time we ever had any type of conflict, but it was resolved easily and only lasted about an hour . . . I was [working] and I was getting my separate check. . . . I had visions of saving it

---

[1]Statistical Abstract of the United States, 1980 (101st Edition). Washington, D.C.: U.S. Bureau of the Census, 1980.

for a year and doing something really big with it. . . . He said, "If you get to that miserly situation and you're not going to spend a dime of your money, you're going to be in trouble. . . ." It would have been wrong to try to feel that I was saving up for something for me.

A mother of nine first responded that money had never been a serious problem for her family. Then she admitted that "it gets discouraging, I think everybody would like to not have to watch it so closely." Another mother proudly proclaimed that "money hasn't been a problem with us because I'm really frugal. . . . You get along with what you've got and are just happy about it. . . . If we had a million dollars, I'd still be that way, because that's me."

Several mothers expressed a firm belief in a "pay-as-you-go" economic policy. Some shared the philosophy of Leslie and her husband who said that, on principle, they avoided debt on anything but a car and the family home. "We pay our tithing [church contribution], house payments, and utilities," she said, "and avoid debt like the plague."

The average age at marriage was 22 for the women interviewed and 24 for the men they had married. Both of these ages are very close to the national averages for age at first marriage. However, a great departure from the national average was the length of time most of the husbands had spent in university and post-graduate education.

Apparently frugal management of household finances was learned by many couples during those college years. As one mother reflected on the past, she described her mastery of deferred gratification: 'We probably did without more than a lot of couples do, but our goal was to get through school so we'd be able to get what we wanted later on."

Help from relatives. Several women said that their parents, their husband's parents, or both sets of parents helped them become established in their homes. In two cases the parents had purchased the building lot or made a gift of a down payment on a home. In other instances parents had loaned the couples money to facilitate the purchase of a home, and these loans were eventually repaid.

In two cases the mothers described a very secure financial lifeline to parents. One wife said that her father had assured them that if ever they were down-and-out, "no one needs to lose their home." Another wife indicated that her mother-in-law was a reliable source of financial assistance, in the form of gifts and cash which could be invested for the future. Still another mother-in-law paid her son-in-law's college tuition while he completed his Master's degree, and financial burdens attending illness or death in the family were sometimes eased by money from parents.

Gifts at Christmas and on birthdays also take the edge off unrelenting financial demands upon parents of large families. Some grandparents send money or clothing to assist Santa in his obligations. Even when there was little direct financial aid, the dresses, nightgowns, bathrobes and swimsuits sewn by grandmas provided sizeable savings for hard-pressed families.

In addition to gifts of clothing, a few in-laws also provided very generous amounts of food. One mother gratefully described her "Idaho connection." "My in-laws have a huge garden every year, and she [grandmother] cans beans and beets in tin cans (you can take them to a cannery up there) and she'll bring us green beans all the time. They also will supply us with potatoes." Nor is assistance to large families provided only by grandparents. In one family, an aunt provides access to her apricot trees, and a sister extends similar access to cherry trees and a raspberry patch.

Of course, grandparents who lived near our focal families were often helpful in babysitting and otherwise providing grandparental counsel and support. It was also heartening to learn how frequently mothers or mothers-in-law travel long distances to help families with a newborn baby. A variation on this theme is the sending of children to "Grandma's." One mother explained, "I know that there isn't a time when I don't call my mom and say I'm sending some of the children that she wouldn't just jump for joy." This same woman also expressed gratitude for her father who "flies up" to help her husband with his bookkeeping and "general upkeep of the house."

Striving for Self-Sufficiency

Sewing. One activity associated with self-sufficiency and frugal money management was sewing. The amount of sewing done, the specific items sewn, and the attitudes toward the whole process varied widely among the families. A few of the mothers claimed to sew substantial proportions of the entire family wardrobe, "everything from their coats to shirts and dresses and pants and everything." Such families were a small minority, however. About one-third of the mothers said they sewed a lot for their daughters but seldom for their sons. The challenge of sewing trousers for growing boys seemed to represent the threshold where mothers who sewed left off sewing for their sons. Some mothers said they made the clothing their small children wore, but did little sewing for the older children. However, two mothers said they sewed for their sons but not their daughters. In these families, the first children were all boys, and the mothers had early become accustomed to sewing for boys rather than girls. In about one-fourth of the families, mothers and high school home economics teachers had taught older girls to sew, and the girls were reported to make most of their own clothing.

A mother of seven explained that in addition to sewing, she found remodeling used clothing very useful:

> I do a lot of knitting. I take my mending to the ball park and mend socks, and I'm surprised women don't mend socks, they'll throw them away, and I do a lot of mending. A lot of people give me a lot. This is quite an affluent area and so people in my ward have been really good to me, and I'm not too proud to take clothes.

About one mother in five said she didn't do much sewing. Reasons given included a self-assessment of little ability or personal interest in sewing. One mother who had formerly done a lot of sewing, said she quit from sheer boredom. A compatriot of hers explained why she didn't sew much:

> I can't get excited about sewing for boys; I used to sew a lot more for my little daughter when she was young. She's been lucky to have cousins, who have given her clothes. But I feel like the way the prices are getting, I better start sewing again, even for myself. But I haven't sewed too much.

Other homemakers said they compensated for not sewing "by shopping for sales and being very careful."

Feeding the masses. The climate in Utah Valley, with its hot days and cool evenings, is ideal for growing fruit, and a majority of our respondents had fruit trees. However, there was great diversity among the families in their reliance upon gardening projects. At one end of the continuum were nine families with fruit trees and very large gardens which were said to provide for most of the family needs for fruit and vegetables. At the other end of the horticultural spectrum were families whose mothers described their gardens and gardening in terms like these:

> It used to be pretty large, but the kids think that it's "the drag of the year," so it's become more or less Mom's and Dad's operation and it's dwindled each year. It's gotten smaller and smaller.

> I told you my husband isn't really helpful in the garden. I have berries, and we have planted fruit trees, but my vegetables die when I plant them. . . . The children don't know what it's like to have fresh baby carrots for dinner, and it breaks my heart. . . ."

Two other mothers said they had given gardening the old "college try" but with less than optimal results. One mother sheepishly confided: "I'm glad the Prophet, President Kimball, said we were to <u>plant</u> gardens, not <u>harvest</u> them." Another explained how her horticultural efforts had been only partially rewarded:

> We canned our green beans. We had a whole row of green beans, and we <u>still</u> have green beans. We had lots of potatoes. We're just learning how to be farmers, though, and we didn't realize that you're supposed to dig them all up. We left a lot in the ground to freeze.

Generally speaking, the degree of the husband's involvement seemed to determine the size and success of a family's garden. Most mothers had energy sufficient to cope with duties within the domicile, but were hard pressed to nurture a large garden in addition to managing the household. A case in point:

> We have five acres, and that's a lot to take care of. We planted it all. I'm in charge of the picking, with the children. My husband never picks any of it, but he's in charge of the rototiller and going down the rows. Then last year I was having such a difficult time with my pregnancy--that was when I had my miscarriage. He took over and he took the children out early and he'd go out and weed. . . . He had never weeded the garden until last year.

184

Canning. The amount of produce gleaned from gardening is reflected in the very impressive amounts of fruit and vegetables bottled, frozen or dried by these mothers. To the typical family of four, a food storage room filled with 1,500 jars of fruit, jams, juice and vegetables is almost beyond belief. But for a family of eight or ten, that amount constitutes just enough so the family needs buy no fruit or vegetables during the year.[2]

We didn't attempt to inventory the families' food storage programs, but several women proudly volunteered the size of their storage in terms like, "hundreds of quarts of tomato juice--the kids juice tomatoes with a vengeance." Others spoke of having canned "100 quarts of peaches," "200 quarts of beans," and of "potatoes by the hundreds of pounds."

About half of the mothers said they canned extensively, and most of the others canned small quantities of fruit jams and jellies. Of those women who did can extensively, many bottled fruit but few if any vegetables. Seven mothers said they froze large quantities of fruit and vegetables, and one mother had two freezers which she tried to keep stocked with produce. In addition to freezing and bottling, six of the mothers dried large quantities of fruit.

Those families who did little canning, freezing and drying used other means to reduce their food budgets. Said one mother:

> I am not a great canner, but I am trying to be better. I am not a great freezer either. But we try to keep up on our year's supply. We have got plenty of wheat and things like this. This year we are trying to increase the size of our garden and these poor little plants, bless them, they're a little scraggly because of the wind, but we are going to try and put up tomatoes and things like that from our own garden. Besides that, during the summer months we sort of like to live off the garden and that helps save on grocery bills and stuff.

Other families purchase food in large quantities at considerable savings. Some mothers shopped for groceries only once a month, and one family made bulk purchases on a semi-annual basis.

_____

[2]Mormons are encouraged by their leaders to have at least a year's supply of food.

One mother explained that in addition to canning nearly all the produce needed by her family she ground her own wheat for bread and wheat cereal. She concluded, "We could get along very well if the stores closed."

In the continual quest for self-sufficiency another family was contemplating the purchase of a gas generator to produce electricity, "so if we had to, we could keep the freezer going and have light a couple of hours a day."

Two fortunate families had all of their meat provided by parents who ranched. Still another family reduced its meat budget by raising their own rabbits for food. A fourth solution to rising meat costs adopted by some families was to eat meat very sparingly. In another family the father allowed a client to pay for his professional services by filling the freezer with pork products.

Children's Costs and Contributions

The degree to which children earned their own money varied considerably. Half-a-dozen families gave their children an allowance on a regular basis. Another ten families had a system whereby children were provided with money as the need arose. The remaining families, the majority, practiced some version of the principle, "If you want things bad enough, you'll earn them."

In one family the older children helped their father with painting, cleaning, and maintaining some rental units that supplemented the family income. The smaller children met their financial needs with the assistance of a very creative mother who kept a supply of greeting cards on hand. According to her description of the system, "whenever the little children need money I just tell them 'go to work' [selling cards]."

A common job for children was delivering newspapers. Three families were involved in two paper routes each, and six other families had one paper route. In this latter group was one route of several hundred papers that was handled by the mother herself rather than the children.

Two mothers said their children earned money by taking responsibility for the care of one or more fruit trees. The children were allowed to retain most or all of the money from the sale of the fruit. One of these families also sold garden produce.

In three of the families, sons had animal-raising projects (including lambs, calves, and rabbits), and the proceeds from selling the animals were used for "anything that is expensive or out of the ordinary." The typical "occupation" of daughters in their pre- and mid-teen years was babysitting. Children aged sixteen or older often held part-time jobs in local firms.

Perhaps the most ambitious contributions made to a single household were those of two teenage boys who had jobs as building custodians while they were in high school. With the money they saved they purchased a building lot. The older son then built a house on the lot, and sold it for enough profit to support himself and his brother on their missions [voluntary two-year church service].

Saving for the future. Several mothers emphasized the importance of teaching children how to save for the future, especially for church missions and education. Here is one exemplary plan:

> We figured out how much money it would take to save $2,000 by the time they are 19. So Thomas, this little seven-year-old, puts in like $15 a month. If he puts in $15 a month from now until the time he is 19, he will have $2,000. We pay half on his Sunday clothes. So they have two savings accounts, one is for their mission and one is just for something they are looking forward to.

Another mother explained that children in her family aren't expected to contribute to the family budget. Said she:

> I've wanted them to feel that if there's something they really need that we'll buy it for them. All of them have little bank accounts that they put money in besides accounts that my husband and I have for them, and trust funds and so forth that the grandparents have for them.

Revenue-sharing. Two of the 41 families had an interesting program of "revenue-sharing" among parents and children. One mother explained how their negotiations proceed in terms of one of her older daughters coming to her with a proposal: "Now, Mother, this is what I need [laughter]. This is what I want! If I earn $25, will you match it with another $25?"

In another family the process works more or less in reverse order, with the children contributing to a combined family purchase.

> Most of the time they just have to help because that's part of being in our family. Now the other day we were talking about getting a popcorn popper, but they're about $30.00. . . . We have popcorn fairly often and William [the father] said, "Well, maybe you children would like to put in a dollar or two and I'll make up the difference, if you can pay for about half." We didn't feel we could pay $30 on a popcorn popper. So we'll see how that works out, if they want to do that.

In order to make sure the children understood the need for careful budgeting and for contributions toward personal items, one father brought his paycheck home in cash. The children watched as he took the stack of money and distributed most of it by placing the needed amounts on top of the various bills due that month. When he finished, the stack had greatly dwindled. Then he said, "Now this much we have left to buy our food, any clothes we might need, and anything else." Seeing the family income thus disbursed made a strong impression on all the children, but especially upon a seven-year-old daughter. She saw the limited amount of money remaining and said, "Well, I guess there really isn't enough and you can't buy me a lock for my bicycle this month, can you?" Then she began to cry. Her parents explained that if she wanted to spend some of her own money, they could contribute also. But the lesson of limited family resources and the need for children's help had been forcefully made.

The age of independence. Sometimes born of economic necessity, and other times merely as an outgrowth of parental concern for teaching good work habits, several children were more or less placed on their own at a rather tender age. One mother explained that her sixteen-year-old had two jobs, and said, "I notified him that he has to buy his own clothes and pay for all of his expenses this year, and he is willing to do that."

Another mother said that her son had been buying "everything for himself" since he was twelve, and that his younger brother, then approaching twelve, "will be expected to do the same."

Another mother told how she taught financial independence.

> My boys have always worked and bought their own
> clothes. And they pay for their school lunches. I
> haven't had to pack lunches and they wouldn't eat them
> if I did. These kids like $35 pairs of shoes, $20
> pants and $8 shirts. I said, "Fine, you buy them,
> because we can't afford it."

Working Women

Full-time homemakers with more than half-a-dozen
children at home can be justifiably baffled when asked: Are
you a working woman? Granted that the 41 women we
interviewed were all hardworking homemakers, we asked
whether they worked for pay outside the home either full-time
or part-time. Thirty-six of the 41 had worked full-time
sometime during their marriage. However, most of them quit
working when they began having babies. Eight of these
mothers had taught elementary school, six had taught high
school, and three had taught at the university level. Three
others had held full-time jobs in kindergartens or child care
centers, and two more had worked as housekeepers. Four
had held positions in the secretarial-clerical field, two had
worked as full-time sales representatives. Other occupations
represented in their histories were accountant, librarian,
nurse, therapist, music teacher, researcher, cashier, and
restaurant employee.

During the year preceding the interview, two of the
women had maintained full-time employment. Four women had
worked full-time within the past five years, and seven had
worked full-time at some point during the past ten years.
Eight women had been employed outside their homes on a
part-time basis during the past year. Given the extensive
training and generally impressive employment credentials of
most of these mothers, it seemed that most were full-time
homemakers by conscious choice rather than because of limited
alternatives.

Views of working women. The mothers who were not
working for pay were generally not critical of mothers who
did. A mother of eleven, in reference to working mothers,
said "That is their business. If they want to be there and
they are happy, and that is their thing, I am not going to
tell them what to do. It is not my business." Another
non-employed homemaker concurred: "I think it is great,

189

if that is their bag. I think we ought not harrass them
[working mothers]." Another mother confided that personally
she wouldn't work unless she had to, "but if somebody else
wants to, I guess that is their business."

A mother of nine was not critical of working mothers "if
there is time and it does not hurt the marriage." She
continued, "I can't see why she should sit home and dust
when she could do something that she felt was more creative
with her time." However, she did think it was a "terrible
mistake" to work when there were young children at home
"unless there was no other way." Several mothers expressed
empathy for women whose financial needs made working
absolutely imperative.

A mother of seven confessed that she had a secret
desire to work mornings and be home in the afternoons when
the children come home from school. "I think that would be
perfect," she said. Another mother with eight children at
home described her experiences on both sides of the fence.
She, too, had wanted to get away from her domestic duties
and escape to the wonderful world of working:

> A lot of women feel like they have to get away
> for a little while to gain their sanity. I can
> understand that, too, because that's part of the
> reason why I went back to work. It just seemed like I
> was cooped up with those two little girls all day
> long, and they demanded so much out of me I just
> thought "I've got to get out of here or I'm going to
> go crazy!" But then after I got out I wanted to quit.
> But I really think that a mother needs to not think of
> her own selfish ways and needs to stay home with the
> family. . . . But you can't just really say "Oh
> you're a terrible person or mother because you work,"
> because we don't always know the situation.

Advantages of Employment

Asked about the advantages of working for pay outside
the home only four women emphasized the additional income.
Most spoke of the benefits of increased self-fulfillment and a
chance to interrupt routine activities by going to work.
Several mothers also remarked that "there aren't any
advantages" to working outside the home.

Material gain. Among those mentioning the added income
was one who conceded that "having more money to spend

would be an advantage to working. Your kids might be dressed better, you might have more food in the refrigerator, more material items, maybe." Another explained that she had to work part-time because her husband's salary had not kept pace with inflation. Her working, she said, helped the family contend with a "financial bind right now."

Another mother said that she knew families "that wouldn't eat, and the family I grew up in was one of them, if my mother hadn't worked."

A sense of fulfillment. A mother of ten children explained that her husband was "dead-set" against working mothers. Her own feelings in the matter were, "I'm just wasting away; I've forgotten what I went to school for." She did concede, however, that her husband encouraged her to do things "to develop myself so that I don't just dry up and blow away." She had worked intermittently and gone to school occasionally since being married, and had found both experiences fulfilling.

Another by-product of working is a sense of independence and security. Said a mother of ten:

> I think that a woman can get a lot of satisfaction from earning her own way. There's a lot of security in knowing that if I had to I could. It's worth a lot of life insurance to know that you could support your family if you had to. So, having marketable skills I think is absolutely essential for every woman. But I think if it's a job she enjoys, that it's perfectly legitimate to do just because she likes to. It's all right to do it because she enjoys the money, I suppose.

Work as variety. One mother told us that a great advantage of working was to experience "a change and a new kind of perspective on the pressures of raising a family." She continued, "I think that if you get out of the home, you can look at yourself more easily." Another homemaker revealed a tinge of dissatisfaction when she described the advantages of working in terms of "being out of the house; I would probably come home happy," she said, "somebody says a change is as good as a rest."

Linda, mother of nine, voiced strong opposition to the view that working meets women's needs for diversity and fulfillment:

I get back to the basic philosophy that this life is not a place for escape, it is not a place for saying, "This is too hard on me, I am going to go someplace else." The thing to say is, "This is hard for me. I am going to work at this until I master it. I am going to grow capable of meeting the situation." There is no growth to getting away from important responsibilities of life. I have worked and I found it to be a stifling experience.

Association with adults. To some mothers, having to spend one's time almost exclusively with several small children was a mixed blessing:

Oh, I think that every woman needs a certain amount of time when she can talk with people her equals. When you talk to children all the time, and I've noticed this in my life. . . . Like one day John and I were driving down the street and there were no children with us, and I said, "Oh, look at the choo choo train!" We looked at each other and he thought the same thing, "Look at the choo choo train?" That's not a very fascinating level of conversation to be on, and you get so you're thinking like kids and you need an adult so that you can just not die mentally.

Part of the advantage that comes from frequent association with adults is the opportunity/need to look presentable. Two mothers said that they thought employed mothers were fortunate to be able to have a more elaborate wardrobe than the typical full-time homemaker. One mother of seven said that her friends who worked "seem to keep themselves up well, they really keep their hair up and dress nicely, more so than women who stay home all the time."

Disadvantages of Working

Less time for children. The most frequently mentioned disadvantage of working outside the home was the perceived detriment such an arrangement would be for the children. Over half of the mothers linked their rejection of outside employment to their love for their children.

Some working mothers, and fathers as well, justify their time away from home with the rationale that they spend quantity time with their children in lieu of quantity time. Linda didn't buy that argument at all. Here is her pointed response to the issue of quantity versus quality:

The people who advocate mothers working say that it is quality time, not quantity. For the life of me I cannot see how they can force quality time into the time that they have. Maybe the quality time is needed at 9:00 when they are not there. There is nothing to say that the child is only going to need his mother at those hours when she is home. I think there should be somebody loving and warm and nurturing there all of the time. I think children need that. I don't think mothering can be an evening-time job. I think it is a full-time job. Even if you are home, I don't always think you are able to meet their needs. There is a lot better chance if you are there than if you are not there.

Another mother said she couldn't see how working women could find time to give each child special attention:

When you have so many children, they each need individual time spent with them. Even if you just pick them up and rock them just for five seconds, just to get that contact. They need that loving feeling, and if you can spend more time than that you need to sit down and read to them and talk to them and find out their problems and really stay close to them, I feel. If you are so busy working I don't see how you could do that.

Sensitive to the persistent needs of her own nine children, Eva argued that working women are "not available to take care of immediate stresses and concerns and emotional problems that the children are having; when they need their mother, she isn't there." Laura spoke with experience about the challenges working women faced, for she had taught school and left her children with a sitter. She described a dramatic change in her children after she quit teaching and became a full-time homemaker again: "I know the difference it made in them. I was home with them and was more patient with them and they didn't have to go to the babysitter."

Here is another statement tying maternal employment to negative outcomes for children.

Even when the children are all gone to school or grown, I don't like the idea [of a mother working] personally. I think when the Prophet says that you should be in the home, that's where you should be, and I think there's a good reason for it. When a child calls up sick from school, there's no one to come home to; and just being there when a child comes home, just knowing that a mother is there is a great comfort to a child, because even though they don't need her, they always come in and say, 'Mom, where are you,' then they'll go out and play. Knowing mother's there is some kind of comfort to them. Maybe you'd end up being at odds with your children if somebody else was instilling principles different from yours in them as they grew up.

Half a dozen of the mothers expressed more concern for the working mother than for her children. One mother confessed that she could not understand how some women were able to manage working for pay while also rearing children:

[Motherhood] is just a full-time responsibility for me and it's not a distasteful one. I think that people who don't know what motherhood is all about are just missing the most satisfying things in life. But on the other hand, I do agree with a woman's need to feel fulfilled and to do things that are increasing her talents and feeling like she's accomplished something.

Another mother sympathized with working women who, she said, were sacrificing some of their "most enjoyable years":

I think women are as intelligent and capable and talented as men. It's good to go use that talent in helping someone and furthering something if in so doing you're not neglecting something that's much more important, like staying home with your own children. I don't see how they can do it. They're giving up the most enjoyable years of their whole life, and the hardest, most grievous things that I've ever witnessed are women who have problems with their kids.

Sherrie, mother of seven, took a similar view: "I feel it's important for a mother to be home if circumstances are good for her to stay at home with her younger ones. I wouldn't want to miss out on the growing-up years."

Reflecting upon her brood of ten, Jenny confessed that "from personal experience I just couldn't be anywhere else but here right now." Karen took a bit more sympathetic stance toward the plight of the working mother:

It's fine for the others. I mean, full-time
would be very difficult if you have very many
children. But, of course, I really have enjoyed being
with my little ones when they are little and spending
time with them. I feel sorry for a woman who has to
miss that, but I know often it's a necessity. . . .
I'm glad I don't have to. I have a friend who has
worked. . . . It's heartbreaking when her little one
has a cold or something and she has to haul her out at
seven in the morning to the sitter, no matter how she
feels. . . .

A few women took a very firm stand against working
mothers. Laura felt a sense of urgency for mothers to be
home when the children are home. She contended that
mothers who need to supplement the family income can and
should find work which can be performed within the home. A
possible example of such work is the large--300 newspapers--
early morning paper route one mother did each day. She
completed the route early enough that she was home to be
with the children during the day.

Another mother who had evaluated the pros and cons of
working had concluded that the financial advantages were
illusory:

In some ways, when your family's raised it's a
nice breaking ground for a person. But I truly and
honestly feel that you're not that much money ahead
for the woman to work when she has a family. She
loses more than she gains.

Working when children are older. Seven or eight women
said they thought about going back to work full-time when
their children were all in school or had left home. One
mother confided that "as soon as the children get in school if
I can find something to do that will not keep me away while
they are home, I will be much happier working than I would
just be at home alone."

Jenny said she had no future plans for working after
her ten children were all in school. However, she added she
favored the option for those who desired it:

I can see that a woman who spends time rearing
her children could anticipate a career later and
probably should be prepared for it. Once your
children's needs are taken care of, there's no reason

why a woman has to stay within four walls, particularly.

Another mother had aspirations of becoming an architect when her children are grown. "But," she continued, "just to go out and get a job--no. I can't think of anything worse."

One other homemaker vacillated between her future roles as a grandmother and as a school teacher:

> I kid about this a lot, but I think with six girls I'm going to have a lot of grandmother missions. I'd sure have a special time though. Who knows, some day I may have to go back to teaching. I enjoyed teaching, but I don't have any plans. At least, it does give me a security to know I can fall back on it. I'm sure I'd have to go to school to brush up and get qualified.

Sarah had discussed the possibility of going back to work when the children were grown with her husband, whose response had not been enthusiastic:

> He just thinks that I ought to be home. I say "What do I do after the kids are gone?" He says, "What will I do when I come home to an empty house? What do you want anyway?" I mean I don't see that I'm so important in the home after the kids leave. I'd like to go into nursing.

Despite her own practice of supplementing the family income with part-time work, another mother strenuously contended that "a mother should stay home."

> That may seem very dogmatic, but I do. I think that a woman should try very, very hard to live within the means that her husband can provide. No matter what it is. I feel like if she's put in a position where she's the breadwinner that the Lord will give her [sufficient], you know, when there's nothing else. I think if she's got young children at home she should have help to stay with those children. Maybe there's a pride factor in her working. I think she really needs to relook at it because like I say, I think the thing you have to save is the children. The children need the mother! The baby-tender, the nursery, the neighbor, nobody loves that child like the mother. I don't care if it's even the grandmother. Besides you

miss so much. It's just too fun to miss all that.
So, I'm against working mothers.

Carol had reservations about women working, based on
her own childhood experience. Her father had died while she
was a child, and her mother had to work to support the
family. As she recounted past memories she said, "I know
what it was like, and there weren't very many pleasant
memories." Another homemaker candidly confessed that she,
herself, would be a better mother today if her own mother
had spent more time at home as a role model. As it now
stands, she says, "there are acts of motherhood that I have
had to struggle with. I think if my mother had been home so
that I could have seen them, I wouldn't have had to
struggle."

Loss of freedom. We mentioned earlier that 36 of the 41
mothers had had a previous taste of working while married,
even though for most of them this experience had occurred
several years earlier. Unlike many mothers who anticipate
returning to the job market some day, some homemakers saw
working outside the home as an encroachment on their
freedom. One of these women confessed: "I myself don't
enjoy working. I don't enjoy being under that kind of a
rigid schedule all the time." Another mother extolled the
virtues of being "just" a homemaker: "If I want to paint or
if I want to practice the piano or something with minor
interruptions here and there, like fixing meals, I'm free!"

Coming home exhausted. A few "non-working" mothers
said the greatest problem of maternal employment was the
sheer lack of physical energy to manage both roles well.
Said one mother:

> I have never worked as a mother, but I think she
> [working mother] would be too tired to come home and
> eat with the children, that would be really hard. And
> then the work load, the washing and ironing and
> keeping the house clean, I just think it would be
> tremendous for her to have to do those things. I
> think she should be home when the children get home
> from school. I can't think of any advantages except
> she would have a lot of money, I guess.

Added another:

> You can have your children trained to take care
> of the housework, but you've still got things to do
> when you come home. I don't think you could have all

the emotional and physical strength you need to deal
with your family, nor the time! Something would have
to be sacrificed someplace.

The real costs of employment. Carol disagreed with the
perceived financial advantages of working. In her view,
working was more costly than rewarding in several ways:

> Problems of a working mother are the added stress
> on the income. I mean the mother then must increase
> her wardrobe. She must have transportation. Then
> there's the care for the children. Then there are
> situations that arise when the children call and need
> a mother, and she's not there, and that really can
> cause some pretty serious problems with the children.
> I think sometimes it puts undue stress on the husband,
> when the woman works, because there are sometimes
> feelings of competition and so the husband sometimes
> drives himself beyond where he really ought to, to
> maintain what you might call a head of the household
> attitude. Then there also has to be some arrangement
> made with the homework, since mother is outside the
> home, and certainly can't be expected to take care of
> everything when she gets home.

Summary

In order to meet the financial demands of their large
families, one-fourth of the mothers work part-time and two
mothers work full-time. Several of the families receive
periodic assistance from relatives in the form of substantial
gifts, loans, and sharing of food commodities and clothing.

In order to maintain their self-sufficiency, one-fourth of
the families grow much of their food in their home gardens
and orchards. About half of the mothers do extensive
canning, freezing and drying of fruits and vegetables. In
one-third of the families the mothers sew a substantial
proportion of the children's clothing.

Although only two women are now working full-time, the
majority of the full-time homemakers were supportive of
working women. The perceived advantages of working for
pay included the increased financial resources, personal
fulfillment, a change of routine, the opportunity to associate
with adults, and the ability and incentive to "keep themselves
up" in terms of their personal appearance.

The greatest perceived disadvantage of working outside the home was the loss of time with the children. Some mothers indicated that full-time employment encroached upon their individual freedom and depleted their physical energy. However, many said they might go to work when all their children were in school, or had left home.

There were several instances of attitude-behavior conflicts, where mothers were working for pay but seemed to reject the image of working women or disliked the financial necessity that made it essential for them to work. One wonders whether the personal and family strains associated with their work in relatively non-remunerative part-time work, such as paper routes or waitressing, are greater than those that would attend better-paid semi-professional or professional employment on a part-time basis.

Chapter X

WOMEN AND THE CHURCH: ATTITUDES AND PERCEPTIONS

* * * * *

Mormon women are supposed to feel happy and
blessed no matter what happens. Armed with a
tradition of strength and dominance, programmed by a
dogma of conformity and acceptance, faced with a
changing world and annoyed by observable paradoxes
between espoused ideals and practice, many Mormon
women are in conflict and unhappy. But church
teachings tell them that they must be happier and
healthier than other women and therefore better able
to handle adversity.

--Robert H. Burgoyne, M.D.,
and Rodney W. Burgoyne,
M.D. [1]

The encounter between Mormon theology, church practice,
and the lives of Mormon women is a complicated topic
deserving book-length treatment. It was not the primary
focus in our survey of mothers of large families, and as a
result the treatment in this chapter and the next is
superficial and limited in scope. Even so, we believe there
are some useful insights in the mothers' views of how Church
practice and activity affect their lives.

Near the end of the interview was a series of questions
on women's perceptions of the LDS Church and their roles in
it. Among these were:

---

[1]Robert H. Burgoyne and Rodney W. Burgoyne, "Belief
Systems and Unhappiness: The Mormon Woman Example,"
Dialogue 11 (Autumn 1978), p. 51.

--How do women in the Church perceive themselves?

--How do women view themselves and their roles in the
Church?

--How do they think their husbands and ecclesiastical
leaders view women's role in building the Kingdom?

--Do they perceive adequate two-way communication
occurring concerning their needs and problems?

--Are there any expectations from Church leaders and
other members which create frustrations and stress for
you as a Mormon woman?

--What problems are Mormon women facing today?

Women's Essential Contributions

The typical responses to the questions about their
satisfaction with women's roles in the Church was an
acceptance of the status quo, an affirmation that the way
things were was the way they were intended to be.   Most
mothers indicated that a majority of LDS women were happy
with their roles.   Said one, "I think most women feel good
about the things they do and that they can do in the
Church."   Another took pride in women's essential place in
the functioning of the Church:

> I hope they [Mormon women] would see their role
> as being very necessary, that the Church will run
> smoothly if they will do their job correctly.   I think
> there is a lot of room in the Church for a creative
> woman. . . .   Women can be very creative in teaching
> the gospel to young people.   I think in Relief Society
> there is a lot of room for creativity for a woman if
> she will take it and do it.

This mother had accepted the definition that a woman's role
was in teaching young people or other women, and that the
appropriate outlet for her Church service was in these
"auxiliary" organizations.

There was also a frequent expression of the idea that
women made it possible for the men to fulfill their
lay-assignments in the church.   Sometimes the notion of
"supporting each other" was stated in equalitarian terms, in
the sense that if a woman had a responsible position in the

Church her husband should support her, just as she should support him if he had the responsible position. A mother of ten explained her feelings in these terms:

> I think the men couldn't accomplish what they have without the women. I think there is a need, a great need, because I think if there is not support in the home from the woman, the man can't function in the Church. . . . If I have responsibilities and I have a nonsupportive husband, then it's going to be difficult on me. I think women are important and men couldn't get along without us. Let's face it.

There was considerable emphasis on how important the woman's role was. A mother of ten explained "They [Mormon women] can only feel really good about themselves [if they understand] how special and precious they are and how important they are and how necessary they are and how vital their contribution is." When this mother was asked whether Mormon women really felt that way, she said, "I'm sure there are women who don't feel that way, and I don't know where the fault lies in that, if the fault lies in what they hear, or how they're treated, or how they think they are treated. I have never felt mistreated."

Satisfaction with the role of wife and mother was sometimes tied to gratitude at being a member of the Mormon church and having the blessings that come with that membership, and often their view of the Mormon women was expressed in a Biblical statement that they saw themselves essentially as "helpmates for their husbands." Most of the mothers, in one way or another, echoed this statement by a mother of eight.

> I think most LDS women feel like they are pretty blessed and that they are pretty fortunate to be LDS and to have the things that they do have. I don't think they are being slighted in the least, I think they realize where their position is. Most of them believe that their position is to be a partner, not necessarily a lower partner, but a partner with their husband. And I think that in general, women feel like they are no less, no lower than men, just equal.

Asked how women in the Church perceived themselves, another woman said, "I think they are satisfied to be queen of the family," but she humorously expressed some ambivalence with that status when she added, "or the top mop, however you want to look at it."

A mother who said she was worried about some tomboy attributes in her daughter said, "I think the most important thing is that a woman shouldn't forget what her real role is in life, and why she really is here and what the real meaning is, and what the word "woman" means. It's a helpmate for the husband." Here is another variation of the "helpmate" explanation:

> Well, I for one see I'm a helpmate to my husband. He is the leader of our family and I like it that way. I'm a leader in some things. Some things he doesn't even see or even want to be responsible for that I'm responsible for. But in the main direction of our family he's the head and that's how I see myself, as assisting him. And though he may be the head, we may have decided together what the goals would be. Together we work with the children, or with the family, towards those and . . . I help him and I help my children that we may all come together with it. . . . Certainly as an LDS mother, I hope my thinking is clear that teaching my family about the Savior, teaching them about the gospel, directing them to eternal life is a major goal. And my being home and my being with my family and my teaching and reading and praying and disciplining is all directed toward that goal, and that's my job.

Attitudes of Mormon Men about Women

Many other revealing comments about what was a woman's "job" were given in response to the question on how Mormon men viewed women's roles. The most frequent answer was that men who lived their religion recognized that women's roles were as vital as their own, although different. Explained one mother:

> They [men] are not going to get there [to heaven] without their wives, so it's kind of a joint effort. They [women] don't have the Priesthood callings to make all the decisions and things like that, but you need the woman there to carry out the program.

The view that women were essential contributors to successful Church programs was expressed many times. In its strongest form, this perspective boils down to the idea that it is the women who push Church programs along.

> I think most men realize how vital women are in
> raising the children. And even in Church functions,
> it's like the Bishop said, "If you really want
> anything done in the ward, turn it over to the Relief
> Society." And I think they [men] realize how valuable
> they [women] are. Even though men have the
> Priesthood, the women run it [the Church].

Also worth mentioning in this regard is the statement by
a non-Mormon mother on the high expectations she saw being
imposed on Mormon women, and--perhaps in consequence--
their dominant role in the creation and maintenance of Mormon
Church life:

> I think there is a tremendous amount expected of the
> LDS woman and the men may think they run the church,
> but they don't. Because if it wasn't for the LDS
> women that are very faithful, the Mormon Church would
> not be particularly strong. It's the women. How do
> you like that blasphemy?

In response to a probe which asked if the men put
pressures on women to perform certain roles and to stay out
of other areas, a mother of seven said that although that was
not the case in her own family, she thought it was in many:

> I think a lot of men in the Church, they have a
> facade that they want their family to be this nice,
> beautiful, exemplary family. So if their wives are
> not beautiful examples in every area, then this is
> upsetting to them and they don't accept that. This
> one lady that was really in depression was really not
> coping with it. She didn't know what was wrong with
> her, but he had a hard time coming to the counselor,
> because of the facade of "Oh, oh, we're a troubled
> family, my wife is having trouble." So the men need,
> just like the women need, to accept themselves, they
> need to accept their strong points and their weak
> points.

Another mother said that she thought that most men in the
Church would like their wives to be "just good mothers and
good wives and to stay home and do what they're supposed
to."

> And yet, I'm sure that if a man loves his wife he
> wants her to be creative and to have these outlets and
> outside interests. I mean, I do have my outside
> interests. I don't believe you should just be home

204

every second of your life and all you think about day
in and day out is your children and your husband.
You've got to have some interests that are yours to
make you interesting. I mean my reading, I talk over
with my husband the things I'm reading. He probably
thinks it's really dumb that I belong to a book club.
It's one night a month where he has to stay home and
watch the kids if he's home. But you've got to do
things that make you an interesting person, too.

Here is a statement by a mother of eight reflecting the
husband's pressure to stay in the home, managing the family:

Now, in my home what has been very important to
my husband, and I'm sure this has been what has geared
my life a lot, has been to be a good mother. He
panics if I am gone from home too much. He doesn't
view involvement with outside activities as a sign of
accomplishment. He views within the home what I
accomplish as the most important role I can do. I am
sure if he hadn't have viewed that and felt so
strongly that I would have done other things outside
the home. But as I look back now, I am glad that I
haven't, because I think I would have sacrificed my
children . . . which I couldn't have lived with
knowing that I maybe should have been home earlier and
maybe this [bad thing] wouldn't have happened. Yet he
has been supportive, in the last few years especially.
He enjoyed my association with music and the choir,
and he complimented me much on that. I think men have
their ideas of women just as women have their ideas of
men. I have known men if they hadn't been so
supportive of their wives, their wives would never
have accomplished anything. Their wives are
outstanding women, and yet if their husbands hadn't
taken over in areas, they couldn't have had time, or
they would never have been able to accomplish or vice
versa. Some men are happy that their women are active
outside the home and the accomplishments they make.
Some men even encourage their wives to work outside of
their home. I think many women work outside their
home because their husbands encourage it.

Although a few husbands may encourage their wives to work
outside the home, a more frequent perception was that most
men preferred their wives to stay in the home. A mother of
seven said, "I think they'd [men] like a woman who is a good
homemaker and a good mother to their children. My husband

hasn't really said that he'd like me to get out and work or anything like that." Another mother agreed:

> I think they [men] see their [women's] roles also as being mothers and wives, raising children; I feel that men and women are in agreement [on women staying in the home].

These mothers of large families did not reject the traditional woman's role of wife and mother in the home. Some of them found certain role prescriptions a little binding, but generally they said they were satisfied with their place in life, and felt they had chosen the roles they now filled. Support for this conclusion is evident in typical responses to the question, "How do Mormon women perceive themselves?"

> How do I feel about being a Mormon woman? I feel good about it. There isn't anything I'd rather do or be. I feel like it has the answers to whatever I need.

> As far as myself, I feel perfectly content with what is expected of me in the Church and as a woman in the Church. I don't know, I don't feel that I could ask for anything more.

Defensiveness and Discrimination

Although the respondents generally felt content in their roles as women in the Church and "mothers in Zion," there may be a thread of defensiveness running through comments about Mormon women and how they were treated. Most were anxious to have it understood that they did not consider themselves second-class citizens. They saw woman's place in the family as different from, but not inferior to, man's place.

Only a few women mentioned feelings of subordination or negative treatment by men in the Church and they defined the problem as one of local people being out of line or misguided. One woman said that she felt that the Church leaders viewed women's roles as being what they should be. Asked what those roles were, she said, "Equal to a man except the roles are different. But I think that there are probably some men in the Church that feel that they are superior to women." Several of the mothers stressed that they felt they stood side-by-side with their husbands, and did not feel discriminated against:

I really don't see women's roles as a problem
compared to the man in the Church because the man has
the Priesthood, but a woman stands side-by-side with
him and shares that Priesthood. She has the beautiful
role of being the mother, which to me is every bit as
important as the Priesthood role. Therefore, I feel
that women in the Church should feel much better about
themselves and their roles than women outside the
Church, because they actually have something to attain
and something to work for.

Rather than being degraded by their separate-but-equal
status, they were satisfied or actually preferred the status
quo. Said another:

I think most of them [Mormon women] are happy.
They accept the role of being the non-Priesthood
holder. We accept Church doctrine pretty much. I
think most women in the church are satisfied. They
don't want to wear the pants, they want the husband to
be the patriarch.

The interviewer asked this woman if she thought that
some women viewed themselves as second-class citizens and if
there were men who had that negative view. She answered:

Yes, I think I have seen women who viewed
themselves that way, that felt like they were nothing
but an extension of their husbands and were just there
to bear children. And if their husbands were wicked,
they were literally going to be judged by what their
husbands did, that they wouldn't get any higher than
their own husband. I have heard women say this. I
was aghast, but they believed it. And I think they
were misguided, but that was what they believed. I
have seen women on the other end of the spectrum also,
that realize that we are going to have to stand alone
when we are judged and we are responsible to develop
ourselves and can't lean on anyone else.

One woman expressed some resentment about men's
perceptions of women:

I think sometimes the men . . . think that we
should just sit home and "make coffee." I use that
expression as the domestic kind of thing. Another
lady I met over here, she had been working for the
Republican Party for years and years, and she said she
was treated that way, as someone to make the coffee,

but not to use her head. And sometimes in the
Bishop's meetings and stuff like that, the women are
the ones who end up having to do it, as I said, the
dinners and put on this and that, but the men think
that we shouldn't be consulted on policy things. . . .
So there's some resentment there. I don't think about
that too often. I'm just a Sunday School teacher and
a Primary teacher. Nobody consults me about anything.

A more typical reaction was that the popular perception
of the subservience of Mormon women was inaccurate and
masked a different reality.

Most of the time we give a great deal of lip-service
supporting the Priesthood, but most of us, I think
underneath that really [know]that sometimes it is the
women that are running things. I mean, have you ever
seen the Elder's Quorum put on a dinner? You know
what they do? The Elder's Quorum President says,
"Dear, I need to put on a dinner," and then
the . . . wife does it.

This mother then described another woman who had claimed a
possible superiority of Mormon women over Mormon men
during a local meeting.

We divided into groups of six and there were me and my
best friend in one group and then we had two BYU girls
and a very conservative woman who seemed to me a
little dimwitted. No matter what anybody said, she'd
go, "Well, what about the children?" She said that as
if anytime you had a feeling of your own worth, you
were neglecting your children. But anyway, the sixth
woman, she's the wife of a BYU professor that
everybody knows . . . she's a former Relief Society
President. I expected her to be very conservative
about home and family, but she sat down and said,
"Sometimes the men in the Church make me so mad. They
try to run everything." She says, "Why don't they let
a woman be Bishop, we could get everything
straightened out." Very radical, things I wouldn't
even say. And here's this middle aged woman, mother
of five daughters or something . . . so I thought,
there's some feelings underneath that we have. I know
if you work in the Mutual, everybody knows that the
women in the Mutual carry the men's end of the ward as
a general rule, even though the men are nominally in
charge. So I think we can't help but resent that
sometimes. I think part of it, of course, is that the

men have full-time jobs on top of their Church work
and so the women are home more and able to do more for
the Church. But we end up doing an awfully lot of
it . . . and that's why I thought the meeting was so
good, because in a million years I would not have
expected this woman to start complaining about
all-male Bishops.

Here are two other defensive reactions to the notion that
Mormon women are treated as inferiors or subordinates:

I don't think that being a female member of the Church
is in any sense of the word a substandard level, not
at all. I feel that Church philosophy, Church
teaching has put the woman on a high position, due
mainly to the fact of her raising a family or her
being more or less the motivating force of
personalities they raise. I think very much they have
been given a very high rank in those terms.

A lot of people say that the Mormon Church is a man's
church, and that women are rather subservient. I have
a hard time seeing that. On the outside, it looks as
if that is true, but look within the ward and see how
it operates, you so often see that if a job is going
to be done, you give it to a woman. It is true.
There are some good men, but women in the church are
the ones that make it go, I think. It is women who
are perfection-conscious, it is women who also do a
lot of petty things that men would not do, the
whispering, the gossiping and a lot of things like
this that men are quite immune from. Oh, there's
some, but women carry the perfection thing just a
little bit too far, I believe. I think women are the
ones, to a large extent, who rear the families of the
Church, to too large of an extent. They are the ones
that teach the children. . . . I think women in the
Church probably might have a lower opinion of
themselves than they ought to. Just because they do
not have the Priesthood, and they do not, this does
not reflect upon their status in any degree.

As was emphasized in the first chapter, in some
characteristics, notably family size and educational attainment,
our respondents are not representative Utah mothers. Their
views about women and the Church may take on added
meaning if placed in the context of responses to statements on
sex roles by a random sample of Utah women surveyed in 1981
as part of a study conducted by Brigham Young University's

Family and Demographic Research Institute. In that survey, respondents were asked whether they agreed, disagreed, or were unsure about several statements. The sample of adult Utahans was cross-classified by gender and religious preference. As may be seen in Table 10-1, over one-fifth of the Mormon women, compared to only two percent of Catholic and Protestant women, agreed that "The only really satisfying role for a woman is as a wife and mother." About one-fifth of Mormon women agreed that "Women should be happy to take second place to their husbands," and that "it is the man's job to make the major decisions," compared to six and twelve percent, respectively, of the non-Mormon Christian women. Almost two-thirds of the Mormon women agreed that, "Femininity is a woman's greatest attribute," and over half agreed that "The saying, 'A woman's place is in the home,' is generally correct."

Although on all of these items the Mormon women were more "traditional" or home-centered than other Utah women, the fact that only one-fifth agreed that the only really satisfying women's role was being a wife and mother, that women should be happy to take second place to their husbands, or that men should make the major decisions, means that four out of five Mormon women are either unsure about their roles in these matters, or do not feel that their religious beliefs dictate subordination to their husbands or that the traditional wife and mother role is the only satisfying option for women.

Of course, among our mothers of large families, there was a clearer consensus that the wife and mother roles were all-important, and that the women who concentrated on being wives and mothers should not feel defensive or like second class citizens because of that choice.

Perceptions of Change

A basic acceptance of traditional role definitions did not preclude these women from being aware of, and often vocal about problem areas in Church organization. Several of the women said that things were changing in the Church, and that women's needs and interests were more frequently considered. They pointed to the recent change in the Sacrament meeting (worship service) procedures that allowed women to give the invocation or benediction. One mother personally had experienced a growing acceptance of women as teachers of adult theology classes. She said that she had

Table 10-1

AGREEMENT WITH STATEMENTS ON SEX ROLES, BY RELIGIOUS PREFERENCES, UTAH WOMEN, 1981

	Mormons (N=299)*	Catholics and Protestants (N=51)*
The saying "a woman's place is in the home" is generally correct.	54%	18%
The only really satisfying role for a woman is as a wife and mother.	21	2
Femininity is a woman's greatest attribute.	63	33
A man should not be expected to look after a baby under normal circumstances.	30	2
Women should be happy to take second place to their husbands.	21	6
Looking after children is just as much the father's job as the mother's.	81	96
It is more important for a wife to help her husband's career than to have one herself.	58	20
It is the man's job to make the major decisions.	22	12

*These are means; number of cases varies by one or two from item to item because of non-response.

substituted as a teacher of the Gospel Doctrine class in Sunday School, and that one of the men in the class had seemed very agitated to have a woman teaching that class. A few weeks later, someone read a statement from the New Testament about women not speaking in the Church, and this man publicly stated that it was clear to him that women should only teach other women, and that men should teach men. She said that since that encounter she had watched the man, and she felt that he had mellowed; now he could accept women praying and doing lots of things in the Church. Still, she said, "I know some young men who think that their wives should just stay home and cook, but not many. I guess I circulate with a pretty select group, but I think for the most part, men [that I know] are very supportive of their wives." A mother of eight gave her opinion about how women's participation, and the definitions of women held by Church members, had changed.

> For the majority I think the feeling is—it used to be—that women were to be quiet and just be supportive and not really have a lot of leadership or a lot to say, that men were to lead out. But that's changing, and I think that men are accepting it very well. I remember when the women were asked to pray at sacrament meeting—and for many years it was never done—it had happened maybe two times when they came and asked me personally to offer the prayer. And I said, "Oh, I couldn't pray [publicly]." It was just such an unusual thing for me that I wasn't sure I wanted to do that, because I had just been happy with having someone else take care of it. If you asked me to do that, it put a strain on me. Now it's been going on for several months and it's just a matter of common happenstance. But I think it was important that it happened, because it opened some people's eyes. Maybe the one man who thinks that women don't make any useful contribution, maybe it would tend to open this person's eyes. . . .

Here is another account of how that simple change in Church procedure, having women pray in sacrament meeting, affected a woman's self-concept.

> I confess that I've had a hard time seeing women pray in sacrament meeting, and it really is difficult for me. When it was my turn, my husband had to say, "Yes, she will." Then he turned to me and said, "you need to get hold of that, dear." That's strictly a cultural thing, because I grew up with the women not

doing that, and I have to reorient my thinking on that.

One of the questions on the Church and women was whether the respondent thought that women in the Church had adequate two-way communication between them and their husbands and between them and Church leaders. The usual response was that the women's needs were largely satisfied by communication with her husband at home; her link to the church hierarchy was through the Priesthood of her husband. A variation of this answer was to affirm that existing channels, whatever they were, met the mother's needs. A mother of ten said:

> I think that there's adequate [communication] for me and my needs, but my needs are solved by the Priesthood in my home. I've never . . . needed to call on a Bishop or home teacher. We've always just solved it here. And for women who do not have the Priesthood, I don't know how they feel about that.

Among the women who said that they communicated with their Church leaders as much as was necessary was a mother of nine who said:

> Right now the brethren in the Church leadership are very concerned about women's roles and women's perceptions of themselves and that kind of thing . . . I think that the women I know see two-way communication occurring. . . . Oh, I think that a lot of women still feel there's a lot of educating to be done in the Church and that kind of thing. But, they see it's moving in the right direction. Some women don't see us moving fast enough. I don't tend to have that particular problem. I think the people like President Kimball [current President of the Mormon Church] are moving just as fast as anybody can, and you have to run to keep up with him."

Another woman who took a positive stance said that in her experience people had been willing to listen and take her seriously:

> Sometimes you hear a little aside, "You know, Bob, these women, you never can satisfy them," things like that. "They always want this and that and everything," then the other side of that, "If it weren't for the women, nothing would ever get done around here,". . . . But, I think, with the

213

Priesthood leadership I've had to deal with, bishops
and stake presidents, they have been really sensitive
to my needs. . . . I think that essentially, the
leaders of the Church are concerned about the needs of
women. Just like this thing with the prayers, making
that a vocal thing, I think that that was a nice thing
for them to do. I think that the Church generally has
a great and high respect for women and their role.
The ones who are in high positions do, anyway.

There was some concern voiced that men didn't
understand women's roles, and that certain needed changes
were slow in coming. A mother of seven related this issue to
the fact that it was women who do most of the changing of
babies. Many of the Church buildings don't have "cry
rooms" for young children, and the mother used that as an
example of needed change and inadequate communication:

Take the cry room, for instance, I think if it
were the men holding the babies in Church, they would
have done something about that a long time ago. If a
man has ever gone into a cold restroom to change a
baby he would know what I mean. I think that if men
had to struggle with a child in Church, they would
have more cry rooms and they would facilitate women
more. I think if men were the mothers who had four
little children at home and were calling women to
their fourth and fifth demanding Church job, they
would know the responsibilities that women feel. I
think sometimes that they don't know the pressures and
the demands that a woman feels.

Sex stereotypes and images of women. Some of the
answers to the question on communication between Mormon
women and men revealed stereotypes about the nature of both
men and women. A mother of eight told us that she didn't
think men were as sensitive to problems as women were. And
she quoted a Relief Society president who had said, "We can
get these women on the ball, it's just the men we can't get
moving." This mother continued:

And I really think that men are not as sensitive to
the problems of people in general. Not just men or
women, but just people in general. Women seem to know
what's going on when somebody needs help quicker than
men do.

One woman revealed some personal sex-stereotypes when she explained why she thought that men would rather work with men than with women:

> Particularly in the executive positions, you find out too much about people and about their problems. You hear too much, women complaining about other women, or complaining about the Priesthood not doing their job, not holding up their end. Some things get to be very petty and maybe it is because of the needs of the person [woman] and they are frustrated in trying to carry out their own responsibilities because everybody else doesn't fall into line. Men are a little easier to work with because there is not so much of that. If somebody falls short, they simply will go on from there and they won't let it bother them. They don't have to call two or three friends and say, "Did you know that he didn't . . . he wasn't there at the right time, and he didn't do his share of the work." Things are a bit more straightforward when working with men. But, also, I think the sensitivity is missing there [among them] and the caring about people as well as getting hurt too much.

A mother of nine said that she felt that if all people were straightforward they could communicate. She hadn't had problems dealing with men with whom she had worked in youth organizations. However, men were different, she said, and you had to know how to deal with them:

> If you want to work with a man [within the Church], I feel that you have got to respect his time and his judgment and not go to him like a whining child, but more or less as an equal. "We've got this problem and you're the person to help us. What are your feelings on it?" I never had any problem working with men, but I do know women who have a great deal of problems because they don't relate straight across but on a little different basis. . . . I think it very largely depends on the woman. Maybe this is what a lot of women don't realize . . . a man does not perceive his job quite the same way that a woman thinks he should. . . .

Another woman justified women's exclusion from some leadership positions on the basis of her psychological makeup. However, most of her explanation was framed as a quotation from her husband, and she saw his point of view as essentially blocking women's opportunities.

I read in the paper last night that Utah is the lowest
state in the Union . . . to have women in leadership
positions in the school system. The lowest! Now I
was really quite [surprised]. I just know that my
husband will say that women that he has worked with
cannot take the pressures as well as men can. They
crack up, I mean the women have their monthly cycles
and they are sick today. They don't seem to be able
to cope with the humdrum as well as the man, and that
is all he has told me. Even the older women; they are
going through the change of life or they are not
feeling good today. . . . Some men . . . rise to be
leaders; . . . now women have been taught to be more
whiny and complainy, . . . murmury. His opinion is
that very few women can really cope with the pressure
of the outside world. Now if that is a man's
attitude, women don't have a chance. . . . Truly, you
don't see women as the deans of the colleges. I don't
know why, maybe our makeups are really different.

Some women come to terms intellectually with the
differing role prescriptions and rewards by deciding that in
fact, women are inferior to men. One mother said she had
reached this conclusion, and decided that people who tried to
teach otherwise were promoting a satanic doctrine. We have
already shown that the equality perspective is by far the
majority view, that men and women are separate but equal,
that neither can achieve unity or harmony and salvation
without the other, and that in building a celestial family unit,
neither sex is superior. The alternative espoused by this
mother is that the hierarchy evident in the fact that men bear
the priesthood and that women are necessarily directed by
priesthood authority is a reflection of some eternal verity,
that women are in some way inferior. But let the mother
explain it her way:

Well, I was reading in the [scriptures]. . . .
It said that wherever there is one--it was talking
about the planets--wherever there is one planet, there
is always going to be one higher. You are never going
to find the highest one because there is always one
greater. So it said likewise, when there are two
persons, there is always one greater than the other.
I can't remember if exactly it used the word persons,
but what I am saying is maybe men are greater than
women. Maybe they are, maybe that is a priesthood
thing.

Teachers are higher than deacons and priests are higher than teachers and elders are higher than priests. Maybe it is that woman is lower than man. Even though we are from his side, so to speak, to be a companion and a helpmate to him. . . .

Some things we just have to accept and maybe that is something, that we are not to be to the level of the man. . . . And yet you don't hear this doctrine outside of the Church. The doctrine [outside the Church] is of equality, and so I think in a way, it is a little damning. In other words it is a satanic thing that puts the thoughts in the woman's mind that she is equal, whereas really I don't think we are equal. I think the man is above the woman. And it is just a law and I don't think it can be changed.

Unless I wanted to choose to be a man [in the pre-earth life]. And I am sure that if women had that choice, then I could have chosen to be a man. Now I can't remember that. But if I did have a choice, then how can I complain, if I at one time had a choice? So I think it is just a matter of just understanding and saying, I accept my limitations as a woman and I will respect the man, because I don't think we are equal. I really don't. If we are equal, then there is no patriarchal order. We may be equal in callings. Like saying two boys are going to clean this room and one does the windows and one mops the floor. You say which job is the greatest? I couldn't say. They both need to be done. In saying which job is the greatest, the priesthood or bearing the children, which is the greatest? I don't think you can say--they both need to be done. But I think you can say that man is above the woman. Just like God the Father is above Jesus Christ, they are not equal. He is still above, I don't know, that is just the way I look at it.

The Ideal-Reality Gap and the Supermom Syndrome

The Church-related challenge that surfaced most frequently as the mothers talked about themselves was the discrepancy between what they were and what they felt they ought to be. Their images of the ideal wife-mother-homemaker-Church member, based on parental or peer models and augmented by statements from Church leaders, both local and general, often differ drastically from the actuality they see in their daily routines.

217

The relationship of women to the Church often translates into self-comparisons not only with ideals stated by male Church authorities, but also with attributes of "supermom" exhibited by other women. The "supermom syndrome" was introduced in a previous chapter. In the context of a religion whose ideals for motherhood include the maxim, "No success can compensate for failure in the home," it can be very oppressive to struggling mothers who recognize their imperfections. Several of the women said that they felt there was too much comparing of self with others. Asked how Mormon women perceive themselves, a mother of seven said:

> I think they perceive themselves as imperfect, where those around them are perfect. I think we are very critical of ourselves, because we are only judging those around us on what we see in this one little situation. And they look good, they definitely show the very best, and we know all our faults in all situations. So, I think we are very critical of ourselves, we are very judgmental.

Not long before our interviewing there had been a television presentation on depression among Mormon women. Several of the mothers had seen the film, and referred to it in framing their answers about how Mormon women viewed themselves. Said a mother of eight:

> Well, after seeing that movie they put out not too long ago about women and depression in the Church, I have my doubts. But I think generally speaking, most women in the Church have a healthy attitude about themselves and what they are able to accomplish. A lot of them are bogged down with the fact that they feel like they should be doing so many things that they are not getting done, just because the leaders of the Church tell us that we should be doing genealogy, we should be doing temple work, we should be doing a myriad of things. They [Church leaders] don't mean that you're supposed to do all of those today, tomorrow or this week. They mean we should have those in mind to do as the time becomes available to us. So I think that a lot of women, especially those who have just been converted, within the last five or six years, have the idea that they are not accomplishing what they should be because they think they should be doing all these things right now.

Another mother highlighted Mormon women's pain at continual comparison with the ideal supermom, and pled for self-acceptance and a reduction of the burden of guilt Mormon mothers seemed to carry around with them:

> The women sometimes see themselves as "supermoms" and that theory has got to go. You can't be everything to everybody and you need to say that "I'm good in this area and I'm poor in this area." And you are going to have to accept that. I may be one that will gather my kids and go on a picnic. Okay, well, that's a good thing, but maybe somebody else, that isn't their thing. But maybe they're out in the backyard, doing scientific experiments with their kids, or maybe they're going to the library, or maybe they're exposing their kids to music, which is a weakness in my family. I'm not exposing my kids culturally. I'm not strong in that area. I'm strong in the athletic area. I've got to not feel guilty that I'm not giving my kids piano lessons. I think we just need to realize that we are not super in every area. Some of us aren't too good of a cook, so we just kind of rush through that little ordeal every day. Let's not feel guilty that we're not super cooks, and quit feeling guilty over the things we are not. Let's be happy in the things that we are. You know, a kid will grow. A child that's loved will grow in most any kind of circumstances. You're not going to mar that kid because you didn't read to him in the first grade. It's better if you can, but if you don't, that's not going to be detrimental to that kid forever. We need to accept ourselves.

The following response on the image of Mormon women shows how closely aspects of the mother-wife role are tied to religious directives. "Supermother" and "super Mormon" are alternate sides of the same coin:

> We should see ourselves as queens and princesses in the household of the Lord, children of our Father in Heaven, and very important in the overall scheme of things. But sometimes, I think, because of that, we see ourselves as failures, because we don't meet up with our own expectations of what we should be. There is the supermother, Super Mormon image which all of us have of grinding your own wheat, making all of your own clothes, having beautiful, well-cared-for children, and everything. Your husband is happy and you support him and send him off to be the bishop, and that sort of thing. And in reality, it is just not that way. The world is still here, and very few of us

can do all that. We see someone else being good at one thing or another, "Oh, I wish I could do that," and someone else is good at this, one is a good cook and one is a good seamstress, but they may not be both. But you feel like you should be all things to all people, plus the great Relief Society Visiting Teacher, and the great Primary teacher, and all that as well. There is a lot of pressure, which probably comes from within, more than from the hierarchy of the Church, to outsupermother all the other supermothers.

Note the self-deprecation of the next mother's comment that "a few of us can't quite measure up." The solution she recommended: do what you're good at.

[How do Mormon women perceive themselves?] Oh, golly, little homebodies I guess. I don't know. And anyway there are so many different women in the Church, that's hard to say. . . . They think they should be home and a loving wife, and supporting and doing all these good works. A few of us can't quite measure up. . . . I know I've been to Relief Society sometimes--this is before I got my tough skin--and gee, you're supposed to do it this way, you're supposed to do all these wonderful things, and really have your act together. You can get very frustrated, because you realize you're not doing all these things: you're not having intellectual discussions at dinner, your house is not filled with creative projects that you do in your spare time, you're not reading your scriptures fifteen minutes a day, you're not devoting all your time to P.T.A. or whatever. Somewhere along the line you have to realize that nobody's doing all those things, and you just have to do the things that you're best at.

The near-consensus about the "superhuman" demands on Mormon women was quite impressive. The pressures ranged from the challenge to be a well-rounded personality through the need to manage a large family essentially alone because one's husband must be "supported" in his church callings and employment, and on to the reflections upon the quality of motherhood implicit in the public performances of one's children.

The need to be well-rounded was seen as a particularly important challenge to Mormon women:

Mormon women have a challenge to be a well-rounded person first. All women don't feel that way. I mean, we feel like we are never-ending, so we've got to keep increasing our talents and our abilities and our preparedness for anything that happens in life. Even our physical body, our minds, emotions, everything, we feel like there has to be a well-rounded woman. Then as far as family, we feel like we've got to keep our family together. I mean, that's forever.

The amount of time spent by one or the other of the marriage partners doing Church work was also seen as a peculiar stress on Mormon women:

Our Church, in particular, demands a lot of our time and I think women in the Church can feel resentful about the amount of time their husbands spend in Church, or that they [themselves] have to spend.

A variation of this problem was the need for coordination:

I think another problem Mormon women face is trying to coordinate their large families with all the Church meetings that they have to go to and all the Church meetings that their husbands have to go to. Because, so many times, especially if their husband's in leadership, they're left with those children a lot in meetings and just at home. There's also a lot of meetings for children that they have to go to, that mothers have to go to and attend and see what they're doing and the activities they have to go to . . . and I think that mothers--Mormon women--also have a problem of learning gospel-type things, scriptures and things like that and teaching their children that so they can talk sensibly with men. It seems like men always seem to know it all and the women spend so much time talking about babies and they don't know anything.

As to the mothers' vulnerability to perceptions of the quality of children's performance and its reflection on the maternal self-image:

Well, I mentioned Sunday mornings. If you have eight children, the two-and-a-half minute talks [sermonettes children give in church meetings] come up very often, and how your children perform is a kind of

221

reflection on you, I think. I think you are very vulnerable through your children, unfortunately, or fortunately. And when things aren't going well for them, for one of them or all of them, it kind of affects the whole plan. How they perform in public and react to other people is a reflection on the home life. So, we really are under pressure to have things go well.

A mother of eight complained that sometimes the emphasis on the externalities, on having a home look nice inside and outside, got in the way of wise time and money management. The public facade of order, peace, and cleanliness may hide a reality of stress, perspiration, and irritability:

I know it is really hard to do all of the things that are expected. We have large numbers of children and many ladies don't have money to hire help. If you can have someone to come in and wash your windows for you, scrub your carpet, life is a lot easier. I think it is a very stressful time, where we put a lot of pressures on one another just by bragging about how much canning we did, how much time we did helping this person or that. We are still expected to keep our houses up and have our children be intelligent and knowledgeable. . . . Last night in Relief Society we had a demonstration on canning, and the home economist who happens to be in our ward showed a movie. There was this lovely lady with her hair all combed and the kitchen sparkling, smiling as she lifted the jars out of the canner and singing a song to her little girl. I think that is the image that we like to put forth to women. We all know that you get hot, sweaty and stressful. It isn't fun to work all day, and yet sometimes we won't admit these things to ourselves, or that we lose our temper. I have a terrible time getting 60 quarts done in one day.

The Dissatisfied Minority:
Uncertain, Confused, Depressed

There was general recognition among our respondents that some Mormon women were experiencing role stress and problems of identity and self esteem. Most Mormon women, it was said, were comfortable with who they were and what their roles were, but there was a minority who were having trouble. One woman explained some of the difficulties in terms of federal programs which had devalued motherhood.

I know that a lot of women feel kind of lost and
floating around.   With all of the nonsense that's
coming from the federal government on limiting
families and what-not, they're taking away where women
ought to be excelling. It's the most rewarding thing
in the world . . . to know and understand these
things.

That some women did view themselves as inferior was
seen as a problem.   A mother of nine put it this way:

I have really been concerned that some of them
[Mormon women] see themselves as inferior.   I mean
it's an inferior role that they're playing to a
priesthood role.   That isn't true as far as I'm
concerned.   Other women in the Church perceive
themselves as persecuted by the Church, although they
know they're not inferior, but they think that some
people in the Church think they are. And some women in
the Church have what I would think of as a more
healthy view of themselves. . . .   And that is, that
their roles are just as important as anybody else's
role that happens to be a little different.

Another woman contrasted her own satisfaction with the
restlessness and depression she perceived among some other
women.

I can't speak for very many [Mormon women].   The
ones I associate with generally feel very similar to
the way I feel about life being a delightful challenge
and children being very enjoyable.   But that may not
be typical.   I think there is a lot of depression, and
a lot of women who feel downtrodden, so to speak.   I
really don't have a lot of experience with those to
really judge.

A description of perceived uneasiness or confusion among
the women of the Church came from a mother of ten who
thought that most Mormon women had good self-concepts, but
that they were enduring trying times:

I think most of the women I associate with in the
Church are mothers, and get their greatest
satisfaction out of home and family, even the ones
that work.   Still, I think their goals are centered in
their families and in their [families'] lives.   I'm
sure that there are some women in the Church who have
a lot of questions about who they are right now,

because we have had mixed messages about who women are
for a long time. And the role models that have been
set up, even in terms of the women that are the
leaders of the Church, are a little mixed-messaged
too, because they are very active outside their
home. . . . I keep hearing that there is a lot of
confusion among women in the Church, but I don't see
it a lot in the women I associate with, in my friends
and in my own family. I think we just pretty well go
on and do our thing and take care of our families, be
happy and enjoy life.

Another response to the questions about the
self-perceptions of Mormon women and their feelings about
their roles was that there is a diversity, and that what
women felt depended on their circumstances. A mother of
seven said that in her experience, there was a lot of
difference by neighborhood:

I have lived in various kinds of wards
[congregations], and I think the perceptions are as
varied as the women are. I see some women who
consider themselves chattels to their husbands, who
had to do everything their husband said. They were
unhappy and yet they would say, "We have to do what
our husbands say," and they couldn't communicate with
their husbands. I think they just figured they were
like doormats to their husbands, very unhappy. I have
seen other women . . . who are the most outstanding,
competent, articulate, accomplished mothers, wives or
in their own professional careers that you could ever
imagine. So I think they are all over the lot.

A mother of seven said that the people she knew were
trying to "follow Church doctrine and it varies in degrees;
some are a little more assertive than others, and yet they
would like to think that they are following Church doctrine."
She continued:

They don't feel put upon and downtrodden. They
are doing what they are doing because they want to be
doing it. I know some that are having an awful
struggle with it. There is a gal that lives over
here. She's got four children now, and up until this
year she taught, at least part time, on a college
level. They just moved here, and for the first time
she is not teaching. She's just home with these four
and they just drive her right up the wall. She can
hardly put the thing together. I guess she is doing

it because she feels like that's what she ought to do,
but she's having a really tedious struggle with it.

A few mothers attributed the sense of dissatisfaction
among many Mormon women to the influence of the media.
Said one:

> There are so many people telling us what we
> should be like . . . we read so much in the paper, in
> magazines and on the news, that you should be
> rebellious about the situation. I think through the
> media that women have been brainwashed a little bit
> [into believing] that they are dissatisfied with their
> roles, but I don't think that they really are. But I
> think due to the propaganda and all of the articles,
> it makes you wonder. . . .

Coping with depression and dissatisfaction. What the
dissatisfied Mormon women need, according to most of the
respondents who offered a "prescription," is patience and
understanding. If they truly understood, the argument was,
they wouldn't be depressed or upset. Time and again the
notion surfaced that if women really understood and held
appropriate values they would have fewer problems. The way
they view themselves and their priorities, it was frequently
suggested, depends on how strongly they believe their
religion:

> It depends on their testimony of the Gospel. I
> would say as a whole, most of them catch a glimpse of
> the family being an eternal situation, and I think
> there are very few who wouldn't do almost anything if
> they really felt it would bring about a positive
> result. I think that our avenues of getting there
> just vary greatly.

A mother who explained that her role as wife and mother
was a growing, learning process emphasized that first of all
she was herself; second, she was a co-partner with her
husband; and third, with her children, she was responsible
to help them learn to grow to independence. But she
recognized that in some ways, even the children were equal
to her in the sense that they also were individuals who were
trying to "become themselves." As to the frustrations of the
motherhood role, she admitted that the children's growth was
slow, and that mothers also had to learn step by step.

> Some women really feel deprived and they feel maybe
> even worthless, or they feel burdened down in all

> these things, but if they do as they are told . . . I
> need to qualify that . . . if they do as they are
> commanded and they attend the things that they are
> commanded, and the Church programs are followed,
> they'll learn, if they go to the Temple regularly.

For her, the problems of women in the Church were
resolvable if the mothers followed the counsel they received
and attended to their Church assignments.

Most of the suggestions for helping mothers experiencing
dissatisfaction or frustration with their roles were
"psychological solutions," in that they had to do with
changing the attitudes and values of the women themselves,
or changing the way they did things so that they were
"better organized." There were a few, however, who
expressed a need for "structural" solutions, or changes in
the demands made upon women. One type of structural
solution would be reduction in the demands made by Church
organizations upon families. Such demands were seen as
particularly heavy outside the Utah-Idaho region, where
Church members are a majority of the population:

> I think that the Church needs to back off and I
> think that we need to get across to the local leaders
> in the mission field that we need to have the Church
> serve the families and not the families be serving the
> Church. . . . When they have brought this up and try
> to say something about it, they [local leaders in the
> mission field] just say, "We all have to sacrifice for
> the Church." Well, to me then, the Church becomes
> like a government, that we just become like a
> bureaucracy that feeds on itself. I think the local
> leaders in these areas need to get the word that they
> are demanding too much of people and their time. From
> what we saw, the members of the Church are losing
> their children from the Church. I know some tragic
> stories that just kill me, of kids that I know that
> are not active in the Church and their parents were
> gone constantly for meetings, and meetings, meetings,
> meetings, meetings. I think they are starting to get
> this [message] in Salt Lake [Church headquarters], but
> I wonder if it is trickling out into the mission
> field. From what I have seen, I know when programs
> come through from Salt Lake, for instance, they were
> going to cut back something, the attitude of our stake
> president was, "Well, our stake isn't going to do
> that." I think they are so afraid, because they have
> large rolls of inactive people and they see the

statistics and they panic and they think they have got to redouble their efforts and what it does is just place a huge burden upon the members that are active, that are trying to carry the load in those stakes.

A structural solution that individuals or families can adopt without changes in Church practice or policy is to set priorities and consciously, purposefully avoid meetings defined as middle- or low-priority.

> You just have to try to never eliminate or cut out things in which the children are involved or they are participating in, and they need somebody to be there to see what they are doing. But anything else, I just don't go to it unless it's really, really important. There's been church meetings that I should have gone to, Relief Society functions that I should have gone to, but you just can't. You just have to eliminate them. . . . And my problem is a lot harder because my husband is gone so much and many times I have to go to things that he could attend [if he weren't gone], and so I just try to go to what I have to, [and do] what has to be done.

Here is another perspective on the method of prioritizing to cut down over-commitment and its attendant stresses:

> We try to keep things under control . . . I think you have to evaluate the various programs, not the Gospel, but the programs, auxiliaries, and different things, in light of your own family's needs. So, if it is not a benefit to your family for your son to make a Cub Scout race car, then I don't think that is really going to damn you all [if you don't partici- pate]. . . . So we just try to evaluate things, one at a time as they come along, and use the programs to benefit our family. We do use Family Home Evening extensively. We try to go to church together as a family, always to Sunday School. We don't always all make it to Sacrament Meeting, because if the baby is asleep we might leave someone home, that sort of thing. And then encourage the children in their Primary and Sunday School, talk about their lessons, amplify on them that week in the family and that sort of thing. So that the Church is an asset to us and not a problem. But I think we can allow ourselves to become the victims of other people's scheduling.

Although they recognized problems and areas needing change, the women in our study were committed to the LDS Church with it's attendant cultural values. They defended their equal but different status with men, their roles as wife and mother in the home, and described their essential contributions to both family and Church. In the next chapter we will consider more specifically how these women feel about their involvement with the organization of the Church.

Chapter XI

WOMEN AND THE CHURCH: INVOLVEMENT IN THE ORGANIZATION

* * * * *

The purposes of the Relief Society are "to
manifest benevolence; to care for the poor, the sick,
and the unfortunate; to give assistance at time of
death; to give guidance and training to the sisters in
homemaking arts and skills; to foster love for
religion, education, culture, and refinement; to
develop faith; and to study and teach the Gospel."[1]

As they discussed their perceptions of women vis-a-vis
the Church, most of the mothers made reference to the
organizational aspects of the Church and their feelings about
involvement with particular programs. Although participation
was seen as important and valuable, reasons for activity and
views about appropriate levels of involvement varied
considerably.

Attitudes about Relief Society

Insights into the women's attitudes about their role in
the Church may be seen in their responses to questions about
the women's organization of the Church, the Relief Society.
Most said that the Relief Society was an important
organization that filled many of their needs. Most said they
liked the association with the other women that it facilitated.
There was some concern that sometimes Relief Society lessons
lowered the self-esteem of the women, by the continual stress
on the ideal ways of doing things. There were also a few
negative comments about the impracticalities of the lesson

---

[1]Relief Society Handbook. Salt Lake City, Utah: The
Church of Jesus Christ of Latter-day Saints, 1976, p. 1.

material and of the homemaking or handicraft activities. But the dominant attitude was one of support and appreciation for the organization.

Over three-fourths of the mothers indicated general satisfaction with the Relief Society. Almost half said that it was meeting their needs, and the others said that it provided valued association with other women, independent of the topics or lessons being presented. Here is a sample of the appreciative comments about Relief Society:

> For one, I find that the others have a lot of the same pressures that I do and you hear it. And two, it gives me a social outlet with special friends. For three, it gives me the spiritual uplift I need and I want and I'm looking for. And I just don't miss because it's great . . . it's the biggest help to me. I am not discouraged coming home from a motherhood lesson when I know I haven't done everything they said, because to me I find that I've heard other women and they're having problems with so and so, too.

> I think it is stimulating. You go there and you come home refreshed. I mean it gives you a boost to get out of the house. I think it is definitely inspired. I think if the Church didn't have the Relief Society, you would find a lot more male domination than you do, because you have the Relief Society. I mean, if you could imagine the Church without the Relief Society, there would be far more problems than there are now. I really enjoy it.

Among the comments of women who stressed the social benefits of Relief Society more than the content of the lessons were these:

> Relief Society is a place where people go and where women understand one another and where you are able to do something just for yourself and by yourself and with others who are like you.

> It's the sisterhood and the fellowship and the contact. . . . We care for one another and serve one another when there's a need. . . . It can create some stresses if people feel pressured by the things they have to do for an organization, but I think that can be controlled as you learn your own strengths and weaknesses and your own time limitations.

I like the association. I think it is fun to sit by a grandmother on one side and somebody who is my contemporary on the other side, to visit with them and listen to their experiences, the things that they have learned and the things that they are so willing and open to share. There are so many good ladies to become acquainted with and to have as friends, and that is when you can really get close with them.

I go just to talk to adults, almost even more than to hear the lesson, even though they are good . . . it is just to get to rub shoulders with your own kind, with people that speak your language. I think that some of the things that they do on work days [Homemaking "work meeting"], I just would not even want to bother with, and that is not very nice to say, but I don't.

Sometimes the Relief Society organization was contrasted with the E.R.A. movement, and seen as an alternative. Here are two such responses:

I think a lot of it with the ERA and this sort of movement is self-esteem. Just that the woman is important and your calling as a mother is vital and you are really making a contribution to society, because there are some, the really radicals, that [think] if you are a mother and not working, you're not worth much and you are not doing your part to contribute to society. If you have a large family, then shame on you, and that sort of thing. And I think Relief Society can build self-esteem and make us feel important.

I love it, I really do. I think it is the greatest thing that anybody could ever have and I am only sorry that they do not have it in Protestant Churches, because I really feel that with the variety of programs that they have, they are offering so much. You wouldn't have a women's movement if you had Relief Society, because these gals have a place to learn to grow. The biggest problem with the women's movement is that they are reaching out to the women that have not grown. They are reaching to the woman whose husband has gone ahead into business, been out in the business world, and she is stuck home with the kids. She gets to feeling like, "I am a dullard, I have no education, I haven't done anything." But I blame her, and I blame him because he hasn't encouraged her in the first place. He hasn't said, "What have you read lately, dear? What newspaper have you read? What article can we talk about? What can we communicate about? What can I do to get you into society?"

That's one way a working mother has an advantage. She's out and she comes back to her home and she brings back her vitality that a woman at home doesn't have. Well, Relief Society provides that vitality, it really does. It provides the opportunity for women to learn new things, to learn new ways. But it also gives her a vent. There are spiritual living lessons, there are cultural refinement lessons, with compassionate service, with social relations, and mother education techniques. It gives her new ideas and gives her a chance to communicate with other mothers and find out what is happening instead of complaining constantly.

Some of the mothers had negative comments about the handicraft or "artsy-craftsy" aspects of the Relief Society. Others made critical suggestions about lesson topics and Relief Society programs. Typically these comments were in the vein that sometimes the lessons were good and sometimes they weren't, or sometimes a program involved useful activity and sometimes it didn't. A more critical view was taken by only a few of the women. One complaint was about the lack of intellectual stimulation.

I think the lessons are kind of shallow on a lot of things, and for me to be really interested in the subject I have to go into it more. If I want to know about Japan, I go take a class on Japan or Guatemala, or whatever. The little hour lessons are too shallow for me to feel that they are any intellectual stimulation. There are other benefits to it, but when they get up and say, "Oh, I keep my mind alert going to Relief Society," I thought, "Honey, You're dead now, if that's keeping you alert," because it's just kind of surface stuff. . . . Some artsy-craftsy things just aren't for me.

Here is another woman's complaint about the emphasis on handicraft:

I feel we spend too much time on little dingy things. Who cares about tole painting? I get so sick of tole painting, I could just. . . . [They need to do] things that can make a difference in your life, and not just superficial little frills. Well, they had a class on rug-making, and they said that in case it comes to the day that we have no carpets, we are ready with rug-making. Well, now listen, if we have no carpets, who cares about rugs?

Another criticism was that the Relief Society was more idealistic than realistic and tended to shade things or present just the nice side. A variation of this view was that the lessons sometimes didn't get down to the real issue:

Some of the lessons are a little weak. I think they could get down to the real nitty-gritty sometimes. . . . I think Relief Society could become a little more realistic. Sometimes you don't even like to go to Relief Society because you come home and feel so guilty because you're not doing that. . . . They need to play down the guilt roles. If you're not doing this in your family, if you haven't done this with your children, if you haven't done this with your husband, you should feel terribly guilty. If you're not terribly organized in your home, you should feel guilty. Somehow they have got to present the fact that you don't need to feel guilty about things. They need to say, "You're at Relief Society. You're really doing what you should be doing. You're really trying." They need to pat you on the back once in a while and say, "You really are trying. You really are doing a good job." There are a lot of people in this world that are doing terrible things. At least I'm going to Relief Society, at least I've made the effort to go. So they need to play down the guilt role and they need to be more realistic about life itself and not look through rose-colored glasses.

I have really found that the Relief Society has just been a valuable education tool in my life, a valuable spiritual tool. I think it has just kept me on top spiritually when at times I haven't been able to get much spiritually out of the Sacrament meeting or Sunday School because I am holding children. It's been a valuable tool, I have learned so many things from Relief Society. . . . I wish that we could have more lessons that are dealing with today's issues.

Time Pressures: Church Callings and Family Time

Let us remind the reader that all of these women were active church members. All except one attended church services at least weekly, and only two (five percent) did not

LIFE IN LARGE FAMILIES

have a current church assignment or office of some kind. Forty-one (of whom one was Protestant) held a total of 59 church positions, with 16 having at least two formal assignments and four women reporting three or more positions. These positions involved teaching children in Sunday School and Primary or administrating and teaching in the Relief Society. It may be recalled that the husbands of these women were also very active in church affairs, often holding important local administrative positions.

"Supporting" the husband in his calling. Large families make unusual time demands on parents, both for the provision of economic support and for teaching and caring for the children. Responsible administrative or teaching positions in the Church also are time-consuming, and the amount of parental time spent away from home in Church activities may be a salient factor in family life. The impact of Church-related time demands may be particularly heavy in large families, where a father's Church responsibilities may leave to the mother an even larger share of the burden of children and home care.

The mother's attitudes about the time they and their husbands spent in Church activities were explored via some direct questions on the topic. Relevant to the interpretation of these findings is the fact that most Latter-day Saints who have Church callings view those callings as calls from God, although the specific call is often issued by the local bishop. The parent in a large family is thus faced on the one hand with a call from God to devote considerable time away from the home and, on the other hand, with the injunction that "no success can compensate for failure in the home."

In response to the question, "How do you feel about the time your husband spends in church activity?" the typical response was an affirmative expression of support for the husband or support for the Church by "lending" the husband to Church activity, followed by an explanation of why it was important to do that. Those explanations generally fell into one of four categories, the first being that the callings were what the Lord wanted the husband to be doing and so, of course, the wife felt good about that and didn't want to stand in the way. A second explanation was that the wife felt good about the time her husband spent in Church activity because there were so many other negative things that some husbands did, and she would be very ungrateful to complain when her husband was engaged in such a good cause. A third justification was that the Church activity helped the husband to grow, and that the entire family profited from that growth.

234

A variation on this was that the husband's Church activity set a good example for the children. Finally, there was the feeling that although the husband held the calling, he tactfully and carefully involved his wife and to some extent the family in his calling, so that they shared in the blessings that came from his performance.

Here are some statements of support for husband's church activity that illustrate these four justifications for father absence.

1.   --"It is what the Lord wants him to be doing":

>   It has never bothered me. I've always been able to support him when he's going doing Church work. That's been fine with me, because I want him to be a success, and I want the Lord to be able to trust him and use him in any way the He sees fit. . . . I think that it's a matter of my attitude how the children feel about it, because I remember when our little boy said, "I don't mind when Daddy's gone on Sunday," he said this one time, "because I know he's doing the Lord's work," and I thought, "That's really neat."

>   Before the bishopric was changed, my husband was a counselor and I hoped he wouldn't be the bishop. I didn't want that For a while I resented the time he was spending. Then I had a spiritual manifestation that was what he should be doing, and since then I've had no problem accepting it. I don't mind him being gone. I do not feel that I or my children are being ignored. Like I say, we have our time in the evenings which I really enjoy. I'm glad that he's doing what he is.

2.   --"There are so many worse things he could do":

>   When you ask me that, it reminds me that my brother has been a bishop, and I guess he was really away a lot. Well, it's in California and there is a lot more distance and travel time involved, and her mother said to his wife, "Don't you get lonesome? Don't you resent the time?" She said, "Well, I'm so grateful that this is what he is doing, because there are other things that might not be desirable that he could be engaged in." And it's true. We're fortunate that they are [busy in Church work].

He could spend it all there [all his time in Church activity] and he wouldn't mind, because that's the best way for him to be, the best place for him to be. When my husband was branch president [bishop] up at the university he had to be gone mostly all day Sunday. I felt a lot of pressure from having to handle everything all day Sunday, and I'm sure I said, once in a while, "Can't you come home for this or that?", but I liked it in him. It's a good place for him to be.

3. --"We all grow from Church activity":

It's something that you have to be aware of, number one, that you feel that way [resentful]. When you realize that, then I think you need to sort out the problem. I heard someone say, "If you want someone to be active in the Church, you must not resent the time he spends being active in the Church." That statement helped me a lot. I think you can't feel guilty if you're feeling this way, because surely it comes out once in awhile. . . . I think these are sacrifices, and sacrifices are what makes one grow, and to have everything handed to you on a gold platter is not necessarily growth. These are the things that make us grow; you do them.

You know, at first I was a little resentful of the fact that, "Gee, he's so busy during the week, why do they have to take him on Sunday, too?" You can feel this way. You can gripe and feel negative about it. Or you can say, "O.K., he has been called, and he knows he's been called by the Lord," . . . you know, we've been faced with things we don't necessarily want to do or accept. There's a lot of things we don't want to do in this life. We have to learn to obey. . . . I still kind of kick against the pricks, too, when I'm trying to take the whole gang to sacrament meeting [by myself] and gritting my teeth, you know. Then the next three or four weeks, I leave one of the older kids home with the little ones and enjoy the meeting. We've done a lot of that.

4. --"He involves us, we enjoy sharing the calling with him":

I don't resent the time at all. Well, I think part of it is because he makes me so much a part of what he's doing in the Church. We do a lot of brainstorming together. When he was scoutmaster, we did a lot of brainstorming of what fun scout activities could be done. When he was bishop we did brainstorming of what ward activities or what youth activities or such could be done. He didn't betray confidences that a bishop has, but there are times when he would say, Honey, how am I going to handle the problem?"

I think there are a lot of parents who are not aware of what their kids are going through, so we have brainstorm parent meetings. He came to Relief Society a couple of times and said, "Hey, sisters, I need to talk to you about what's happening in your homes." That was a result of our brainstorming together. There were times when he called meetings after Sacrament Meeting for all parents of teenage children. I've always been very much a part of what his calling has been. That does two things. That makes me a contributing part of his job, and then as we plan an activity and he goes and does it while I stay home and keep the home fires burning I anxiously await his return to say, "Hey, how did it go? Did it work or didn't it? What are we going to do to make it better next time?"

There were also some negative responses, but generally the negative responses were statements about past attitudes, perhaps that the mother used to resent the time her husband spent or had selfishly tried to keep him at home or had been jealous of the time he spent away. The definition of the situation for these formerly "selfish" or "resentful" mothers was not that the husband had spent too much time away from the family, but rather that there had been something wrong with the attitude of the mother herself in not understanding and supporting him as she should.

Only one or two mothers were critical of the situation itself, rather than of their own attitudes. These women suggested that people with young children shouldn't be called to time-consuming positions, or that it was impossible for people to manage large families and to carry out their major Church callings as they should. These criticisms of a structure which seriously competed with the family for the father's time, with the result that mother had to cope with the children without his support, were really quite rare. Usually a mother explained that what resentment she had felt, the complaints she might have made about her husband being away, were in a previous period when she had not yet worked through what her role was and what being supportive really meant.

A case of dealing with stressful reality by redefining the situation was the mother who said:

> You have your moments when you have things that he could be doing. For example, we moved into this house . . . and when we moved in it was just a frame, and the lights weren't hooked up and the water wasn't on and things like that . . . so it wasn't a finished product and still isn't . . . but when he went in to be bishop [six months after moving into the house] everything stopped as far as getting things done, and . . . while he was bishop he did not have the time . . . so there were moments when I would feel, "Golly, if he were just here look at what we could accomplish." But then I would think of it in the overall perspective. Things that he accomplished in the time he was giving to the Lord were far more valuable than putting a shelf here or putting a door there, or things like that. At the time, while you are living the experience, you are frustrated by it. When you think about it and evaluate it and see how it fits in, you realize that it was just a stumbling block for you that you had to overcome.

Here is one of the mothers who defined her need for her husband as selfishness. In this relatively rare instance the man had been released from an administrative calling because of pressure at home:

> Well, he's not very busy right now. Well, he just quit most of his [Church] jobs last year too, because I just had to have him. When he was home he had to be helping me or he had to be working. But one year, it was a few years ago, he was Elders' Quorum President, and oh that was hard, because Sunday was supposed to be the day that I thought he ought to be home with the family, and that was the day when he did most of his work. During the week he had to work at these other jobs and so he couldn't do much then. He just spent all day long doing Elder's Quorum work. It was really hard, because I just felt I needed him home, and I felt like I was just taking care of the whole show by myself, and all the kids by myself. And sometimes I feel like I ought not to be so selfish, but it sure was hard. But right now he does have a couple of jobs, but they're not major jobs like that.

They still keep him busy. It still seems like he has
to leave more often than I want him to.

Still another mother expressed her desire for her
husband's association in lieu of his Church service:

> I am fortunate in a way because he doesn't have
> any desire to get out and do things with men friends,
> so there has never been that kind of pull. When we
> were first married, I was a little bit resentful of
> his being away on Sundays for different things if I
> were home alone. I think I was a little bit jealous.
> Maybe that was what it was, that he was in more demand
> that I. . . . It doesn't bother me anymore. . . . I
> want him to fulfill his callings well. I would feel
> badly if he didn't. I would feel like I had to nag
> him.

For some families having father away from home is
defined as helpful stress-reduction time. A mother of ten,
whose husband was away at least two nights a week, said
that those were the times that she used to get close to the
children:

> That time I use to help the kids with their
> studying, their school work, and what not, if they
> need it, or we sew. It just gives me some times with
> the kids. He's not quite so easy going as I am, and he
> gets frustrated with all the confusion--even if it is
> organized confusion!

A mother of seven whose husband's Church calling
required him to attend Church services in other congregations
said that she generally felt very positive about the time he
spent. However,

> There are days when the kids are acting up that I
> think, why can't I go listen to him talk and let the
> kids go to our ward? Just send them off to this
> corner and I'll go with him. [Then I remember] if you
> want to get to the Celestial Kingdom together, you are
> going to have to share him there. He's not going to
> be sitting holding my hand when we get there, so
> Church responsibilities are important. I don't think
> they should become so important that the family is
> neglected. There are people that are so dedicated and
> try so hard that they do neglect their families, and I
> think that's wrong. The family needs to get the prime
> attention.

The mother's Church assignments. When questioned about their own Church callings, the women were similarly positive. They said they enjoyed their Church jobs, they learned from them, and they found them rewarding and challenging. However, when talking about their own Church callings there was more criticism about structure, about meetings being held for the sake of meetings, and about stresses from competing family demands. Some mothers said they occasionally had to let Church assignments go or rush through them in order that they might devote time to family.

It was with respect to their own callings, rather than to their husbands' Church assignments, that women tended to make the point that the purpose of the Church was to strengthen families, and that if they had to choose between their Church callings and the family responsibility, they had to choose the family. Most made sure that a bishop fully understood their situation before he formally gave them a calling, or before they formally accepted.

Perhaps we should be reminded at this point that these mothers' statements about Relief Society and time spent in Church callings do not represent the attitudes of Mormon women generally. Data on Mormon womens' feelings about these matters simply are not available. Although we lack a context in which to place the mothers' reports, it is very likely that they are far more positive about traditional family roles and about existing Church programs than Mormon women generally. After all, most of them are leaders or frequent attenders at Relief Society, and most are wives of local Church officials. In other words, these women are highly committed to and very active in the Mormon Church. In general, they were accepting rather than critical. To the degree that they voiced concerns or made constructive criticisms, these should be interpreted as the perceptions of the hard-working, committed, faithful members of the Church rather than the complaints of the disaffected.

The notion that the parents of young children, both male and female, should be called on less frequently for major church positions was voiced several times. Speaking of men's callings, a mother of seven said:

> I think there are times when we need to use some of our people in the ward whose kids are gone to college, those who have a little more time than a young father who has young kids at home.

This woman also said that she had reservations about church responsibilities that kept her away from home in the evenings:

> At night when my husband is home and my family needs me here, and I need to be here, I'm not thrilled. Yet I realize that in a Mutual Association [youth organization] you need to have someone there too. I honestly feel strongly that they need to call someone who has kids of Mutual age, not a mother who has young children. . . . When I was in Relief Society . . . in the nursery, I loved it. I got along beautifully with that, because it was during the day. I could take my kids and we would be fine. Primary was fine with young mothers, but night time when you have got kids to get into bed, no. . . . I really feel that that is something else, but even night time Relief Society, when you have young children to get into bed is a real hassle.

Another mother found both the time and the financial demands of some of the church programs a little too demanding:

> I feel that for our family that I would rather have some of that time as a family to do things as a family. . . .
> . . . it's going to be a fine line to really balance it out, because I think definitely sometimes we are hurt as a family, because we've got too many outside [activities]. . . .
> With people who are having financial trouble, the church can really put a lot of stress, especially in the teenage area, or in the Relief Society area, or anything. You know, a two dollar luncheon, or a three dollar [and] fifty [cent] luncheon doesn't seem like a lot, but to some people that is a lot. I think the Church is going to have to watch these types of things.

A mother of eight said that she thought she saw an evolution in church programs toward increased home-centeredness:

> I can see the day is coming now where the teaching will be more and more at home. I can see the need for it. When I was being raised everything was activity out in the Church. I was glad and I think it solved the problem at the time, but I don't know, the

241

last three or four years, we have felt the weight of
our family more and even more, so now in the past two
years we do not have time to give to the church jobs
that we had before. I can see that we have got to
spend less time in [Church] activities, and more time
concentrating on the home and teaching our own
children. I can see this happening not only in our
own family, but other families are doing this. . . .
I have always loved meetings, but I find it more
difficult and more difficult, because the more we are
away from our home, the less strength the home is and
that's not the purpose of the Church. . . . There is
so much demand from the world, I don't know what it
is, but I feel the pressure from the world is stronger
than it has ever been before. . . . I think that we
have to be very careful in our meetings, and the
activities that require the children outside the home.

How does one deal with the conflict between church
assignment and family? There is a strong norm in the
Church that one does not seek assignments, and one does not
voluntarily withdraw from them. One waits until one is
released by the authorities. However, here is a mother who
was able to balance that norm against the increasing
pressures she felt at home:

There are some jobs that I think it would be well
to keep away from women, unless there is a special
need for them at that time. Now, before my son was
born, I was a counselor in the Primary, and it took a
great deal of time. Particularly, if you know the
people well, and if the teachers have needs and feel
free to call you. I was spending a lot of time on the
telephone, plus a lot of other things. It was
demanding, and I felt like with another child that I
really couldn't do justice to my family and a new baby
and that job. I don't believe in asking to be released
from jobs. I don't believe in seeking them or getting
out of them, but I did talk with a member of the
bishopric about that, and told him how I felt, and I
was released.

Here is another mother's account of how she found it
necessary to turn down a Church job:

If everybody gives as much as they can give, then
we're all learning and progressing, so I feel good
about it, whatever I can do. I don't have a large
church calling, because I just know that I can't spend

that much time. So I wouldn't want to <u>not</u> do a good job, so once I did turn down a job, because they'd asked me to work with the Cub Scouts, and it was just when I'd had a new baby. I really felt that it was just too much for me at the time, and so I just said I thought it would be too much. I didn't feel bad about it. My husband didn't want me to do it either. At the time it was really too hard.

Another mother said that her experience in the Church has convinced her that often people's callings were too demanding, or that people define them in demanding ways, to the detriment of their families. She said that sometimes it was important for people to be able to say no:

The things that I am doing have allowed me to spend time with my children, to spend time with my family, and to do the kinds of things that we talk about in Church, and I have got time to do them and feel good about it. . . . I probably have as strong a testimony as anyone you will ever see, and I grew up to give my all to the Church, but I finally reached the point where I could see that it was having a negative influence, that it was counterproductive to the family. I found myself in Relief Society one day just almost bitter because I thought, "Who has time to go home and practice any of the things that we have been preaching in all these lessons? We don't have time to write even thank you letters . . . to people who are doing things because we are so busy preparing the next lesson and doing the next thing." . . . I have seen it both ways now.

A mother of twelve described the responsibilities of helping others that she faced, even though she didn't have a formal position in the church at present:

Sometimes I feel like I do more for the Church . . . I feel like I'm making more cakes for the Church than I am for us. Usually when we do something like that it's for the Church instead of for us. But sometimes I think it's a little more than I want, and other times it's fine. It seems like we have a lot of banquets in this ward. But usually I'm not involved very much because people just don't ask me to. They're usually pretty careful about giving me something easy, so I can't really complain. Most people do more than I do.

LIFE IN LARGE FAMILIES

Several of the mothers remarked that they didn't spend a great deal of time in their church callings, and some indicated that, because they had several children, they received some degree of protection or special concern about time-consuming callings from their ward leaders. Others said that they had standard church callings, but that the callings didn't take too much time, either because they were very well organized, or they had had that calling before and knew how to do it without inordinate preparation time.

A mother of eight who had a time-consuming administrative calling was asked about the time she spent away from home. She responded:

It just goes along with the job. I don't resent it. I'm careful not to use more [time] than I absolutely have to use. We eliminate meetings that aren't absolutely essential, but we use the time it takes to get the job done . . [my children] are very supportive. They wouldn't be, I am sure, if my husband wasn't so good to take over and step in. We have just been blessed with some really special children, in that way. They like me to put my church job first . . . they seem to be really proud that I am doing the things that I do.

If there is an overriding principle that governs church-family competition for parental time among these families it is that, if one accepts a church calling in the proper spirit, somehow things work out for the best. A mother of ten, whose husband had been a bishop for many years, explained about those years:

Something happened during those years that was really interesting. Somehow he had more time with us. He was gone a lot, but we just knew when he'd be gone and just planned around it. There is just something that happens, something that happens when you have a real responsibility in the Church that helps you to organize the rest of your life better, or something. But it's a good time and when you're busiest it seems that you can manage the best at home [emphasis added].

The Transmission of Religiosity: The Mormon Mother's Challenge

The mothers' answers to the query about the problems Mormon women face reveal the permeating influence of the Church upon their perspectives and problem definitions. They were concerned about the lack-of-fit between external or worldly standards and Church standards, and the resulting difficulty of living up to their ideals. Some see the problem in terms of the difficulties of rearing children properly in a world where the prevailing standards often reflect sin, immortality, and corruption. A mother of ten said her major problem was "worldy more than anything."

> I mean economic and moral and just plain trying to keep your family on the straight and narrow pathway when the outside world is just closing in on you. I think this is our pressure.

The idea that the Mormon mother was responsible for the faith and righteousness of her children was stated in a variety of ways. Here are some illustrations of the way the mothers perceive this central challenge of their existence:

> There is the problem of keeping unspotted from the world and keeping your family righteous . . trying to counteract all the worldly influences which people have.

> I think there is a polarization taking place. When I was growing up there was a great big middle glob of people kind of wishy-washy, and now you're either good or bad. And as we are moving closer and closer to the Second Coming [of Christ] it is going to polarize more, this real division where you are either doing what you should or you are not. And so there is going to be more pressure.

> Probably the biggest problem that we have to face is rearing our children . . . I think the world has let teens down. I think the world has really let our teenagers down. For example, we have a teenager, and the standards that we used to have, there were some things that were definitely taboo in our culture as I was growing up. There were some things you just definitely didn't do because you knew culturally that wasn't accepted, and that isn't the way it is today. . . . One of the biggest problems that we have

to face today is the problem of how to live in a world and yet not be part of the world.

There's so much evil around that comes into the home, I mean television, language, anti-God types of things. . . . these kinds of things are pressures that Mormon women face.

Part of the reason that this is such a problem to Mormon women, according to some of our respondents, is that the women measure their success by their children's lives. Two mothers reflected:

I think it is really challenging because I am not a working mother, I am a home mother. I stay home all the time. It is hard sometimes because of the changing morals and the world is so much different from when I was little and growing up. You have to just watch so carefully to see what goes into their [children's] minds and things like this. That is the big challenge, to try to keep them true to the Church. That is how I measure success, too, if they remain loyal to the Church. We would like the boys to be missionaries and, of course, we want all of them to get married in the temple. And if this would happen, then, of course, I would consider myself successful.

I think that the burden that we as Church members carry, because we're taught that we need to teach our children correct principles, and then when that child particularly falls away, and falls away so deeply you feel, "How have I failed?" . . . . I think it's a real hard problem for parents, the complete guilt that sometimes they feel when the child still has free-agency. And you can't take that free agency away from them.

Another mother similarly recognized the problems of raising children in the world, but noted that there were also stresses associated with life in Utah Valley, where the social pressures sometimes ran too much the other way:

I think outside of Utah County or Utah, you don't get any support for having a big family, or staying home, and so that could really be hard . . . you've really got to be strong. You can't just drift along and think they'll turn out all right, because the peer pressure is against you. That's why I do appreciate Utah County . . . so I think Mormon women outside of

Utah have that problem trying to keep their families
in line. I feel a stronger pressure to conform in the
Church here, less tolerance for crazies . . . I
sometimes think that we don't have too many different
people out here. We're all pushed into a mold and if
you don't conform you are kind of ostracized in a way.

All May, Indeed, Be "Well in Zion"

The Church-related problems of Mormon mothers have
been considered at some length. To keep things in
perspective, we should say that, given their worldview, these
are the problems that most of them choose to have and they
assured us they can "live with them." For most of the
mothers, the alternative problems they perceive among other
women are more intimidating, more depressing, than their
own.

The phrase, "all is well in Zion," is a Mormon cliche
drawn from a scriptural statement to the effect that when
people think "all is well in Zion," all may not be well. Many
of the mothers are sure that the present situation is not the
best of all possible worlds. Even so, they seem convinced
that things are better in "Zion" than elsewhere. Let us
conclude this chapter with four quotations making that point.

I have too much to be thankful [for] to feel any
pressures . . . I haven't noticed any pressures as a
Mormon woman.

I think [among] members of the Church, men are
probably some of the finest husbands in the world,
because they do have a lot of respect for their wives,
they appreciate them.

[I've heard] some real horror stories about women
that felt put down and not accepted. But I've seen
such a change in the generations, I just don't know
very many men that don't believe that a women should
be as knowledgeable as a man about the scriptures or
anything else . . . I hear this. . . . But when I
stop and look at the women I know, my close friends
and the people I associate with, I don't really see it
in their lives. Maybe we're a fortunate group.
Financially, I suppose we are . . . we don't have a
lot of [financial] pressures. . . . But for the most
part the women I associate with are quite comfortable,
I think, in their homes. They're happy, they're

comfortable in their roles and understand their roles, and understand their husbands' roles. We had this workshop on depression, but everybody there kept talking about "well, these other people," or "I know there are these other women," but I didn't see anybody there that was relating an awful lot to what they were saying about it.

I don't think that Mormon women face as many problems as women out in the world do because of the fact that Priesthood does have this extra respect for women in the Church. It's very seldom, for instance, that you hear of men and women who are active in the Church that will have a beating problem, or neglect problem, or things of this nature. If they are active and doing as they're supposed to do, generally speaking, in most cases the women don't really have a problem.

Chapter XII

THE MATERNAL SEARCH FOR MEANING

* * * * *

. . . happiness invariably accompanies a meaningful
life. Consequently, by engaging in meaningful
activity, a person enjoys happiness as a by-product.
                                    --William S. Sahakian[1]

Viktor E. Frankl, a survivor of the Nazi holocaust and a
retired Viennese psychiatrist, recently wrote:

Western society, due to its technological
progress, has the capacity--at least in principle--to
satisfy all needs of humankind except one: the need
for meaning. . . . The struggle for survival is over.
But the question of survival for what? is still open.[2]

For many mothers of large families the endless economic
constraints, the pursuit of precious privacy, the search for
solitude, the deprivation from desirable adult company, and
the seemingly endless task of maintaining a household for ten
or twelve or fourteen people still constitute a daily struggle
for survival. And what is the outcome of this enterprise? In
most cases, according to the women we interviewed, the
end-products are a sense of satisfaction, feelings of personal
well-being, and the gift of a meaningful life.

---

[1]William S. Sahakian, "Logotherapy--For Whom?" in J. B.
Fabry, R. P. Bulka and W. S. Sahakian (Eds.) Logotherapy
in Action. N.Y.: Jason Aronson, 1979, pp. 3-4).

[2]Viktor E. Frankl, "Foreward" to Logotherapy in Action,
p. ix.

In his best-selling book, Man's Search for Meaning, Frankl described a pervasive psychological malady in modern society; perceptions of an "existential vacuum" characterized by a sense of emptiness and boredom.[3] Indeed, the addiction of many homemakers to TV soap operas, alcohol, and numerous prescription and over-the-counter drugs all confirm Frankl's assertion that boredom and loss of meaning in one's life induce more patients to pursue psychotherapy than do traumatic events.

One manifestation of an absence of meaning to life is the so-called "Sunday neurosis," which Frankl depicts as a:

> . . . kind of depression which afflicts people who become aware of the lack of content in their lives when the rush of the busy week is over and the void within themselves becomes manifest. Not a few cases of suicide can be traced back to this existential vacuum.[4]

Not being one to identify a problem without suggesting a solution, Frankl prescribes a strategy for finding meaning in life which consists of (1) doing something for someone else, (2) developing and experiencing something of value, and (3) learning how to bear unavoidable suffering.[5]

Frankl's disciples in different professions have extended and codified his seminal work by identifying principles which seem to govern the relentless search for fulfillment in life. Six of these principles are stated below in a slightly modified form. Each is related to what has been learned about the lives of Mormon mothers of large families.

1. <u>Meaning can be found in apparently meaningless activities</u>.

For some women the thought of bearing and caring for more than six children, let alone a dozen, represents the ultimate in subverting self-fulfillment. Others may inquire,

---

[3]Viktor E. Frankl, Man's Search for Meaning. N.Y.: Simon and Schuster, 1963, p. 169.

[4]Ibid.

[5]Ibid., p. 176 ff.

"How can anyone find changing diapers and doing housework to be self-fulfilling?" Some career women avoid domestic drudgery in their quest for self-fulfillment, and still they do not achieve happiness. Sahakian contends that the reason that happiness is so difficult to achieve is that "most people confuse happiness with pleasure."[6]

For the 41 fertile mothers in our study, being tied down by domestic duties did not directly constitute self-fulfillment. Some were quite vocal about the non-fulfillment inherent in cleaning a house, only to find it in disarray a short time later. However, this apparently meaningless activity may help seven or eight children learn to work, to share, and to cooperate in a joint family enterprise. The by-product is that mothers have something, or someone, to pull them out of bed each morning. Their self-fulfillment is an indirect result of their helping several others to find fulfillment.

In a previous chapter one mother unwittingly described her own personal discovery of meaning in her life when she said: "You work your tail off . . . and you think, 'Oh, what am I doing, I'll never get through this.'" She then explained that after the children received excellent grades in school or performed well at a recital she realizes, "This is what I am working for."

2.   Situations in which one feels irreplaceable elicit meaning in one's life.

The mothers we interviewed occasionally felt ignored and unappreciated by their husbands, children or by society at large, but none of them expressed the feeling that they could be easily replaced. In fact their irreplacebility was underscored by a few who indicated they never adopted the sick role because "mothers just can't afford to get sick." With so many other people depending directly upon them, it appears that these women are quite immune to an existential vacuum or lack of meaning in their lives.

3.   Men and women have an inherent capacity for "self-transcendence."

----

[6]Sahakian, p. 4.

In other words, people find meaning in their lives through reaching beyond themselves "toward people to love and causes to serve." This self-transcendence was particularly evident when these mothers of large families were asked if they ever suffered from the so-called "child care burnout syndrome" often experienced by professional child care workers. Notwithstanding the fact that the professional workers can leave their obligations behind after an eight-hour shift, while mothers are perpetually "on call," these mothers denied any serious problems of burnout. Many confessed to being physically exhausted on occasion, but they were emphatic about the rejuvenation inherent in a mother's love for her own children.

Inasmuch as children are a genetic and social-psychological extension of their parents, the accomplishments of children in work and play, or simply their natural "unfolding" into maturity, gives proud mothers a substantial psychic pay-check. A mother of one or two children can be proud of each child's growth and development; when the accomplishments accumulate among eight or ten children, maternal love and pride may be correspondingly enhanced.

4. People have the capacity of "self-detachment" and the ability to objectively observe themselves and their life patterns, and to make changes in the direction of their goals.

We were impressed with the feelings of internal control over their own lives manifested by most of the 41 mothers. They seemed to feel that they had chosen their present circumstances, and their decisions to bear several children were generally seen as very conscious choices, even when these decisions involved "letting nature take its course." Thus, none of them seemed to feel victimized by circumstances beyond her control. Nor did any of them exhibit delusions of maternal grandeur in perceiving themselves to be "supermoms." Indeed, their perceptions were quite to the contrary. Some of the women expressed disdain for the accolades heaped upon them on Mother's Day. Others insisted that they were ordinary women engaged in an ordinary homemaking venture merely on a larger scale than that experienced by most other women. And most of them were able to stand back from the fray and objectively appraise areas in which they and their families needed to improve.

5. Every person has the "defiant power of the human spirit" that enables her to take a stand in all situations, to focus on growth and to search for the specific meanings of life.

Even within the state of Utah where larger families are more common, mothers with seven children are a small minority. Less than one percent of Utah families have a college graduate mother who has borne seven or more children. Not only are they deviant in a statistical sense, but many of these mothers had felt deviant in social context, having been subjected to occasional ridicule or criticism about the size of their families.

In the face of this social censure it became a way-of-life with some mothers to marshal the "defiant power" mentioned above. Recall, for example, that when one mother was asked: "Don't you know where babies come from?" her standard reply was, "I sure do; isn't it marvelous?" Another mother, when asked, "Are those all your children?" replied with a twinkle in her eye: "No, we left several others at home!"

Sometimes the pressure was not exerted by strangers in restaurants, or on the street, but by one's own relatives. Even under the threat of in-law ostracism many of these women defiantly continued to bear more children. One mother of ten children mentioned that questions like "Don't you know when to quit?" merely served as an incentive to prove that it is possible to have a large family and a good family. Many mothers stood firm in the conviction that large families provide a superior environment for teaching children how to accept responsibility and get along with others. Others perceived themselves as "professional mothers" doing what they liked to do. Some had intentionally abandoned previous roles as career women, and emphasized that they were mothers by choice.

6. Tension is part of human existence. To be healthy, a person need not achieve "adjustment" or equilibrium, but must face the unavoidable tension, of life with daily exercises that will strengthen one's spiritual muscles. The healthiest tension is that between what a person is and the vision of what he or she might become.

Deeply committed to both a religious and personal ethic, these 41 mothers all seemed to know what they were supposed to be doing with their lives. They didn't expect others to copy their life-styles, and they readily admitted that rearing a large family was no easy task. But their repertoire of techniques for coping with stress seemed to be quite effective in most cases.

In his analysis of the U.S. Constitution, T. V. Smith observed that the Constitution doesn't guarantee happiness, but merely the pursuit of happiness. Sometimes we must be content with the happiness of pursuit. So it is with these maternal managers of large conjugal corporations. Their homes are never quite spotless, are seldom quiet, and are rarely free from stress. But such households cohere members in a common cause. The collective quest for elusive perfection goes on, monitored by the mother who, though she feels unequal to the task, finds meaning in the struggle. The spirit of "We shall overcome" pervaded the interviews, and a mother of nine neatly capped that sentiment when she said:

> When you have an understanding of the great potential that you can become and that is ahead of you, and you're happy together, there's nothing to stop you. Knowing you love your kids--It's just great, it's a fantastic life, and we can overcome so many things. That would be the overall view of what I would hope to leave you with, and the feeling of how I feel and how we all feel.